D0020793

Mortgage
Rip-Offs
and
Money
Savers

Mortgage
Rip-Offs
and
Money
Savers

**AN INDUSTRY INSIDER EXPLAINS
HOW TO SAVE THOUSANDS
ON YOUR MORTGAGE OR RE-FINANCE**

Carolyn Warren

BICENTENNIAL
1807
WILEY
2007
BICENTENNIAL

John Wiley & Sons, Inc.

Copyright © 2007 by Carolyn Warren. All rights reserved.

Published by John Wiley & Sons, Inc., Hoboken, New Jersey.
Published simultaneously in Canada.

Wiley Bicentennial Logo: Richard J. Pacifico

No part of this publication may be reproduced, stored in a retrieval system, or transmitted in any form or by any means, electronic, mechanical, photocopying, recording, scanning, or otherwise, except as permitted under Section 107 or 108 of the 1976 United States Copyright Act, without either the prior written permission of the Publisher, or authorization through payment of the appropriate per-copy fee to the Copyright Clearance Center, Inc., 222 Rosewood Drive, Danvers, MA 01923, (978) 750-8400, fax (978) 646-8600, or on the web at www.copyright.com. Requests to the Publisher for permission should be addressed to the Permissions Department, John Wiley & Sons, Inc., 111 River Street, Hoboken, NJ 07030, (201) 748-6011, fax (201) 748-6008, or online at http://www.wiley.com/go/permissions.

Limit of Liability/Disclaimer of Warranty: While the publisher and author have used their best efforts in preparing this book, they make no representations or warranties with respect to the accuracy or completeness of the contents of this book and specifically disclaim any implied warranties of merchantability or fitness for a particular purpose. No warranty may be created or extended by sales representatives or written sales materials. The advice and strategies contained herein may not be suitable for your situation. You should consult with a professional where appropriate. Neither the publisher nor author shall be liable for any loss of profit or any other commercial damages, including but not limited to special, incidental, consequential, or other damages.

For general information on our other products and services or for technical support, please contact our Customer Care Department within the United States at (800) 762-2974, outside the United States at (317) 572-3993 or fax (317) 572-4002.

Wiley also publishes its books in a variety of electronic formats. Some content that appears in print may not be available in electronic books. For more information about Wiley products, visit our web site at www.wiley.com.

ISBN 978-0-470-09783-0

10   9   8   7

To Brandon Warren
because you loved me and believed in me enough
to let me quit my day job and travel to New York.

CONTENTS

CONTENTS

Contents

CONTENTS

Contents

PART II
Tips for Homeowners Who Are Refinancing

CONTENTS

Contents

CONTENTS

ACKNOWLEDGMENTS

To all the hardworking loan officers—whether I've met you or not, whether you charge high prices and junk fees or not—I acknowledge you as awesome salespeople who work in one of the most stressful businesses there is. Honor to all the wholesale AEs who move heaven and earth to make a deal work, and especially to Michele who taught me so much about the business.

I am indebted to Audrene who first hired me, and to Allison, who said, "You can do this." And especially to my dear friend, Saundra, who is quite possibly the world's best processor and underwriter and an extraordinary photographer. A special thank you to Rick Cashman, my first friend in New York, for helping me close loans in the East and win the Maui contest.

Thank you Dee Splater and David Sharp at Alpine Mortgage Services for letting me join your team of rock star mortgage professionals. Hugs to all my friends there: Kimberlee, Pat, Tom, Jim, Dustin, Alan, Tina and Eric, Gayle, Susan, Karen, Michelle, Brenda, Tracy, Paul, Veronica, Holly, Hannah, Katrina, Larry, Kathy, Kaulana, and Barb. And to my friends at Precision Escrow: Karen and Liesl. High fives to all my friends at First Franklin, especially to my team, Pat, Kelly, Lori, Dana, Christa, and Vu.

Much appreciation goes to my agent, John Willig, who said, "I like this project" right from the start and remained enthusiastic throughout; and to my editor at John Wiley & Sons, Richard Narramore, who has brilliant ideas for titles and organization. And many thanks to the entire professional team at John Wiley & Sons, Inc. Thank you Steve Harrison for hosting the National Publicity Summit in NYC.

A special acknowledgment to the brilliant minds I admire so much—writers and businesspeople who gave me advice and encouragement: Clayton Makepeace, Bob Bly, Michael Masterson, Matt Furey; Kenneth Harney; and Brian Kurtz and Marjory Abrams.

Thank you Maggie, Gwen, and Joe for feeding Francie when I went to New York to meet my agent.

ACKNOWLEDGMENTS

To my loving and supportive family, thank you for your prayers and for believing in me: Barbara Jean and Gus, Donald Lee, Wendy and Brian, Kimberly and Ryan, Sherrie and Dan, Bonnie and Earl, Bev and Dick, Deanne, Brieanne, Theresa, and Tina. And to my husband Brandon, who values truth above all else. May God watch over you and bless you as you pursue your own dreams and fulfill your ministries.

Many secrets are told over lunch—casual comments, candid confessions, things that would never be said to an outsider. Little things like slipping 40 bucks to the gal who locks in interest rates. Or big things like making 40 grand off of one deal.

This particular day, I was dining with a loan officer at Michael's Broiler on the eighteenth floor overlooking Lake Washington and with a clear view of the Seattle skyline.

"Forty grand. That's amazing," I said, cutting another piece of my filet mignon. "How did you do that?"

The loan officer tapped his linen napkin to his lips and smiled proudly.

"It was a 5/1 ARM with an interest rate of six and a quarter."

"Aha," I responded. Perhaps I raised my eyebrows a tad, but nothing more. I understood perfectly. He had sold his client an adjustable-rate loan that had the interest rate of a 30-year fixed-rate loan. By selling the client a rate significantly over par, the officer was able to pocket a big back-end commission from the wholesale lender.

"Did you broker out the loan?" I asked this because I wanted to know if his client, the homeowner, had any idea how rich his loan officer was getting off him.

 Loan officers increase their commissions by giving you a higher interest rate than par.

"I did it 'in house,'" he said matter of factly.

Even better, he had a legal loophole for not revealing his windfall to the client, a windfall his client would pay for each and every month for the life of his loan. "That's the beauty of correspondent lending," he said. "You don't have to disclose your YSP [yield spread premium]." He finished up his mashed potatoes and expressed his pleasure about the absence of garlic.

"How long did the loan take to close?" I asked.

"Three weeks. And I had four other loans last month. But this month I plan to do more."

Our lunch was almost over, but I had one last question. "How long have you been in the mortgage business?"

"Two years. Two more and I expect to retire," he boasted.

I mentally did the math and figured he was right. Four years of charging clients for secret back-end commissions that big could net a loan officer enough to quit the business and get on with perfecting his golf game.

Unfortunately, this is not an uncommon story. I know from years of personal experience that this kind of price gouging is rampant in the mortgage industry. Charging a higher interest rate than par is just one way for loan officers to collect extra pay. Most people are aware that there are also unnecessary "junk" fees.

Are You One of the Savvy Consumers?

Most homebuyers or people refinancing their loans know there are financial booby traps waiting, so they're on the lookout for scams and junk fees. Nevertheless, they're still paying way too much. On average, homebuyers are shelling out an extra $1,225 up front, and they're taking a higher interest rate than necessary, to boot. They're much like the senior couple who was signing for their refinance one rainy afternoon.

As a licensed notary, my job was simply to get the papers signed properly for the loan officer. I saw that there was a $2,000 bogus discount point. (The couple wasn't getting a discounted interest rate by paying the fee.) I also noticed there was an unnecessary $395 Processing Fee. But, again, that wasn't any of my business, as a signing agent. The couple happily signed away. Then we got to the $19 Flood Certification Fee. Suddenly, the wife threw down her pen and said she wasn't going to pay that $19.

"Flood certification is a requirement in the state of Washington," I explained. "The mortgage company must show that the property is not in a flood zone and therefore does not need flood insurance."

She still objected, "But we're on a hill."

I said, "I understand. Most people around here are. But it's a state requirement, so there's no way around it."

"Well, I'm not paying it; $19 for nothing is ridiculous," she said adamantly.

I found it astonishing that she was happy to pay the unnecessary $2,000 and $395 fees and yet the $19 was a stumbling block she refused to get over.

Clearly, even people who are aware that scams and junk fees exist need to know which fees are fair and which are not. The question is, who's going to tell them?

How are you going to find out what's real, what's fair, and what's bogus when all the most important secrets are kept behind locked lips? The loan officers who are laughing all the way to the bank and slapping high-fives with one another behind your back aren't going to tell you. "If they're stupid enough to take it, it's their fault," one loan officer said to me.

Even the many articles and books written by talented reporters who interview and research professionals in the mortgage industry can't reveal all the rip-offs. How could these writers find out what's going on in secret when no one is talking? Not even the loan officers themselves know everything that goes on. The wholesale lenders who provide money to the mortgage brokers have plenty of sneaky little secrets all their own.

Like what? Like bribes. And false "sales." And loans for "important people," who are essentially getting cuts in line ahead of other loans. Like certain documents "disappearing" from loan files, so a loan that got denied at first can get approved instead. This is just the tip of the iceberg, and it's all very interesting, especially if you or someone you know happens to be buying a home or refinancing.

How to Use This Information to Save Tens of Thousands of Dollars

I wrote this book to keep you from becoming a victim to any one of the many rip-offs in the mortgage industry—rip-offs meticulously designed to steal your hard-earned money. It is organized to be a quick and easy resource, to help you can save the maximum amount of money possible:

- Part I, Chapters 1 to 8, takes you through the homebuying process, step by step. By browsing the chapter titles and subheads you'll see what information is included there. That way you can dive right into the parts that are the most pertinent to you. This isn't a novel, so there's no need to read the chapters in order, unless you choose to do so.

- Part II, Chapters 9 and 10, specifically addresses refinancing, because the majority of homeowners who refinance are paying too much. What's worse, some are putting their greatest asset at risk and don't even know it. It's as if they're playing a game of "chicken" with their financial future.

- Part III, Chapters 11 to 16, covers unique situations, and in the process reveals some juicy secrets from inside the "inner circle," meaning wholesale lending.

In addition, I'm offering these extra benefits to buyers of this book, on my personal Web site, www.AskCarolynWarren.com:

- Ask me a question and get a personal answer within 48 hours.

- Download, free, the "Credit Investigation Request" to easily dispute credit without having to compose a letter.

- Take advantage of a $30 discount on my "Ten Point Check-Up and Personal Loan Recommendation." (I guarantee you will save at least double the $67 cost—or else it's free.)

- Access free updated mortgage information.

What Is the Difference between Retail and Wholesale Lending?

As in other industries, mortgage lending has both a retail and a wholesale side. Retail includes banks, mortgage companies (also called direct lenders), and mortgage brokers. You can go to any of these three for a loan. If you go to a bank or mortgage company, they will use their "own money." If you go to a mortgage broker, your loan officer will shop the wholesale division of these same banks and mortgage companies, as well as others that are wholesale only, to get your loan. Some mortgage brokers have their "own money" to lend, as well as the ability to shop wholesale. Clearly, then, a mortgage broker has the most options.

Loan officers—who also like to be called mortgage consultants or loan specialists or other fancy titles—work in banks, mortgage companies, and mortgage brokerages.

The wholesale representatives who provide their services to the loan officers are called account executives. It's their job to help loan officers and to bring in business for their company.

My Credentials

I started my career in lending by working for a large, national mortgage company. It was a direct lender, so it had its own money and didn't shop wholesale. After two years there, I wanted more options, so I went to a mortgage brokerage. (I also had short stints at a finance company and another big national lender—short, because I couldn't tolerate their pricing shenanigans for long.)

I worked very hard at the mortgage broker shop for about seven years. Then, feeling that I needed to round out my career, I moved "inside" to wholesale lending, and spent almost two years there as an account executive. I worked "behind closed doors" with the manager and sales manager, underwriters, loan account manager, and the people who locked in rates, drew loan documents, and funded loans.

During this decade, I also served as a licensed notary public and worked freelance, signing loans for many companies, on call.

"Am I going to be in your book?" a loan officer asked when I told him I was writing about mortgage rip-offs.

"I won't reveal names," I answered.

"Oh, good!" he replied, obviously relieved.

Then one day I'd had enough. I knew it was time to expose the secrets and share vital information with the public that had been hidden for too long. I decided that the best way to get this information out was in a book; and I confided in one of my friends—a processor and underwriter for many years—what I was planning.

"Be careful what you say, or you could lose your job," she said. Wise counsel. But I didn't want to be careful about what I said. I wanted to tell all. So I respectfully submitted my resignation and got to work on the book you're holding now.

Eight-Step Guide to Getting the Best Rate and Protecting Yourself from Most Common Scams

CHAPTER 1

Step 1:
Boost Your Credit
Rating and Prequalify

Unless you just won the lottery, you need a good credit rating. Without it, you'll be at the mercy of higher rates, bigger fees, and fewer options. Or worse, you could find yourself sitting on the curb with all your belongings piled up next to you, and nowhere to go. That's exactly what happened to a family I'll call the Happys. The Happys were so happy they'd found their dream home, they made an offer, signed an agreement, and gave notice to their landlord. They weren't worried about a thing—not even their credit—because they had a prequalification letter for financing in hand. They were happy, too, because the builder was going to get the home finished just before Mrs. Happy was due to have her baby. But, alas, their financing hit a snag when the lurid details of their credit came to light. Consequently, their prequalification could not be turned into an approval. Frantic, they went online and shopped every lender imaginable, but no one would grant them a loan.

"Why won't anybody take a chance on us?" wailed Mrs. Happy. "We're good people, and I'm about to have a baby!"

What she failed to realize was that the mortgage business is not about taking a chance on good people. You can be a saint from heaven and still get denied if your credit report is ugly as hell. The mortgage business is all about making money for its investors, and these investors want to *invest* their money, not gamble with it.

"Perhaps your landlord can let you stay longer while you clean up your credit?" I asked, being one of a long line of loan officers she'd come begging to.

 Mortgage companies have to pay their investors. They can't afford to gamble on people with good intentions and a poor payback history.

"No, he's already rented it out to someone else for next month. We have no choice but to get out, and we have absolutely nowhere to go. I've got my entire house packed in boxes, ready to move, but I can't seem to find a loan. I didn't think our credit was *that* big a deal." Ignorance about credit does not equal bliss.

Last I heard, the Happy family was anything but, as they were forced to move three states away to bunk up with the wife's dad. You might think this story is ludicrous, but it's true, and some version of it happens to someone every day. That's why you must take care of your credit as your first step; otherwise, your prequalification letter won't be worth the ink it took to print, and you could find out what it means to be homeless.

✐ NOTE
If you know your credit is outstanding, you can skip ahead to the shaded box titled, "Look Who's Selling Your Credit behind Your Back!" You'll want to know about this slimy practice and what you can do to prevent it from happening to you. ✐

What Credit Score Do You Need to Buy a Home?

If you want a conventional loan with the lowest rate, you need a score of 620 to pass lenders' automated underwriting programs (defined below). I'll explain how this works and mention some exceptions. If you don't need this information, skip ahead to "How Lenders Rate Credit."

Lenders pull a *trimerged credit report* that contains data from the three credit bureaus (Equifax, Experian, and TransUnion) with a credit score for each. Your numeric score comes from a complex algorithm based on at least 40 components from the information in your credit file. It's an industry-specific score that's been created just for mortgages. The purpose of the score is to predict how risky it will be for a lender to extend you credit.

Mortgage companies go by the middle score. If your scores are 560, 589, and 650, your score is considered to be 589, for example. Other rating factors include the following:

- Lenders do not average your scores together.

- Each person has his or her own score; married couples do not share a score.

- Your scores will vary with each bureau, because not all creditors report to all three bureaus.

The loan officer or a loan processor inputs your application into a specific lender's computerized underwriting program. This program, called *automated underwriting* or *desktop underwriting (DU)*, reads the information, looks at your credit, and spits out a verdict lickety-split, as follows:

- *Accept.* This means you're approved as long as a live underwriter looks over your paperwork and agrees that the figures you've provided match your pay stubs and other information. The program also provides a list of the documentation that is required for the final approval, which is done by a real underwriter.

- *Review.* This means the computer isn't certain and wants a live underwriter to make the call. If you get a "review," your loan will go in line and may take a few days to get the verdict. So if you're wondering, "Why is it taking so long for me to get an approval when my neighbor got one in an hour?" this could be the reason.

- *Denied.* If the computer turns down your application, your loan officer may appeal the decision or go to a different wholesale lender. (If your loan officer works for a bank or direct lender, then he or she has only that lender's own loans to pick from and can't shop around for you like a broker can.)

✐ NOTE: EXCEPTIONS
Nonconforming (or subprime) lenders don't follow these rules, because they have different investors and their own

guidelines. They'll accept credit scores lower than 620. One lender takes your highest credit score (rather than the middle one) with a 10 percent minimum down payment and a higher interest rate. ✎

> The credit score is an index of risk. It is an unbiased indicator of whether a consumer will repay a loan on time. Scores range between 400 and 850, approximately.

If your score is 620-plus, lenders will look to see if you have any other factors that could cause a denial, such as a recent bankruptcy, foreclosure, judgment, or tax lien. It's something of a pass/fail system with computerized underwriting (called *automated underwriting* or *desktop underwriting*). Whether your score is 620 or 720, you pass, and that means you are eligible for the best interest rate of the day. The conventional 30-year fixed-rate loans don't have a better interest rate for people with higher scores, as long as automated underwriting gives you an "accept."

✐ NOTE
If you're getting a Stated Income loan or other nonconforming loan, then your score will make a difference in your interest rate, up to about 720. This is called risk-based lending. ✎

If your score is 720 or higher, you can take your choice of the loan smorgasbord. If your score is 800 or higher, you'll have loan officers exclaiming over you and treating you like a rock star.

Here's a general guideline of how lenders rate credit scores:

720–higher	A	Take your choice of loans at the lowest cost, including risk-based loans such as Stated Income and Interest Only.
620–719	A–	You qualify for conforming, conventional loans. You'll pay slightly more for risk-based loans.
600–619	B	You may take a Federal Housing Administration/Veterans Administration (FHA/VA) loan or even a zero-down loan with desktop underwriting.

575–599   C   You can qualify for a subprime loan, but your interest rate will be significantly higher. Expect a prepayment penalty.

500–559   D   Most lenders will deny your loan; but there are a few "hard money" subprime lenders who will approve a loan if you have a sufficient down payment. Mortgage brokers have access to these wholesale lenders.

490–499   D–   Only the rare subprime lender will approve a loan for someone with a score below 500, and a large down payment will be required—usually 25 to 50 percent. Other conditions will apply, as well.

Additional Notes about How Lenders Rate Credit

Tax Liens and Judgments.   Public records (liens and judgments) must be paid off prior to or through closing the loan. For example, if you have an IRS tax lien that shows up on your credit, it will have to be paid before your home loan can record and fund. This is because the tax lien would be in "first position" on the title to your property and the mortgage would be secondary. A mortgage company cannot take a second position to a tax lien or a judgment because that would put them in financial jeopardy.

Consumer Credit Counseling.   Many lenders regard being in a debt-consolidation program—such as Consumer Credit Counseling, Solutions, and other similar nonprofit organizations—equal with being in a Chapter 13 bankruptcy, because they look at it as a self-made debt reorganization bankruptcy. Most lenders will require that you complete and be out of the debt counseling program before they will approve your home loan. Some require a length of time to pass for the reestablishment of good credit thereafter.

It is my opinion that there are two better solutions for burdensome debt: (1) negotiate payments and settlements with the creditors yourself, or (2) file a Chapter 7 bankruptcy and get the ordeal over with in a few months rather than draw it out for years. (Again, this is my personal opinion. Consult an attorney for legal advice.)

Collections and Charge-Offs. Just because a credit card company writes off a bad debt and stops harassing you, doesn't mean everything is okay now and you can ignore it. Often, an unpaid debt is "charged off," and then sold to a collection company.

A collection company buys a bundle of bad debts for pennies on the dollar. Then it goes to work to collect. It may add on its own fees and may continue to charge interest, causing your balance to rise higher and higher as time goes on. Even if you don't agree that you owe payment to this third party, if it's on your credit report, it's a factor in calculating your score and getting a mortgage. (Read how to handle collections and charge-offs on page 11, under "Nine Steps to Boost Your Credit Rating.")

Bankruptcy. Your mortgage broker can shop the subprime wholesale lenders to find you the best loan available for people who have had a bankruptcy discharged just yesterday. Yes, as long as you're out of the Chapter 7 or Chapter 13, some subprime lenders don't care how long ago it was, and they'll go by your credit score. (Other conditions will be required, however. Your loan officer will advise you, as lenders vary.)

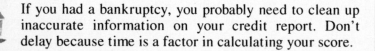

If you had a bankruptcy, you probably need to clean up inaccurate information on your credit report. Don't delay because time is a factor in calculating your score.

The government loans, FHA and VA, require that a bankruptcy be discharged for 24 months, and that you have clean credit thereafter. Credit score is not a factor for government loans.

Foreclosure. Mortgage lenders don't want to see that you failed to pay on a past mortgage. Period. And the fact that your former house was a "short sale" or otherwise amicable foreclosure doesn't cheer them up a bit. Foreclosures make investors very nervous. But don't despair if this happened to you. Just realize you'll need to take some time to rebuild good credit, and make sure you have absolutely perfect payments on everything from here on out.

No matter what your credit looks like today, you must never give up on your dream of home ownership. Your credit score is recalculated at the moment your credit report is pulled, so there's always hope for a better score once the data in your credit file improves.

What to Do if You Have Credit Challenges

What if you have "ugly" credit but still want to buy a house *right now*? Will it take a miracle to get a loan? No, just a large down payment. If you give the investors enough security, they'll make the investment in you—provided they collect a higher rate of interest to compensate for the risk. You might wonder how far that rule can be stretched. Here's an example.

 Giving the lender collateral in the form of a down payment is one way to make up for having poor credit.

As a wholesale account executive, I got a loan approved for a couple who had six pages of late payments and paid-off collections. These people had stiffed everyone from Visa to the pizza delivery guy. It was one ugly credit report! But this lucky family had just inherited money, so they got their loan. The catch was that they had to make a 20 percent down payment and take a high interest rate with a two-year obligation (prepayment penalty).

What's interesting is that the investor wasn't the only one who wanted more money. On top of the lender's high rate, the loan officer jacked up the rate by an additional 1.25 percent so she could collect the maximum back-end commission for herself. Then she added a couple extra points up front, too, because she figured they'd consider themselves "stuck" and wouldn't shop around. So Mr. and Mrs. Lucky ended up paying *triple* for their bad credit, because on top of what the lender required, the loan officer saw an opportunity to take advantage. And that's the way it usually goes.

People with Low Scores Get Ripped Off More Often

Why is this the case? Simply, if you have subprime credit, you're easy prey for loan sharks disguised as helpful, understanding, charming loan consultants. In fact, some loan officers prefer to specialize in subprime loans, because it's easier to make a killing on them.

Folks with subprime credit are famous for not scrutinizing the cost of their loans. Typically, they: (1) fail to shop properly, (2) fail to scrutinize their Good Faith Estimate, (3) don't know their real credit status and believe they're a "D" when they're really a "B," and (4) focus on payment rather than on the true cost of the loan.

Suave, good-looking guys like Jake are in high spirits about helping people with credit and income challenges. I walked into his office one day to see if I could be of service. (I was one of his wholesale lending reps.) Jake leaned back in his leather swivel chair, hands clasped behind his head, and announced with a big, happy smile, "I'm making $16,000 on this loan!" He held up a loan file.

"How are you doing that?" I asked.

"Four points," he said triumphantly.

Not only that, he had two loans he was charging four points on, so by doing just two loans that month, his take was about $32,000. Not a bad monthly income for part-time work.

$$4\% \text{ of } \$400,000 = \$16,000 \text{ commission}$$
$$\text{Two of these loans} = \$32,000$$

You might wonder how Jake was getting away with what looks like highway robbery. I asked him that question.

Smiling, he pointed to one file and then the other and said, "It's because these people have some collections, and these other people are self-employed and can't verify their income. They don't think they can get a loan anywhere else."

He had, in short, convinced them that because of their circumstances he was the only one who could get them approved. Of course, that wasn't true; in fact, any mortgage broker could have done the same loans more cheaply. But these were two typical subprime borrowers, and they were getting gouged.

Jake grinned and said, "I have to scoot now as I've got a game of golf this afternoon."

Good People with Bad Credit. Not all people with poor credit are irresponsible goof-offs. Some have suffered through illness, hurricanes, and other storms of life. These are intelligent people with integrity who need a fresh start.

I don't like seeing good people being taken advantage of, so I'm offering you an easy nine-step plan (*with new information revealed*) to boost your credit score. This is beneficial information for *everyone* who wants to prepare to buy a home. No matter what your past has been, if you follow this simple plan, you will become a homeowner, and the American dream will be yours. So take heart and start today.

Nine Steps to Boost Your Credit Rating

1. *Ignore private Web sites offering free credit reports.* Instead, obtain a copy of your credit report directly from the credit bureaus so you can check for errors. Avoid using other Web sites, because with these "middleman" reports, the information may not be updated and complete. What's more, the credit score is usually 30 to 80 points higher than the score your mortgage lender receives. Consumers who order free credit reports via various Web sites are shocked and upset when their loan officer tells them their actual score is lower. A rep for one of the bureaus told me she receives complaint calls daily, so the word needs to get out: scores from Web sites other than those of the credit bureaus themselves may not be calculated with the same algorithm and can appear higher.

2. *Take immediate action to correct errors with one handy form.* You can compose your own letter or get a handy fill-in-the-blanks form on my Web site, www.AskCarolynWarren.com (offered free to purchasers of this book). In addition, call each creditor who has reported an error, and do the following:

   a. Ask to speak with the supervisor in charge.

   b. Explain the situation and ask to have a letter confirming the correction sent to you right away.

   c. Ask the creditor to report the correction to the credit bureaus also, politely reminding them that it is illegal to report false information. (But don't trust them to do this; take responsibility to send in your own dispute as well.)

   And note that according to the Fair Credit Reporting Act, the bureaus must investigate your dispute and report the results to you within a reasonable time (30 to 45 days).

3. *Get current on credit cards and installment loans.* Get caught up on any past-due accounts, and from this day forward, pay everything on time. The older a late payment becomes, the less harm it does to the score, so time really does heal bad credit.

4. *Get single bad accounts deleted.* If you have good credit overall, with an "uncharacteristic" late payment, contact that creditor and ask to have the "mistake" deleted. Usually, a company will do this favor for one of their long-time good customers. (If a clerk says no,

call back and ask for the supervisor. You're likely to get a yes.) Don't worry, this is legal. The law does not require a creditor to report information; in fact, some companies don't report to the bureaus at all. If creditors choose to have a late payment deleted from an individual's credit file, they are within their legal rights to do so, even if the late payment actually happened. Creditors own the credit information for their own accounts. They may choose to give grace by having a mistake deleted early in order to keep their customer happy and returning to their store. It's simply good business.

Here's an example of how this works. One day a loan officer came to me for advice, because she discovered a collection on her credit report. She was fairly frantic, because she was just about to buy a house. She said she didn't know about the derogatory account until she checked her credit, and this one thing was dragging down her score. I advised her to call the creditor, tell her story, and politely ask to have it removed from her credit. Sure enough, a few minutes later she reappeared in my office, smiling. The creditor was happy to fax her a letter stating the collection was "in error" and should be deleted. Once she explained the situation, the creditor was happy to give her some grace providing she paid the sum with her credit card. This mutual agreement benefited both parties. And why not? This collection was an honest oversight and uncharacteristic of her credit profile. She was not defrauding or deceiving future lenders.

5. *Pay down credit balances that are up to or near the limit.* A balance that is over 50 percent of your credit limit lowers your credit score, even if it is paid on time. I suggest keeping balances below 30 percent for maximum benefit. This is a step you can take to boost your score—pronto. Once your balance is lowered, your score immediately improves.

6. *Keep long-standing credit open.* If you close off accounts you've had for several years, you will lose your "longevity points" and lower your score. You don't have to carry a balance from month-to-month, so don't waste money paying interest. Simply use the card for a minimal purchase ($20 is fine) a couple times a year to keep it active with the bureaus.

7. *Avoid opening new credit. Say no at the checkout counter.* Applying for and opening new credit temporarily lowers your credit score, so

don't apply for a credit card or auto financing until after you've closed on your home loan. If you've got three credit cards, do not apply for another—even if a retailer tries to bribe you with a 10 percent discount on your purchase. (In addition to helping your credit score, this will lower your debt ratio, too.)

8. *If you have old collection accounts with balances, leave them alone.* Don't pay collections or charge-offs before you apply for a loan, or your score will be penalized. The credit scoring system looks at the "date of last activity." So if you make a payment, you update that date of last activity from years ago to now—and your score goes down. It may seem ridiculous that you get docked for paying an old, bad debt, but because that's the way the system is set up you have to play the game that way. Until this is changed, I advise you *not* to pay off old collections and charge-offs (unless they're recent). Many of the subprime lenders will allow you to ignore collections that are over two years old and close your loan without paying them off.

   If one of the conditions on your loan approval is to pay off a collection, it's best to do so through the escrow company or attorney who is closing your loan. Don't pay it off while your loan is in progress. That way you don't have to go through the hassle of providing more paperwork and proof that it's paid in full. It's easy and "clean" when you do it through your closing, and lenders prefer it.

9. *Correct bankruptcy misinformation.* If you had a bankruptcy in the past, you'll probably see credit cards with open balances that were actually included in the bankruptcy. You need to mail a copy of the list of creditors that were included in the bankruptcy to the credit bureaus to fix this, along with the handy form mentioned above.

Don't be discouraged. You can consider this the tenth step in this plan. Don't be downhearted about mistakes in your past. Let go of the emotional baggage and concentrate on your future. I've seen people raise their credit scores by 60 to 100 points in just a few months. The important thing is to take action—*now*. Procrastination is a thief that steals many dreams. It's all in your hands.

Once your credit is squared away, you'll want to find out how much money you can borrow.

Look Who's Selling Your Credit behind Your Back!

We like to think our credit is a personal matter, but someone is toying with your private information without your consent. The credit bureaus have concocted another scheme to make more money. They're selling your private information, including your home telephone number, to bottom-feeding mortgage companies.

When one mortgage company pulls your credit report, the bureaus say, "Aha, someone wants a mortgage." So then they sell your pertinent information to a competing mortgage company who can then call during your dinner and try to steal you away. Can you imagine the nerve? They call them "trigger leads."

A mortgage company in Michigan, for example, pays one of the credit bureaus to tattle whenever a credit report is pulled in the state of Michigan by a mortgage lender. Then someone from the company scurries to the phone, calls you up, and harasses you to switch your business over to it.

A loan officer at a small broker shop confronted another loan officer at a large national lender about trying to steal his clients. The officer at the large firm wasted no time in admitting that her company was doing just that. "It's the advantage of working for a large company," she said. "We can afford to buy these trigger leads, which are very expensive, from the credit bureau. When the bureau notifies us that a person in our state has had their credit pulled by a mortgage lender, we get in touch with them and have a friendly chat. 'How are you doing?' we ask. 'Is there anything I can do for you today? I understand you have a Good Faith Estimate from another company. Let me show you how I can save you money. By the way, where do you work? Oh, that's on my way home, so I'll drop by and get your signature on my application.'"

 To opt out of having your private information sold by the credit bureaus, go to www.OptOutPrescreen.com.

The loan officer from the small broker responded angrily to the discovery of this tactic. How dare this large company "spy" on people having a credit report checked? And how dare it "backstab" him, a fellow mortgage professional?

We all know some companies sell lists of customer names to other companies. Most of us take note of that when we sign up for something online, and we make sure to check the opt-out buttons. But the credit bureaus? Somehow we don't expect them to pass along our private information *without our consent or knowledge* when we apply for a loan. But they do. And you can prevent this disgusting practice by opting out at www.optoutprescreen.com. If a parasite mortgage company calls you, you can send a message with quick "No thank you; I don't do business that way."

Find Out How Much You Qualify For

House hunting is exciting. It's fun to walk through new homes and open houses and imagine yourself living there. But what happens when you fall head over heels in love with the royal master suite with that sunken Jacuzzi tub and gigantic walk-in closet, only to find it's priced just above your budget? You start thinking there must be some way, because now that you've pictured yourself soaking in that queenly tub after a hard day's work, you really have your heart set on it. You're thinking you *deserve* it. So then you look at the new "creative" loans that will allow for the payment you need, even with the bigger mortgage. Only you don't consider that these are also high-risk loans. You're just thinking about how fabulous you're going to feel in that dream house.

Think twice, otherwise you'll be hopping mad two years later when your payment skyrockets out of control and you're faced with losing your home. It all starts with that initial unrealistic desire—because you failed to prequalify first. What's the use of getting your heart set on a house you can't afford? And what's the use of buying a home destined to become your ball-and-chain when you realize that you really couldn't afford it?

 Tailor your desires to your budget, not the other way around.

Don't rely on your loan officer or your real estate agent to set your personal budget for you. Remember, they get paid on commission, and the bigger the sale, the bigger the paycheck that goes into their pockets. Even though there are some wonderful professionals who will advise you not to spend beyond your reasonable means, you have to take responsibility for determining what that is yourself.

The Three-Step Preapproval Process

After you have your credit ready to be checked by a lender, the next step is to get prequalified and then preapproved. Here's how it works:

1. *You get prequalified.* This is a verbal estimate. You call a loan officer and say you're ready to get prequalified. A prequalification is an estimate of what you can afford based on the credit, income, debt, and asset information to give him or her over the phone. You don't need to have your credit report pulled yet. You're just "testing the waters."

   You also need to decide which company and which loan officer you're going to work with, so you're not making a commitment just yet. This is why you won't give out your Social Security number for the credit check. That comes later.

   The loan officer gives you a verbal estimate for the loan amount he or she believes you will qualify for. (The officer can do this over the phone in a 10-minute conversation.) This gives you an idea of what kind of house you can afford. Of course, this verbal prequalification is only as accurate as the information you've provided, so be very careful to give accurate figures for your income and monthly payments. If you overstate your income, you can't blame the loan officer for prequalifying you for too much money.

2. *You compare three Good Faith Estimates and choose a loan officer to work with.* This is an extremely important step, which is why Chapter 2 is devoted to making sure you do it right.

3. *You get preapproved.* This is a written commitment. Once you know you're happy with the approximate loan size you qualify for, and you've selected your good, honest mortgage professional to work with, you're ready to make and receive a commitment. You've established a relationship of trust, and you're done shopping around. Now you're ready for the next five steps:

   a. You complete the loan application, including your Social Security number, and let your loan officer pull your credit.

b. You negotiate the fees on your Good Faith Estimate. (This is explained in Chapter 5.)

c. You sign the Good Faith Estimate and other disclosures for your file.

d. Your loan officer gives you a written preapproval letter or certificate. This is a commitment to lend, as long as you meet all the lender's conditions and nothing changes for the worse, such as losing your job.

e. You give a copy of the preapproval to your real estate agent to accompany your offer.

How Do Lenders Decide How Much Money to Lend You?

Lenders have their own guidelines for calculating how much money they'll lend. This is called your *debt-to-income ratio,* or DTI. Depending on the lender, the total DTI allowed is usually 40 to 45 percent. This means that when you add up all of the payments listed below, it cannot be more than 45 percent of your gross monthly income (income before taxes and other deductions).

Some lenders allow a 50 percent debt ratio; others allow 50 percent but require that you take a higher interest rate, because stretching your DTI is risky. Another lender allows a 55 percent debt ratio and bases your interest rate solely on credit score. (These are all wholesale lenders, and you can get these loans through your local mortgage broker.)

Don't become overwhelmed by these variances. This is precisely why you'll have a good mortgage broker representing you. He or she will handle the details of these underwriting rules and shop the various lenders to get you the right loan.

Which Payments Count for Debt Ratio?

The lender will use the following criteria in calculating your debt-to-income ratio:

- Your new house payment, including property taxes and hazard (fire) insurance and mortgage insurance (if applicable)
- Flood insurance, if required for the location

- Homeowners' dues (if a condominium, townhouse, or Planned Urban Development—PUD)
- Auto loans and other installment loans
- Credit cards
- Student loans that will not be deferred for at least 12 more months

Then, to figure out the ratio, follow these steps:

1. Take the gross income for all borrowers. Multiply it by 0.45.
2. From that number, subtract all your loan payments and credit card payments.
3. What is left is the maximum amount you can afford for your total house payment (using a 45 percent DTI).

Following are two examples that will be useful in seeing how debt-to-income is calculated. Then you can do the same for yourself to see whether or not you have enough income to qualify for a mortgage now or need to pay off some debt first. If you're uncomfortable with a 45 percent debt ratio, use another ratio. In times past, 35 percent was used, but nowadays, lenders are much more generous.

Example 1

Husband's gross monthly income is $3,000; wife's is $3,000.

Total income = $6,000

$6,000 × 0.45 = $2,700 for monthly outgo (including new house payment and debts)

$2,700 for monthly outgo

− 400 auto payment

− 200 total credit card payments

$2,100 left for new house payment

(We'll subtract $300/month for property taxes and insurance and take a 6.75 percent rate.)

This couple qualifies for $277,500. But look what happens, in the second example, if they don't have an auto payment and their credit cards are minimal.

Example 2

Same scenario as above, but with lower payments.

$2,700 for monthly outgo
    0 auto payment
   $\underline{- 50}$ total credit card payments
$2,650 left for total new house payment

Now they qualify for $362,300. This extra $90,000 makes a big difference in the quality of home they can afford.

Get Your Loan Amount the Easy Way, in Private

Use the mortgage calculator at www.mortgage-helper.com to get the loan amount you qualify for. Simply type in the payment you desire and the interest rate. You'll get an instant answer. Feel free to play with different numbers, as you remain anonymous.

However, if you don't like doing any math or research, your loan officer will calculate your DTI for you.

Pick Your Own Budget

If a 45 percent debt ratio doesn't leave you enough cash (disposable net income) to live on, use 35 percent (times 0.35). You and you alone decide where your comfort level is. Some people want more money left over for living expenses such as shopping and travel than others.

What about those higher debt ratios? In my opinion, the only time to take a 55 percent debt ratio loan is when you have more money coming into the household than what you can show on the application. (So, in reality, your debt ratio is lower than 55 percent.) An example of this is when only one spouse is going on the loan (because of credit), but both

Unsure about a Higher House Payment?

Here's your solution. Perhaps you've been paying $1,000 a month for rent and want to buy a house. But you're not sure where your comfort level is. Try setting aside an extra $1,500 a month for a $2,500/month house payment and see if you can live with that for three months. This idea will let you test a higher payment before you make a commitment.

are working and bringing in money. Another example is the person who consistently makes $2,000 a month selling merchandise via online auctions but can't prove it.

Coming Up

In the next chapter, I'll talk about the extremely important decision that too many people leave up to chance: finding a competent, honest loan officer. Just wait until you read about some of the sneaky rip-offs! You'll understand why working with the right professional is critical and why you can't always trust a referral.

CHAPTER 2

Step 2:
Create a Short List
of Three Honest
Mortgage Lenders

"Hey, if they're stupid enough to take it, it's their fault."

When you think about that statement made by a loan officer, you'll agree it's important to select three *honest* mortgage lenders to get a quote from. To help you do that, first, I'll alert you to some common ploys that snare even the best educated and intelligent people. Then I'll sum up exactly how you create your own short list of three honest professionals.

There's no need to wear yourself out calling 10 or 20 companies because my short list approach will get you a better loan anyway. From this list, you'll select your loan officer.

But, first, the "funny business." These days, the mortgage industry has more tricks than a magic show, so you can't afford to be naive.

Tricks to Foil Your Shopping Efforts

Is that a loan officer or a magician working on the financing? I had to ask this question myself when I sat in a training class for loan officers. A certain corporate trainer was explaining how we should handle people who object to high pricing. What were his words of wisdom? He said to vary the components of the loan so people won't be able to figure out which loan is cheapest. His exact words were "compare apples to oranges." Nice strategy—if you've got something to hide.

Sneaky companies strategize on ways to foil your efforts to find the cheapest loan.

The sad truth is that this is a major lender who advertises all across the media. You can combat this deceitful ploy by insisting on a quote with the same terms, *with* the inclusion or absence of prepayment penalty. But I think the better approach is to walk away. My dad used to tell me, "Don't do business with the devil."

One company has its own unique approach to providing you with a Good Faith Estimate (GFE). Instead of the standard form, it has its own sheet that includes a fraction of the information on the standard GFE. The loan officers are instructed to fill it out by hand using green ink. Why green?

✐ NOTE
A Good Faith Estimate is a detailed itemization of all closing costs and fees estimated to be required at closing. It also includes the loan amount, loan type, interest rate, monthly payment, and funds required to close/funds back to the borrower. ✎

"It's the color of money, and that has a psychological effect on people," said the trainer. I had to wonder how many people would take their 9 percent loan with four points and a prepayment penalty, all because that green ink is so seductive. So I asked one of the loan officers, a young, beautiful woman, working for this company, how she sold a 9 percent loan with four points and a prepayment penalty to her client, who happened to be an elderly single woman.

Her answer, "I had to talk a lot, but I finally convinced her that she couldn't get any better because of her credit." (The client did have sub-prime credit, but without a doubt, she could have received a better loan through a different company.)

 Unique formatting of the Good Faith Estimate allows a lender to hide certain fees. I recommend working with a company that uses one of the standard GFE forms that lists all costs clearly.

Back to that green ink. The aforementioned company calls its "substitute Good Faith Estimate" a loan summary sheet; the main problem with it is that it doesn't disclose all the information that a traditional GFE does. Some of the costs are hidden from you until the time of signing, at which point—they hope—you'll be so emotionally caught up in either (1) the cash-out you're soon to get or (2) getting rid of your credit card balances that you'll overlook the high rate and extra fees.

Selling the Sizzle

More than one mortgage trainer tells his loan officers, "Sell the sizzle, not the steak." It's a motto they love to quote, and it's aimed right at you. What does it mean, and why should you be on the lookout for the "sizzle sellers"?

 "Sell benefits, not price," said the high-priced mortgage manager to his loan officers.

When a company knows its pricing is higher than its competitors', it needs to take your focus off pricing and onto other issues. It's tantamount to keeping you from asking about the grade or cut of the steak, instead listening to that sizzle and smelling that delicious aroma. Your mouth is watering so much you just can't wait to cut a piece and savor the flavor. You are focusing on how juicy it's going to taste, so you don't think about whether it's filet mignon or hamburger. You're ready to pay anything just to get a bite of that sizzle.

How does that metaphor translate to loans, exactly? The high-priced loan officers take your attention away from the fact that their fees are double or triple what you could get elsewhere. They take your attention away from the fact that their interest rates are higher. They don't even mention the prepayment penalty. Instead, they get you to focus on how *fast* they're going to get your loan done. How *easy* it's going to be. If it's a purchase, they'll focus on how the payment is low, even if it's a temporary low payment or a terribly risky loan. If it's a refinance, they'll focus on the cash back you'll get. They'll ask you about what you're going to do with the cash, encouraging you to go into all the savory details, so that by the end of the conversation, all you care about is how quickly you can get that money into your hands. Whatever benefits they can sell, that's what they'll focus on. It's all about the benefits—the *sizzle*—not about the overall financial picture of the loan itself.

Special Deals and Secret Loans

If there's "a special deal just for you" or "a special loan just at our company," then there's a man with flying reindeer who slides down your chimney once a year. Lovely fantasies for the naive are just that—fantasies.

When I was a wholesale account executive, our company would sometimes roll out a "monthly special," such as a reduced interest rate Adjustable Rate Mortgage (ARM). Of course, these programs were available to all mortgage brokers, and we wanted to sell as many of them as we could. The whole point of having a special was to increase business.

One month we had a 3.99 percent rate on a 2/28 ARM. (Fixed at 3.99 percent for two years, then turns into an adjustable rate after that, and includes a two-year prepayment penalty.)

 "Special deals just for our company" are actually "special lies."

I called a particular mortgage broker shop that advertises regularly on Christian radio. Posing as a potential homebuyer, I asked what they could offer me.

"We have a special," she said and described the above loan.

"Who is the wholesale lender?" I asked.

"It's a company called First Franklin. They've offered this special *exclusively* to us, because we do a lot of business with them," she lied.

She was so busted! As an account executive at First Franklin, I knew we offered the special to *all* mortgage brokers. Like I said, we were advertising it like crazy to increase our business.

The point is, there is no such thing as a special loan available "only at one company." No mortgage broker has a unique loan that no one else in the city can get.

The Loan They Don't Want You to Know About

One afternoon I heard this amazing ad on my car radio. It said this mortgage company had a "no fee, no down payment loan that the lenders do not want people to know about, because they don't make any money on them." Wow! I just couldn't resist pulling off the road and whipping out my cell phone.

The manager answered, much to my delight. I asked him why they were advertising "a loan that the lenders don't want people to know about" when lenders eagerly wanted people to know about the loans. I also asked him why they were saying they didn't make any money on them when they were making yield spread premium (YSP) back-end commissions.

 There's no such thing as a loan that lenders make zero money on. Mortgage is not a charity.

He did a verbal dance until I told him I was in the mortgage business as well, and I knew all about this 103 percent loan.

At that point, here's exactly what he said, "I know it's not true, but as a marketing technique, it works."

This is an example of why you can't rely on radio or television ads. You've got a better plan with your short list.

The Sticky Trick

Loan officers strategize about how to get clients to "stick." The last thing they want is to spend hours working on a loan they never get paid on, because their clients hop off to another company midstream. But some of them don't want you shopping around in the beginning either.

One of the most effective ways of getting a client to stick is to obligate them with their money. This is why some loan officers collect $500 or more right up front. They ask for fees in advance to keep you from running off. If your loan officer asks you for money before he or she provides you with a Good Faith Estimate, forget about it. Why should you obligate yourself before you know what the loan looks like? This is why I advise against paying an application fee.

One mortgage dude said, "I've never once, in 146 loans, had a borrower change his mind and go with someone else *after* he wrote me a check. The solution to losing clients to competitors is to get a check ASAP."

You don't need one of these loan clowns to represent you. That's why you shouldn't apply all over the Internet and call around randomly for a loan.

Creating Your Short List

With my short list plan, you'll get a better loan with less work, in only three steps:

1. Write down two mortgage companies and one bank.
2. If possible, make one of these a referral.
3. Get a specific name.

Here are the details for each step.

Write Down Two Mortgage Companies and One Bank

This is all the shopping you need to do, because each of the two mortgage companies will be comparing rates from at least a dozen lenders. If you call too many, the loan officers won't think they have a good shot at getting your business, and they may ignore you. They'll think you're a waste of their time. And you'll waste your own time as well.

You can look in your local yellow pages to get two mortgage companies, if you have no referrals. Then you'll pick one bank, preferably the one you already do business with.

Make One a Referral

If you have a friend or coworker who got a mortgage recently—either a purchase or refinance, it doesn't matter—ask if he or she was happy with the loan officer. If so, that person can be one on your short list.

Getting a referral is a fabulous idea, but you still need to shop with two more lenders. And don't reveal to the referred loan officer until after your interest rate is locked in and you have a written lock confirmation. Then go ahead and give your friend credit. Please take this very seriously, because loan officers know that a referred client is a naive client who is not going to compare GFEs. If you call up and gush, "Meredith referred me to you. She said you were just wonderful, and I'm so happy you'll be able to help me too," you're sealing your fate to pay an extra junk fee and probably a quarter to a half percent more in rate as well. Articles in magazines for loan officers, as well as speakers and trainers, tell loan officers to concentrate on getting referrals, because a referred client is easier to work with and easier to make a bigger commission from. "A referred client is not shopping you," is what they say. "You can make more on the back end with referrals."

Personally, I did not charge my referred clients more, and neither do the other mortgage "stars" in the industry; in fact, we often try all the harder to get them a great deal. But how do you know which side of the fence your referred loan officer is on? You don't; therefore, you must still follow the short list plan.

If you're buying a house, your real estate agent may refer you to a loan officer. This referral may be one of your three. Never go to a referred lender exclusively, especially if he or she was referred by another professional in the business, because that professional is likely to get a kickback for referring you. (Yes, this is illegal, but it's common nonetheless. More on that later, in Chapter 15.)

Get a Specific Name

If you don't have the name of a specific loan officer, you'll need to get one. You don't want to be "the luck of the draw" for the person who happens to pick up the phone. If you don't have a name, call and ask. Here are two scripts you can use:

> What is your manager's name please? Thank you, may I speak with Mr. Big?

> Hello, Mr. Big, my name is Carolyn and I'm in the market for a zero-down loan. Can you recommend a loan officer who will give me a Good Faith Estimate to compare with the one I already have?

By stating you want a zero-down loan (or 5/1 ARM or Interest Only, or whatever), you let Mr. Big know he needs to give you a loan officer who's knowledgeable about that particular product. By saying you want a GFE to compare with one you already have, you let Mr. Big know he needs to give you a loan officer who will actually provide you with a GFE—and one that isn't too pricey. You sound like a serious shopper, so he won't think you're a waste of time. You aren't calling a ridiculously long list; you've said you're comparing it with *one* you already have. And, best of all, because the manager has referred you to one of his loan officers, that loan officer knows he better do a good job, because his manager will be asking him about it later.

If you have credit challenges, use the same approach as above, except say:

> My name is Carolyn, and I'm in the market to buy a house (or I'm looking to refinance). Can you refer me to a loan officer who has at least two years' experience in nonconforming loans (or subprime loans)?

The nonconforming/subprime loans are an entirely different ballgame from the loans for people with excellent credit. It's like comparing football to soccer. So you want to work with someone who has at least two years' experience with these type of loans.

Some loan officers don't do subprime loans and you'll get a denial right away. Others don't have experience, but they'd like to take a stab. The problem is that that stab is likely to end up right in your back when a "condition" pops up these novices don't have any experience in dealing with. Trust me, experience is everything in the subprime loan arena, because surprise conditions from underwriting pop up more often that not.

It's possible that the manager will offer to do your loan himself. If so, he can be one of the three on your short list. Don't be seduced by his title into thinking you don't need to compare three Good Faith Estimates. Being a manager or owner of a company does not mean you can get a lower rate from a wholesale lender. Some consumers think they'll get a cheaper loan from the manager, when the reverse is usually true, because a manager may put a higher price tag on his time than a loan officer.

Using an Internet Lender

Should you pick one of the online lenders as one of your three? Let's take Benjamin Franklin's advice and make a yes/no list.

Benefit	Local	Internet
Can you meet face to face to have your loan explained?	Yes	No
Can you go speak with the loan officer in person if an unresolved problem surfaces in the middle of the process?	Yes	No
Can your loan officer attend the loan signing with you, to help explain terms and assist with any errors that show up in the final loan documents?	Yes	No
Is the loan officer familiar with your local neighborhood home values?	Yes	Probably not
Does the loan officer have a relationship with your local escrow company or the attorney who will be signing your loan?	Yes	Probably not
Does the loan officer know your local property taxes and title fees?	Yes	Probably not
Does the loan officer have a local wholesale account executive who will visit in person and help address any challenges?	Yes	No

Are loans from the Internet cheaper? Not necessarily. I recommend using your local loan officer, for the reasons above. At the least, he or she should be in your own state, because every state has its own quirks when it comes to lending. If your loan officer is in an office in California and you're in Pennsylvania, he or she may not be familiar with your state stamp tax, because West Coast states don't have that. He or she may think buying a unit in a four-plex is a "unique property" and risky, because it's not common in California as it is on Long Island.

When an Internet company collects your application online, how do you know if it's really a lender or just a *lead generation company*? That's right, some of them merely collect your application to sell to mortgage brokers. This includes that big Internet company mentioned previously—it sells leads and does loans, so it can make money both ways. When mortgage brokers buy leads, they have to make up for that cost somehow, and it's no small cost. Who do you think is going to pay an extra $1,200 in junk fees to cover the cost of buying your application from the lead generation company? You, of course.

Mystery Shopping Internet versus Local Lenders

I did some loan "mystery shopping" of my own when I was preparing to write this book. I shopped both local and Internet companies. For my first Internet loan, I clicked on one of those appealing pop-up ads. Soon after, I received a call from a loan officer who agreed to send me a Good Faith Estimate. It was the worst! For one thing, he estimated my title fee approximately three times higher than it should be. All local loan officers were within $50 of each other, but this guy was $800 off! It was because he was on the East Coast and had no idea of title fees in Washington State. But wait, it gets worse. For all the other fees, he sloppily put $1,000 on one line and left all the rest blank. He left the interest rate blank. Was he lazy? Did he think I was too stupid to notice? Or did he think this approach gave him a competitive edge? Take a look at the GFE in Figure 2.1 and you'll see what I mean.

Naturally, I had to mystery shop another Internet lender—one that advertises "you'll be the winner when banks fight over you." The slogan is brilliant, but the truth is, every mortgage broker can let banks "fight over you." That's the virtual definition of a mortgage broker—they shop competing wholesale lenders for you. It's their job. It's what they're all about. So don't think that this one big national broker/lender has an advantage over your local mortgage broker. At the end of the day, they all get their money from the same places.

I'll share more loan mystery shopping experiences in Chapters 4 and 5, but I can say now that I did not find any financial advantage to using Internet lenders, and I strongly prefer using a local lender who can help you out, face to face and be there at your signing to handle any last-minute surprises.

GOOD FAITH ESTIMATE

Applicants: Carolyn Warren
Property Addr:
Prepared By:

Application No:
Date Prepared:
Loan Program: **AM100**

The information provided below reflects estimates of the charges which you are likely to incur at the settlement of your loan. The fees listed are estimates-actual charges may be more or less. Your transaction may not involve a fee for every item listed. The numbers listed beside the estimates generally correspond to the numbered lines contained in the HUD-1 settlement statement which you will be receiving at settlement. The HUD-1 settlement statement will show you the actual cost for items paid at settlement.

Total Loan Amount: $ 300,000   Interest Rate: (%)   Term: 360 / 360 mths

800	ITEMS PAYABLE IN CONNECTION WITH LOAN:	PFC S F POC
801	Loan Origination Fee	$
802	Loan Discount	
803	Appraisal Fee	
804	Credit Report	
805	Lender's Inspection Fee	
808	Mortgage Broker Fee	
809	Tax Related Service Fee	
810	Processing Fee	
811	Underwriting Fee	
812	Wire Transfer Fee	
	Application Fee	1,000.00 ✓

No Interest Rate disclosed!

The Loan Officer failed to itemize fees, which will no doubt be added at closing.

This sloppy GFE came via that big Internet Lender.

1100	TITLE CHARGES:	PFC S F POC
1101	Closing or Escrow Fee	$ 350.00
1105	Document Preparation Fee	
1106	Notary Fees	85.00
1107	Attorney Fees	
1108	Title Insurance	1,383.00

Should be about $500, but the Internet Lender didn't know title for my state.

1200	GOVERNMENT RECORDING & TRANSFER CHARGES:	PFC S F POC
1201	Recording Fees:	$ 75.00
1202	City/County Tax/Stamps:	
1203	State Tax/Stamps:	

1300	ADDITIONAL SETTLEMENT CHARGES:	PFC S F POC
1302	Pest Inspection	$

		Estimated Closing Costs	2,893.00

900	ITEMS REQUIRED BY LENDER TO BE PAID IN ADVANCE:		PFC S F POC
901	Interest for	3 days @ $ per day	$
902	Mortgage Insurance Premium		
903	Hazard Insurance Premium		
904			
905	VA Funding Fee		

1000	RESERVES DEPOSITED WITH LENDER:			PFC S F POC
1001	Hazard Insurance Premiums	months @ $	per month	$
1002	Mortgage Ins. Premium Reserves	months @ $ 175.00	per month	
1003	School Tax	months @ $	per month	
1004	Taxes and Assessment Reserves	months @ $	per month	
1005	Flood Insurance Reserves	months @ $	per month	
		months @ $	per month	
		months @ $	per month	

		Estimated Prepaid Items/Reserves	
	TOTAL ESTIMATED SETTLEMENT CHARGES		2,893.00

Look at this! He manually changed the standard GFE form to delete "Compensation to Broker" — Hiding the YSP!

TOTAL ESTIMATED FUNDS NEEDED TO CLOSE:				TOTAL ESTIMATED MONTHLY PAYMENT:	
Purchase Price/Payoff (+)	300,000.00	New First Mortgage (-)		Principal & Interest	833.33
Loan Amount (-)	300,000.00	Sub Financing (-)		Other Financing (P & I)	
Est. Closing Costs (+)	2,893.00	New 2nd Mtg Closing Costs (+)		Hazard Insurance	
Est. Prepaid Items/Reserves (+)	0.00			Real Estate Taxes	
Amount Paid by Seller (-)				Mortgage Insurance	175.00
				Homeowner Assn. Dues	
				Other	

Total Est. Funds needed to close	2,893.00	Total Monthly Payment	1,008.33

These estimates are provided pursuant to the Real Estate Settlement Procedures Act of 1974, as amended (RESPA). Additional information can be found in the HUD Special Information Booklet, which is to be provided to you by your mortgage broker or lender, if your application is to purchase residential real property and the lender will take a first lien on the property. The undersigned acknowledges receipt of the booklet "Settlement Costs," and if applicable the Consumer Handbook on ARM Mortgages.

Applicant   Carolyn Warren   Date   Applicant   Date

Calyx Form gfe2.frm 11/01

Figure 2.1

Big National Lenders versus Local Lenders

Whether you go to a large national bank like Wells Fargo or a small, local mortgage company called Neighborhood Smiley Loans it doesn't matter. Neighborhood Smiley Loans can shop the wholesale division of Wells Fargo Bank, as well as hundreds of others. The more critical issue is the individual person who will be working with you. Is he or she honest, and do you communicate well with him or her?

Listen to Your Instincts

If you have a hunch that something isn't right with any of the three lenders on your short list, then don't work with them. All too often I've heard people lament, "I had a feeling something wasn't right," and sure enough, it wasn't. For example:

- If they don't want to give you a written Good Faith Estimate, they're off your short list.
- If they want cash or your credit card number up front, they're off your short list.
- If they talk a million words a minute and you can't understand anything they're saying, they're not the right match for you.

Also consider these factors: Do they answer your questions to your satisfaction? Are they happy to give you the loan you want, or are they trying to talk you into taking a risky loan you're not sure about? (For example, if you can afford to pay both principal and interest, why should they push you into taking Interest Only, which costs you more in the long run?)

You have to feel comfortable with the person who's going to handle the financing on the biggest purchase of your life. You can't wait until you get to the signing table to act on your instincts. By then, you're in a time crunch, and it's stressful. So, you're going to choose a loan officer you have a good rapport with.

Coming Up

Before you can ask for a Good Faith Estimate, you need to know the type of loan you want. This is one of the critical decisions you'll make about your financing. Chapter 3 gives you the lowdown on loan types, plain and simple.

Step 3:
Choose the Right
Type of Loan for
Your Situation

This chapter is designed to be a resource for selecting the right loan for you, whether that means a 15- or 30-year fixed rate, Adjustable Rate, Interest Only, or other. This information may not be as thrilling as a crime scene investigation, but it could prevent your finances from getting murdered, so it's worth taking the time to read through it carefully. You can skip around to the sections that interest you, just be sure to check out these three:

1. Risky Loans
2. Prepayment Penalties, Good and Bad
3. Biweekly Mortgage Savings: Bargain or Rip-Off?

Types of Loans

I'll begin by briefly defining the various types of loans.

30-Year Fixed Rate

With this loan, the interest rate is fixed, meaning your principal and interest payment do not change. The loan pays off in 30 years.

Take this loan if: You plan to keep the loan for more than five years and you're happy with the interest rate for the long term. If you're conservative and want the security of knowing your payment will never change, you'll like the fixed rate. (Your property taxes may increase, but that is independent of your loan.)

15-Year Fixed Rate

The interest rate for this loan type, too, is fixed, so your principal and interest payment do not change. The loan pays off in half the time as the traditional 30-year fixed, netting you huge savings in interest payments.

Take this loan if: Retirement is in sight and you want to own your house free and clear, or if you can afford the higher payments and want to save tens of thousands of dollars in interest. (This loan is my personal choice.)

40-Year or 45-Year Fixed Rate

Here, too, the interest rate is fixed, so your principal and interest payment do not change. However, these long-term loans have been less popular than the 30-year fixed rate, because time is the borrower's—your— enemy. The longer you stretch out your payments, the more you lose in interest costs.

Take this loan if: This is your only option for getting a start in real estate and you're not stretching price to get a bigger house than what you really need. Also, consider the 30-year fixed Interest Only loan before you decide. As an example, take a look at the two Truth-in-Lending forms in Figures 3.1 and 3.2. You'll notice that the homebuyer pays $207,391 more on the 40-year loan than on the 30-year loan. What could you buy with that much money if you don't blow it on extra interest?

Adjustable Rate Mortgage (ARM)

There are a variety of adjustable rates to choose from. Popular choices are the 3/1 ARM and 5/1 ARM. These loans are fixed for the first three

TRUTH-IN-LENDING DISCLOSURE STATEMENT
(THIS IS NEITHER A CONTRACT NOR A COMMITMENT TO LEND)

Applicants: **CAROLYN WARREN**   Prepared By:

Property Address:

Application No: **WARREN 30 YR FX**   Date Prepared:

ANNUAL PERCENTAGE RATE	FINANCE CHARGE	AMOUNT FINANCED	TOTAL OF PAYMENTS
The cost of your credit as a yearly rate	The dollar amount the credit will cost you	The amount of credit provided to you or on your behalf	The amount you will have paid after making all payments as scheduled
* 6.905 %	$ * 433,115.97	$ * 314,072.00	$ * 747,187.97

☐ REQUIRED DEPOSIT: The annual percentage rate does not take into account your required deposit
PAYMENTS: Your payment schedule will be:

Number of Payments	Amount of Payments **	When Payments Are Due	Number of Payments	Amount of Payments **	When Payments Are Due	Number of Payments	Amount of Payments **	When Payments Are Due
		Monthly Beginning			Monthly Beginning			Monthly Beginning
359	2,075.51	07/01/2006						
1	2,079.88	06/01/2036						

360 months = 30 year loan

This figure is $954,518 on the 40-year loan. $207,391 more!

☐ DEMAND FEATURE: This obligation has a demand feature.
☐ VARIABLE RATE FEATURE: This loan contains a variable rate feature. A variable rate disclosure has been provided earlier.
30 YEAR FIXED

CREDIT LIFE/CREDIT DISABILITY: Credit life insurance and credit disability insurance are not required to obtain credit, and will not be provided unless you sign and agree to pay the additional cost.

Type	Premium		Signature
Credit Life	N/A	I want credit life insurance.	Signature:
Credit Disability	N/A	I want credit disability insurance.	Signature:
Credit Life and Disability	N/A	I want credit life and disability insurance	Signature:

INSURANCE: The following insurance is required to obtain credit:
☐ Credit life insurance ☐ Credit disability ☑ Property insurance ☐ Flood insurance
You may obtain the insurance from anyone you want that is acceptable to creditor
☐ If you purchase ☑ property ☐ flood insurance from creditor you will pay $ for a one year term.
SECURITY   You are giving a security interest in: **1007 WALL ST., BELLEVUE WA 98004**
☑ The goods or property being purchased   ☐ Real property you already own.
FILING FEES: $ **30.00**
LATE CHARGE: If a payment is more than **15 days** late, you will be charged **6.000 %** of the payment
PREPAYMENT: If you pay off early, you
☐ may ☑ will not have to pay a penalty.
☐ may ☑ will not be entitled to a refund of part of the finance charge.
ASSUMPTION: Someone buying your property
☐ may ☐ may, subject to conditions ☑ may not assume the remainder of your loan on the original terms.
See your contract documents for any additional information about nonpayment, default, any required repayment in full before the scheduled date and prepayment refunds and penalties
☑ * means an estimate ☑ all dates and numerical disclosures except the late payment disclosures are estimates.

* * NOTE: The Payments shown above include reserve deposits for Mortgage Insurance (if applicable), but exclude Property Taxes and Insurance.

THE UNDERSIGNED ACKNOWLEDGES RECEIVING A COMPLETED COPY OF THIS DISCLOSURE.

CAROLYN WARREN	(Applicant)	(Date)		(Applicant)	(Date)
	(Applicant)	(Date)		(Applicant)	(Date)
	(Lender)	(Date)			

Calyx Form - til.hp (02/95)

Figure 3.1

TRUTH-IN-LENDING DISCLOSURE STATEMENT
(THIS IS NEITHER A CONTRACT NOR A COMMITMENT TO LEND)

Applicants: **CAROLYN WARREN**   Prepared By:

Property Address:

Application No: **WARREN 40 YEAR**   Date Prepared.

ANNUAL PERCENTAGE RATE	FINANCE CHARGE	AMOUNT FINANCED	TOTAL OF PAYMENTS
The cost of your credit as a yearly rate	The dollar amount the credit will cost you	The amount of credit provided to you or on your behalf	The amount you will have paid after making all payments as scheduled
* 7.136 %	$ * 640,479.73	$ * 314,038.67	$ 954,518.40

☐ REQUIRED DEPOSIT: The annual percentage rate does not take into account your required deposit
PAYMENTS: Your payment schedule will be:

Number of Payments	Amount of Payments **	When Payments Are Due	Number of Payments	Amount of Payments **	When Payments Are Due	Number of Payments	Amount of Payments **	When Payments Are Due
		Monthly Beginning			Monthly Beginning			Monthly Beginning
480	1,988.58	07/01/2006						

[handwritten] 480 months = 40 year loan

[handwritten] This figure is $747,187 on the 30-year loan. Save $207,391 !

☐ DEMAND FEATURE: This obligation has a demand feature.
☐ VARIABLE RATE FEATURE: This loan contains a variable rate feature. A variable rate disclosure has been provided earlier.
40 YEAR FIXED

CREDIT LIFE/CREDIT DISABILITY: Credit life insurance and credit disability insurance are not required to obtain credit, and will not be provided unless you sign and agree to pay the additional cost.

Type	Premium	Signature	
Credit Life	N/A	I want credit life insurance.	Signature:
Credit Disability	N/A	I want credit disability insurance.	Signature:
Credit Life and Disability	N/A	I want credit life and disability insurance.	Signature:

INSURANCE: The following insurance is required to obtain credit:
☐ Credit life insurance ☐ Credit disability ☑ Property insurance ☐ Flood insurance
You may obtain the insurance from anyone you want that is acceptable to creditor
☐ If you purchase ☑ property ☐ flood insurance from creditor you will pay $ for a one year term.
SECURITY: You are giving a security interest in: **1007 WALL ST., BELLEVUE WA 98004**
☑ The goods or property being purchased   ☐ Real property you already own.
FILING FEES: $ **30.00**
LATE CHARGE: If a payment is more than **15** days late, you will be charged   **6.000** % of the payment
PREPAYMENT: If you pay off early, you
☐ may ☑ will not have to pay a penalty.
☐ may ☑ will not be entitled to a refund of part of the finance charge.
ASSUMPTION: Someone buying your property
☐ may ☐ may, subject to conditions ☑ may not assume the remainder of your loan on the original terms.
See your contract documents for any additional information about nonpayment, default, any required repayment in full before the scheduled date and prepayment refunds and penalties
☑ * means an estimate   ☑ all dates and numerical disclosures except the late payment disclosures are estimates.

* * NOTE: The Payments shown above include reserve deposits for Mortgage Insurance (if applicable), but exclude Property Taxes and Insurance.

THE UNDERSIGNED ACKNOWLEDGES RECEIVING A COMPLETED COPY OF THIS DISCLOSURE.

CAROLYN WARREN   (Applicant)   (Date)   (Applicant)   (Date)

                         (Applicant)   (Date)   (Applicant)   (Date)

                         (Lender)   (Date)

Calyx Form - til.hp (02/95)

Figure 3.2

or five years, respectively, and then adjust every one year thereafter. There is also a 7/1 ARM and a 10/1 ARM.

Pay attention to the terms of the adjustments. What is the start rate? What is the maximum cap it can go to? How much can it adjust in a year? Is there a prepayment penalty? Ask your loan officer to point out these terms on your Good Faith Estimate and Truth-in-Lending forms. (Working with a local loan officer will enable you to go over the numbers in person, so you understand it all.) Be sure you read it in writing for yourself, because verbal quotes mean nothing.

Take this loan if: You plan to stay in your house for only a few years. These loans have a lower interest rate than the 30-year fixed. Why pay more? When taking an ARM, pay as few points and as low fees as possible. A short-term loan does not warrant paying a lot up front. If rates are high, take an ARM and refinance when rates come down. These loans are a good choice for many people. I highly recommend them for young couples buying a starter home.

Balloon Loan

This loan has a fixed rate and your payment is calculated over 30 years, but you get a lower interest rate than with the 30-year fixed. The "catch" is the balloon payment. After the agreed-upon time, the entire balance is due. (It may be 3 years, 5 years, or 10 years.) So you have to pay off this large lump sum by refinancing or selling the house (unless you came into a lot of money and have the cash).

Take this loan if: You plan to keep your mortgage for a short time and the current market gives you a better deal with this loan than with the ARM. For example, some years, the 5/1 ARM has a lower rate; other years, the balloon loan has a lower rate, so you have to compare the two. Also consider the likelihood that you'll want to sell or refinance. With the balloon loan, you're forced to do so, but with the ARM, you could go ahead and keep the loan with the adjusted payments without being forced to incur refinancing costs if you do decide to stay longer.

2/28 and 3/27 "Fixed Rate" Adjustable Loans

These are nonconforming (subprime) loans designed to be temporary. The rates are fixed for the first 2 or 3 years, and then are adjustable for the remaining years to pay off in 30. Some loan officers call them "Band-Aid loans," because people use them to get a house when they have "wounded" credit. The plan is to improve your credit so you can refinance when the prepayment penalty expires, and the rate adjusts upward. These loans have a prepayment penalty, but you have the option to buy down the penalty to one year or to buy it out altogether.

These loans are ARMs, but loan officers sell them by calling them "fixed for two years and then adjusts." That's why I've written the heading as I did. It's laughable, I know, and loan officers enjoy chuckling about it.

Take this loan if: You want to invest in real estate now and let your equity build while you clean up your credit. Be aware of your obligation with the prepayment penalty and be willing to keep the loan that long. The prepayment penalties are steep, so you should avoid paying them. For some people, buying down the prepay penalty to one year is a wise choice; usually you need to keep your loan that long before you can refinance anyway. When these subprime loans turn adjustable, the rates can go up suddenly and continue to adjust upward every six months. They are not designed for the long term. Most people refinance out of them as soon as the initial two or three years are over. It's extremely important to establish perfect credit so you'll be ready to refinance into a better conventional loan by the time the 2/28 or 3/27 turns into an adjustable.

Interest-Only Loans

Interest-Only (IO) loans are potentially dangerous in some situations but make sense in others. I'll explain so you can decide whether an IO is for you. An IO loan lets you make a smaller payment, because you pay only the interest due and nothing on the principal balance. This means after five years, your loan balance will be the same as it was on the day it opened. The interest-only payment period usually lasts for either 5 or 10 years. After that time, it becomes fully amortized, so your loan still pays off in 30 years. (It is not a negative amortization loan where the balance goes up.)

 Some financial advisors fear Interest-Only loans set up the homeowner for a possible foreclosure.

When the IO period ends, your payment will go up, perhaps drastically. If you had a 10-year IO, then you have to pay off your original balance within the next 20 years. Paying off your mortgage in 20 years rather than 30 years gives you a significantly higher payment. If your loan turns into an adjustable rate so the interest rate goes up as well, watch out. You could be in for a real payment shock.

Subprime lenders have a 2/28 Interest-Only loan. This is where you get a lower fixed rate for the first two years (with a two-year pre-payment penalty) and get to pay interest only for the first five years. So, after two years, your payment will go up, because it turns into an adjustable rate (but still interest only). After five years, you have to start paying down the balance. This loan is allowed with zero-down payment, so you get 100 percent financing.

Let's say you buy a house for $250,000. After five years, you'll still owe $250,000 and your payment will go up by several hundred dollars per month. What if you can no longer make the payments and need to sell? If you live in an area where the value has appreciated to $300,000, then you have no problem. But if you live in an area where the value has appreciated to only $260,000, then you have a serious problem, because $10,000 is not enough to cover your closing and selling costs, including real estate fees. You will have to bring in cash to the closing table in order to sell.

If you take a zero-down, IO loan, you will not be able to refinance unless the home has a significant increase in value.

If your value has remained flat, then you're in even more trouble. In that case, you don't even have enough equity to refinance without bringing in cash. Then your only choices are to find a way to make the new, bigger payments, or to let the house go back to your bank and ruin your credit with a foreclosure on your record.

If you're taking a zero-down loan, be cautious about an Interest-Only loan. You must know your market. You don't want to get stuck in a financial situation you can't handle. However, if you live in a city where prices are so high, and rising by the minute, and that IO is the only way you can afford to get a start in real estate, it can make good sense. You buy your $700,000 starter home, make the payments affordable with IO, and in five years sell for $1.2 million. You made a smart move, coming out ahead.

It's precisely this market that has made IO loans so popular. In the mid-1990s, almost no one considered an IO loan; but by 2004, the national average had risen to 31.4 percent, and it has climbed higher since then.

> You always pay more in the long run with an Interest-Only loan.

Lenders do not offer IO just to be nice. They offer it because it gives them two financial advantages: (1) They can get *more* loans and *bigger* loans when people who do not qualify for a traditional loan take IO, and (2) they make more money on an IO loan in the long run. You pay more for your house with an Interest-Only loan than on a loan where you pay down the balance every month.

On a $300,000 loan at 6.75 percent, 30-year fixed rate compared with a 7 percent IO, 30-year fixed rate, you would pay an extra $55,532 with the IO loan if you keep it for 30 years. (Most lenders charge an extra .25 percent on your interest rate if you choose IO.)

✐ NOTE

You can compare payments by looking at the box that reads "Total of Payments" on the Truth-in-Lending Disclosure Statements shown in Figures 3.1 and 3.2. ✎

Some loan officers argue that most people don't keep their loans for 30 years; but this in itself is not justification for taking an IO loan. If you keep your IO loan for the 10 years of the IO period, you'll still come out behind. Using the same example above, you'll pay an extra $13,700 in interest payments; furthermore, you'll give up almost $34,000 in equity, because you haven't paid down the balance.

If you can afford the standard principal and interest payment, that's your safer and cheaper choice, but study your own market to make your own decision.

Risky Loans

You are cordially invited to play Russian roulette with your finances. If you care to take a spin and pull the trigger, the following are your choices.

High Debt-Ratio Loans. It's easy to become infatuated with a fabulous home, but your crush will not turn into lasting love if you find yourself strapped with payments that are too high. How far should you stretch yourself? Some lenders will allow you to have monthly expenses that reach 55 percent of your gross income.

 Looking at houses before you've set your budget is a common mistake that leads to disappointment or to making a foolish buying decision.

Taking a loan with a 55 percent debt ratio is only justified when it's not your *true* debt ratio. For example, some people look as if they have a 55 percent debt ratio on their loan application; but in reality, it's much lower, due to the nature of their self-employed business or because they have a partner with a good income who's not on the application. These are the people whom the high-ratio loan is for—not the W-2 wage earner with no real extra income.

Stated Income Loan. The Stated Income loan (a.k.a. "liar's" loan) can be financial death waiting to happen under the wrong circumstances. This loan, formally called *No Income Verification* or *Stated Income,* allows you to state whatever income you like on your application, and the lender accepts it on blind faith (as long as it sounds reasonable for your job title). That gives you a lot of leeway, especially since the lender doesn't verify that your stated job title is even your real job title.

Let's say you work in a restaurant, busing tables, and make $2,000 a month. Then you find this amazing house, and you need more income to qualify. On the loan application, you can call yourself a "senior manager" and state your income as $4,800 a month. The lender will call the restaurant and ask, "Is John Doe an employee of your restaurant?" But he or she won't ask if you're really a senior manager or what your income is. That's the danger of the liar's loan. You can buy a house you don't qualify for, just as long as your credit score is sufficient and you've saved a little in your bank account. (A bank may require that you have a score of 700-plus and six months' of payments in reserves, but a subprime lender may require a score of just 680 and only two months' reserves.)

Nonprime loans are easier to qualify for, but they have a higher interest rate.

But what happens if you can't afford the payments and have to choose between eating and paying the mortgage? What if you thought your girlfriend was going to pitch in, but she changes her mind and moves away? You could find yourself wishing you'd never lied and taken that expensive loan.

With that warning clearly understood, I will say there is a legitimate place for the Stated Income loan. It's a good program for the people who are *not* lying about their incomes but need leeway on paperwork. A perfect example is the self-employed person who has plenty of money but shows too many deductions on his or her tax returns and splits his or her cash flow between too many bank accounts to qualify with documentation.

Because Stated Income loans are riskier to the lender, they have a higher interest rate to offset the risk. Therefore, you don't want to take this option if you could just as well document your income.

Lazy loan officers will put a homebuyer into a Stated Income loan simply because they don't feel like asking for or handling your W-2 and pay stubs. I asked one loan officer why she put *all* her clients into an Stated Income loan. She said, "It's usually only .25 percent higher, so why not?" (Although sometimes it was .5 percent higher.) Another loan officer confessed that he put his clients into the Stated Income loan because, "It's easier for *me*."

I think it's unfair for mortgage professionals to charge a person a higher interest rate just because they don't feel like doing the extra work. It should always be the consumer's choice.

When I was doing my "mystery loan shopping," one loan officer suggested I take a Stated Income loan because I'm self-employed, even though I told him I could fully document my income. "Go ahead and take the Stated Income loan. It's only an eighth of a percent higher," he said.

Sound good? But wait. The wholesale lender he was using offered "No Income Verification" without an increase in interest rate for people who had: (1) a high credit score and (2) a large down payment. Since I had both, I qualified. So this loan officer was suggesting that I take (a) a Stated Income loan when I could easily verify my income, and (b) bumping up the interest rate needlessly to increase his yield spread premium (YSP) commission. The "takeaway" here is that you should not take a Stated Income loan unless you truly need it *and* can afford the payments.

Interest-Only Liar's Loans.   If you overstate your income *and* take an Interest-Only loan *and* put zero down, you've got three layers of risk: (1) no income verification (your true debt ratio may be too high), (2) no reduction of your loan balance, and (3) no equity.

In the wrong market, the "zero-down, stated-income, interest-only loan" will be the bullet that kills your finances and your credit. There's no mystery to that.

Loans That Should Be Illegal

Certain loans have been called toxic, because they'll kill your financial future. You must be careful of a loan that:

- Has a lot of legalese you don't understand.
- Has a special repayment formula.
- Does not require a payment until after you sell your house.
- Is from a "hard money" finance company (i.e., specializes in loans for people who cannot qualify elsewhere and are "hard up for money"). Typically, these loans are very pricey.

Imagine taking a $30,000 loan for home improvements and then finding out that you owe $127,000 five years later. That's exactly what happened to a 57-year-old woman whose loan officer told her she wouldn't have to pay back anything until she sold her home. That sounded pretty good at the time. Too bad the loan shark didn't explain the "pledged value interest" feature that cost her $92,698. The loan officer told her it was "standard loan disclosure legalese" and that she didn't need to read every "boring paragraph." That kind of talk is a red flag in itself.

One weird loan has a clause that says one late payment will put your loan into default status (meaning the lender can start foreclosure proceedings to take your house) and instantly raise your interest rate by up to 5 percent. This isn't normal. This is why you must read your Loan Note, to find out what the terms of default are. Every loan contract spells it out. Normally, default doesn't happen until you are 90 days past due.

Credit Life Insurance.   Although credit life insurance is an add-on to a loan, I didn't want to leave it out because it's a rip-off that comes along with some mortgages. Often, they don't even bother to tell you about it ahead of time. You just see it on your documents when you go to sign, then they'll gloss over it, saying it "protects you in case anything should happen."

If you die, credit life insurance pays off your loan; but the fact is, few people ever use it, so its main function is to boost to the lender's profits. It could easily cost you $7,000 to $40,000 or more, and chances are, you'll refinance out of the loan long before you leave this earth. If you want life insurance, you can find much better deals elsewhere, so I suggest you refuse to sign loan papers that include credit life insurance.

"Pick-a-Payment" Option ARM.   How can lenders advertise a rate of 2 or 3 percent when the market is 6.5 percent-plus?

Notice how they say, "On a $500,000 mortgage, your payment will be just $1,931," and you're thinking, "Wow, I could get into a half-million dollar house!" Then you start thinking about what it would feel like to own two stories on an acre and have a fabulous master suite with a Jacuzzi bath. The more you think about it, the more you get your heart set on this fabulous house with a low, low payment.

How is this possible? Lenders are advertising the start rate for the Option ARM. "Option" because you get four payment options with your billing statement, and ARM because it's an Adjustable Rate Mortgage.

The trick to this super low rate is that it is a temporary, introductory rate that does not include all the interest due. Rates are not at 2 percent, and they cannot offer you a 2 percent loan; but they can let you *pay* just 2 percent now and *owe the rest later.* What you owe for later is tacked on to your loan balance, so each month that you pay just 2 percent, your loan balance actually goes *up.* This is called *negative amortization,* meaning the amount you owe is going up, not down.

Naturally, they can't let you pay partial interest and let your balance keep going up forever, or they'd lose a ton of money. So this seductive advertised rate is like a teaser.

44

He Listened to His Conscience and Quit!

I had a telephone conversation with a young man who quit the finance company he worked for because he couldn't sell its loan products with a good conscience—such as its line of credit with a 21.99 percent rate. At first, he didn't realize how toxic the loans were; all he knew was that he was making $120,000 a year doing what management told him to do, and he didn't even have a high school diploma. Sweet.

Not one homeowner asked to read a Good Faith Estimate before they agreed to the loan. They were too focused on getting cash in their hands.

He wasn't aware of the way the loans worked, and neither were the customers he sold. He never sent out a Good Faith Estimate or Truth-in-Lending form, as required by Federal law. He simply focused his customers on the bimonthly payments without looking at the whole picture. He sold loans that were so pricey they violated Regulation Z, Section 32, which places limits on loan profits, but he never had a single person object. The only thing his clients cared about was how quickly they could refinance and get their cash. Eventually, he realized what he was doing to his clients, and he got out.

"I had to get myself back to honesty," were his exact words.

I asked him why he was willing to come forward with this information. Here's what he said, sounding both remorseful and sad: "I'm trying to redeem myself after what I did."

I actually felt sorry for the guy.

The Pick-a-Payment loan is only for people who know how to invest their money wisely.

When this loan first came out, it was dubbed "the wealthy man's loan," because the concept was that a wealthy "man" would choose to make the minimal payment on his million-dollar home while he invested his

Don't Make These Four Mistakes!

One time I was called to a mortgage office to notarize a refinance loan for a middle-aged couple on a modest income. They were taking the Option ARM so they could get cash out and have a lower payment as well. I saw what they were doing and it made me sick. These people needed to keep their current loan so they'd own their house free and clear for retirement. Instead, they were making four big mistakes: (1) stripping their house of equity with cash-out, (2) starting over on the life of their loan when their retirement years were in sight, (3) going into a negative amortization loan that could take 40 years to pay off, and (4) taking an adjustable-rate feature that could make their payment much higher than what they had now. But they didn't get it. All they saw was their initial low payment and the big check that would soon be in their hands—and that's exactly what their loan shark (disguised as a caring loan officer) focused on.

I was squirming in my seat during the signing. It was all I could do to keep my mouth shut (which was my job—to keep my mouth shut and notarize signatures). But then, right in the middle of the signing, the husband's cell phone rang. It was another loan officer from a different company.

The husband told the loan officer on the phone that he'd decided not to take his loan, because he was signing for this other loan instead, a wonderful loan that had a 2 percent rate. The conversation went on for some time, and I could tell there was something of an argument going on. When he hung up, he explained.

"That was Jim from such-and-such company. He told me not to take this loan, because it's dangerous," he said.

The loan shark rolled her eyes and pulled a face.

"Yeah, I know," the husband scoffed. "I'm saving $400 a month, and he tells me it's dangerous."

The loan shark replied, "He's just jealous that he's not getting your business."

"Yeah, that's right. He tried to tell me my payment could go way up and that I could lose my house to the bank. That's not true, is it?"

The loan shark replied, "Do you plan to make your monthly payments?"

"Yes, we always make our payments on time."

"Okay then, the bank can't take your house. They can only do that if you completely stop paying them."

"That's what I thought," he said, looking pleased with himself. It never occurred to him that maybe he wouldn't have the income to make the payments if they rose to the cap of 19 percent.

Then they had a laugh together about the loan officer who tried to warn the couple about this *wonderful* loan—someone even called him stupid for suggesting it wasn't a fantastic option for this couple on a modest fixed income and virtually no savings. Perhaps this "jealous, stupid" loan officer was really their guardian angel in disguise.

After the signing was done and I had notarized their signatures, the shark swam off to make copies for the people, so I was left alone in the room with them.

The husband said, "I know we'll never own our house, but who cares? With payments this low, the bank is losing out!" Then he chuckled with glee.

I said, "What will you do if your payment goes up? I saw that the lifetime cap was 19 percent. Those low payments aren't going to last."

"Oh, I'm not worried about that. Our loan officer told us she'd refinance our loan for us again if we needed her to."

Yes, I'm sure she would. Another refinance would mean another commission.

The frustrating thing for me is that some people insist on making a bad decision. This man's knight in shining armor had called on his cell just in time to rescue him, but he refused to be rescued. He wanted to believe the fairy tale.

It's a free country, and you have the right to be taken advantage of if you so choose.

money in a market that would give him a higher return. Then he'd take his earnings and pay off his mortgage in one fell swoop before his rate went too high. It was seen as a financial strategy a person who had money to invest could use. Unfortunately, people without money or financial wisdom were conned into taking the loan that was all wrong for them.

One savvy investor reported that he has an Option ARM with a 10 percent maximum deferred interest window before it recalculates into a Principal-and-Interest loan. The first year, he deferred $9,500 in interest. He invested $7,700 of that and realized a 12 percent gain. In his neighborhood, property values appreciated by 18 percent. Clearly, his mortgage/investment plan worked out exceptionally well. Not everyone has his expertise or his luck.

Now that the price of housing has continued to rise, the Option ARM has stopped being called the wealthy man's loan and has become a popular choice for many people who are seeking any way possible to get a start in real estate. There are times and locations where it does make sense, so it's not always a rip-off. My protest is about the loan officers who sell it to people who don't understand the loan terms or see the whole picture. If they think they're "taking advantage of the bank," then the joke is on them. It's foolish to think a lender is not going to profit on your loan. They're in business to make a profit, and they're very good at what they do.

Many variations of the Option ARM exist now, so if you're considering this, you need to shop around. Popular choices are called Pick-a-Payment Loan, CashFlow Option Loan, and Pay Option ARM.

How Does the Option ARM Work? Typically, when you get your billing statement each month, you have four choices for making your payment, and it's this flexibility that's stressed as a selling point of the Option ARM:

1. Minimum payment (Your balance will go up.)

2. Interest-only payment (Your balance will stay the same.)

3. Fully amortized, 30-year payment (Your balance will go down.)

4. 15-year payment (Your balance will reduce faster.)

Ten Questions to Ask When You're Shopping for an Option ARM. When you're considering an Option ARM, you need to be aware of the important terms. Be sure you get answers to the following questions:

1. *How long does that low start rate last?* It may be for one year, six months, three months, or just one month.

2. *How often can the rate adjust?* You should be aware that the rate may go up even while your minimum payment remains the same. In this case, the balance you owe rises faster.

3. *What is the index?* You can check the historic stability of the index your loan is based on. It may be based on London InterBank Offered Rate (LIBOR), Cost of Funds Index (COFI), Cost of Savings Index (COSI), or Monthly Treasury Average (MTA).

4. *What is the margin?* (Very important!) *Also, what is the margin for par?* When your payment adjusts, it will be determined by the index plus the margin. The lender and the individual loan officer may set the margin.

✐ WARNING
One way loan officers increase their back-end commission (yield spread premium) is by putting a big, fat margin on your loan. This increases profitability for lenders, so they pay the loan officer more for a higher margin. One loan officer made a $30,400 commission by getting a 4 percent back-end commission! He did that by putting a putting a high margin on an Option ARM loan. I'm sure the interest rate looked fabulous to the consumer, but I'm wondering if he noticed the margin. One thing for sure is that he could have gotten a lower margin and a better deal by shopping around. Fortunately, not all loan officers are so greedy that they want to make 30 grand off you. ✎

5. *What is the minimum payment cap?* On most Option ARMs, your minimum payment option can change by plus or minus 7.5 percent.

6. *What is the negative amortization cap?* This limits the loss of equity on your home. Just how high can your balance go? Usually it is between 110 to 125 percent of the original loan amount. Once you reach that number, you can't make the minimum payment anymore, so your payment is guaranteed to rise sharply.

7. *What is the lifetime interest rate cap?* What is the maximum your rate can go? (Prepare to be shocked.)

8. *What is the highest your payment can go?* You must not overlook this. Ask, because it probably won't be volunteered. On one Option ARM offered by a big bank, the payment on a $300,000 loan could vary from about $830 to $2,000 per month. Quite a variation. And this was with a low margin of 2.45 percent. Many loans have higher margins, so you must pay particular attention to this.

9. *What is the payment recast period? Recasting* means recalculating your loan payment. Recasting your loan is a way to limit negative

amortization and keep your loan on the original payoff schedule. Option ARM loans are recast every five years (or when the negative amortization limit is reached, whichever is sooner). This recalculation is based on three factors: (1) your outstanding principal balance, (2) the remaining term, and (3) the fully indexed rate. When your loan is recast, the payment will go up to whatever is required to fully pay off the loan over the remaining term. Your payment could go up sharply, because the payment cap does not apply (the payment cap will go back into effect immediately after the recast and will hold until the next time your loan is recast).

10. *Does the loan have a conversion option? If so, what is the fee?* A conversion option will let you convert to a fixed rate for a small fee rather than requiring you to completely refinance. However, having a conversion option will mean your Option ARM has a higher interest rate or higher cost in up-front points (origination fee).

As you can see, there are many variables to Option ARM loans, and you should completely understand your loan before you sign for it. It can be tricky for most people who are not in the mortgage business, so don't be shy about asking a lot of questions. If you don't get a clear explanation, ask again or ask someone else. You can use the fill-in-the-blanks form at the end of this section to make your comparison easier. But before you do that, read through the following guidelines.

Consider an Option ARM If

✓ You cannot afford to get your start in real estate in any other way.
✓ Home values in your area are forecast to rise sharply over the next few years.
✓ Your income is going to increase significantly in the next year.
✓ You are self-employed and you need the flexibility due to cash flow variation in your business.

Do Not Consider an Option ARM If

✓ You're trying to "maximize your buying power"—that is, buying more than you can afford.
✓ You're not absolutely certain your income can handle the maximum payment cap.
✓ Home values are predicted to have only modest gains or remain flat, and your loan is more than 80 percent of the value of your home.

✓ You're on a modest fixed income and don't have large liquid assets as security.
✓ You're trying to refinance because your spending is out of control and you've run up your credit cards. Why? Because you're likely to spend on credit again and get into serious trouble.

Option Arm Loans: 10 Questions

Fill in the answers for three companies under A, B, and C.

1. How long does the initial rate last?
   A. _____
   B. _____
   C. _____

2. How often does the rate adjust?
   A. _____
   B. _____
   C. _____

3. What is the index? How stable is this index, historically?
   A. _____
   B. _____
   C. _____

4. What is the margin? What is the yield spread premium? What is the margin for par?
   A. _____
   B. _____
   C. _____

5. What is the minimum payment cap?
   A. _____
   B. _____
   C. _____

6. What is the negative amortization cap?
   A. _____
   B. _____
   C. _____

7. What is the lifetime interest rate cap?
   A. _____
   B. _____
   C. _____

8. What is the highest my payment can go?
   A._____
   B._____
   C._____

9. What is the payment recast (recalculation) period?
   A._____
   B._____
   C._____

10. Does the loan have a conversion option? What is the conversion fee?
    A._____
    B._____
    C._____

Prepayment Penalties: Good and Bad

People are fuming about prepayment penalties. Like the business owner who got stuck with a lifetime penalty for $43,000 when her loan officer told her it would expire in 18 months. And the married couple who were told there would be no prepay penalty, but then one for five grand popped up when they were trying to refinance. Home owners feel stuck or ripped off, and they're not happy.

The prepayment penalty should be disclosed right up front on the Truth-in-Lending Disclosure Statement you get with your Good Faith Estimate. If there is none, that box will be checked. If there is one, the box "may" have to pay a penalty will be checked. (See the sample in Figure 3.3.)

What Is a Prepayment Penalty and How Does It Work?

A prepayment penalty is a fee you pay the lender for paying off your loan before the maturity date. Some lenders offer a lower interest rate if you're willing to take a prepayment penalty, because it guarantees their investors they'll receive a certain return. The prepayment penalty prevents the lender from taking a loss if you refinance within a few months of taking the loan.

TRUTH-IN-LENDING DISCLOSURE STATEMENT
(THIS IS NEITHER A CONTRACT NOR A COMMITMENT TO LEND)

Applicants	**Carolyn Warren**	Prepared By:

Property Address: **TBD**

Application No: **Warren , C**   Date Prepared:

ANNUAL PERCENTAGE RATE	FINANCE CHARGE	AMOUNT FINANCED	TOTAL OF PAYMENTS
The cost of your credit as a yearly rate	The dollar amount the credit will cost you	The amount of credit provided to you or on your behalf	The amount you will have paid after making all payments as scheduled
* 6.189 %	$ * 477,660.42	$ * 397,300.04	$ * 874,960.46

☐ REQUIRED DEPOSIT: The annual percentage rate does not take into account your required deposit
PAYMENTS: Your payment schedule will be:

Number of Payments	Amount of Payments **	When Payments Are Due	Number of Payments	Amount of Payments **	When Payments Are Due	Number of Payments	Amount of Payments **	When Payments Are Due
		Monthly Beginning			Monthly Beginning:			Monthly Beginning
359	2,430.44							
1	2,432.50							

360 months = 30 years, fixed rate

Surprise!
On this loan, the prepayment penalty
is approx. $9,800.   See below.

☐ DEMAND FEATURE: This obligation has a demand feature.
☐ VARIABLE RATE FEATURE: This loan contains a variable rate feature. A variable rate disclosure has been provided earlier.

CREDIT LIFE/CREDIT DISABILITY: Credit life insurance and credit disability insurance are not required to obtain credit, and will not be provided unless you sign and agree to pay the additional cost.

Type	Premium	Signature	
Credit Life		I want credit life insurance.	Signature:
Credit Disability		I want credit disability insurance.	Signature:
Credit Life and Disability		I want credit life and disability insurance.	Signature:

INSURANCE: The following insurance is required to obtain credit:
☐ Credit life insurance ☐ Credit disability ☑ Property insurance ☐ Flood insurance
You may obtain the insurance from anyone you want that is acceptable to creditor
☑ If you purchase ☐ property ☐ flood insurance from creditor you will pay $ for a one year term.
SECURITY: You are giving a security interest in:
☐ The goods or property being purchased   ☐ Real property you already own.
FILING FEES: $
LATE CHARGE: If a payment is more than   days late, you will be charged   % of the payment
PREPAYMENT: If you pay off early, you
☑ may ☐ will not have to pay a penalty.
☐ may ☑ will not be entitled to a refund of part of the finance charge.

The Loan Officer didn't mention a prepayment penalty. "May" means there is one.

ASSUMPTION: Someone buying your property
☐ may ☐ may, subject to conditions ☑ may not assume the remainder of your loan on the original terms.
See your contract documents for any additional information about nonpayment, default, any required repayment in full before the scheduled date and prepayment refunds and penalties
☑ * means an estimate   ☐ all dates and numerical disclosures except the late payment disclosures are estimates.

* * NOTE: The Payments shown above include reserve deposits for Mortgage Insurance (if applicable), but exclude Property Taxes and Insurance.

THE UNDERSIGNED ACKNOWLEDGES RECEIVING A COMPLETED COPY OF THIS DISCLOSURE.

Carolyn Warren	(Applicant)	(Date)		(Applicant)	(Date)
	(Applicant)	(Date)		(Applicant)	(Date)
	(Lender)	(Date)			

Calyx Form - til hp (02/95)

Figure 3.3

The most common prepayment penalty is six months' interest on 80 percent of your original loan balance. (You're allowed to pay 20 percent off early without penalty. So if your loan is $200,000, you can pay off $40,000 early without penalty.) The penalty may be in effect for two, three, or five years. The full prepayment penalty is in effect until the day it expires. That means if you pay off your loan one day ahead of the expiration date, you'll pay the entire penalty.

To determine the prepayment penalty, use this calculation:

$$\frac{\text{Loan balance} \times .080 \times \text{Interest rate}}{2} = \text{Prepayment penalty}$$

For example:

$$\frac{\$200,000 \times \$160,000 \times .07}{2} = \$5,600$$

 A prepayment penalty usually calculates to be between four and five monthly payments—no small sum.

A rare type of prepayment penalty has a gradual decrease, so if you pay off your loan one month before the expiration date, you will pay less than if you pay it off right away.

Hard or Soft Prepayment Penalty?

There are "hard prepays" and "soft prepays." A hard prepayment penalty means you'll pay the full amount, whether you refinance or sell your house. A soft prepayment penalty means you only have to pay it if you refinance away to another lender; but if you sell your house, it is waived.

However, many lenders will waive your prepayment penalty if you refinance with their company. But that usually means you'll have another prepayment penalty, so it doesn't always make good sense to refinance before your prepayment penalty expires.

✐ WARNING: DON'T TAKE THEIR WORD FOR IT

If you get one thing out of this chapter, let it be this: you must read the terms of the prepayment penalty for yourself. Never take anyone's word for it. ✎

When you're at the signing table, just say, "Show me where it says there's no prepayment penalty," and then read it for yourself. If there's no penalty, the wording will be obvious. If there is one, make sure you notice the time period. You don't want to take a five-year prepay on a loan that has a fixed rate for two years. Those last three years could murder your finances when your interest rate and monthly payment skyrocket.

Some prepayment penalties allow only a short window to refinance without a penalty, such as three months.

I've received far too many emails from people saying their loan officer lied about the prepay penalty, or that they were never told about it, and it hadn't occurred to them to ask. They never even thought about the possibility of being stuck in a loan they wouldn't want later. At signing, they just scribbled happily away without reading anything—you know, that shiny pen thing. People get to chatting and laughing and thinking about how much fun they're about to have when their loan funds that they fail to read the terms of their loan. They're focused on the cash-out they're soon to get or on the new house they're soon to move into. You must not do that.

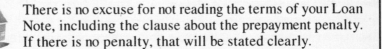
There is no excuse for not reading the terms of your Loan Note, including the clause about the prepayment penalty. If there is no penalty, that will be stated clearly.

Even if you have an honest loan officer, you still must read the terms of the penalty for yourself. Every loan will address this issue, either saying there is none or saying what it is. This is part of the Loan Note itself, and it is a legal contract. As an adult, it is your responsibility to know what you're signing. If you don't know, take the documents home so you can get advice from a professional neutral party. This is not something you should feel shy about doing. Intelligent people who buy multimillion dollar homes often have their attorneys look over their paperwork before they sign, so you're in good company if you do this as well. (I'm not recommending this as a necessary step for people who take average loans and can understand the terms themselves. But if you're uncertain about the loan terms, don't hesitate to exercise your right to get a professional opinion.)

When I worked for a direct lender (a company that had its own money to lend), I did a temporary loan for some friends of mine. They were in a bit of financial trouble, and this loan saved them from going into foreclosure. They had a good plan in place to pull themselves back up on their feet, so the high interest rate (because their credit put them into a high-risk category) was only a temporary situation. They'd be set to refinance in a year. I made sure there was no prepayment penalty on their loan. However, their signing took place while I was gone on vacation.

A year later, I'd moved on to another company, and my friends called to refinance. They wanted to know why they had a prepayment penalty on their loan. I reminded them that I specifically ordered their loan documents without one, so it shouldn't be there. But it was. Confused, I called my former coworker who'd filled in for me during my vacation when my friends signed their loan.

"Sorry about that," he said. "The manager added a prepayment penalty. I guess they [my friends] never noticed it at signing."

I was furious that this had been done to my friends behind my back. But it goes to show you, you can never take anyone's word for it. You never know what can happen.

Good Prepayment Penalties

Can it ever be a good thing to take a prepayment penalty? Sure.

If you have excellent credit, your loan *won't* have a prepayment penalty 98 percent of the time. If you have a score below 620, your loan *will* have a prepayment penalty 98 percent of the time. It goes with the territory of subprime lending. So even if your score is high, but you're taking a subprime loan due to a debt ratio challenge or stated income, you'll see a prepayment penalty on your loan documents.

My only complaints with a prepay penalty are: (1) when it's not disclosed properly, and (2) when it's not in your best interest. Sometimes it is in your best interest to opt for the prepay. Follow the guidelines listed here.

Choose a Prepayment Penalty in These Circumstances:

- You need the advantage of the lower interest rate taking a prepayment penalty gives you.

- You are committed to keeping the loan for the duration of the prepay period, and you will not refinance or sell during that time.

- You've explored the possibility of a one-year prepay penalty as opposed to a longer one.

Biweekly Mortgage Savings: Bargain or Rip-Off?

Save $32,000! Save $54,000! Save incredible money! Take five to seven years off your 30-year loan!

This biweekly payment program is advertised for fees of $400 and $500. It is a great deal for the middleman, but it's no bargain for you. Why? Because you can do it yourself for free. Why should you throw away $400?

Street magicians distract people with flashy movements of their right hand while the real trick is taking place unnoticed in their left hand. In the case of biweekly payments, the mortgage company flashes your savings at you, making you think the "magic" is in the biweekly payment. But the truth is, you save no money by sending in a check biweekly rather than monthly.

Consumers think they're saving on interest, because they're making a half payment two weeks early. They think it cuts two weeks' interest off. But that is not true. If you read the fine print, you'll see they don't even credit your account biweekly. That's right: they take your money and hold it for two more weeks.

But the real reason you save no money by paying early is because mortgage payments are paid in arrears. ("In arrears" here means your payment on February 1 is covering you for January, and so on. Remember how you seemed to skip a payment when you first moved in or refinanced? You weren't really skipping a payment, it's just that mortgage payments are made in arrears. You get to live there for a month, and then pay.) Therefore, paying days or even two weeks early does not save anything in interest.

How Does It Really Work?

The savings comes from the fact that there are two months out of the year in which you would be making three payments rather than two. Thus, you are making two extra biweekly payments (one extra monthly payment) per year. There is no good reason why you should pay a company $400 to make an extra payment per year. I call it a rip-off.

To accomplish the same thing yourself for free, select one of these two options:

> *Option 1 (best for people who are paid every other week).* Calculate one-half of your principal and interest payment. Send in that extra amount on the two months you receive three paychecks.

> *Option 2 (best for people who are paid once a month or twice a month).* Divide your principal and interest payment by 12. Send in that extra amount each month with your payment.

To add further insult, some companies add a monthly administration fee, such as $39, as well. They say you owe them that because you're too undisciplined to send in the extra payment on your own.

Ignore sales flattery such as, "You are a special customer chosen to receive this special offer." What do they think you are, gullible? Don't fall for silly sales pressure tactics like, "Hurry and sign up before the expiration date." Please. As if they wouldn't be just as happy to take your 400 bucks later. These are marketing ploys.

Remember, you are in charge of the terms of your mortgage. If you choose to add to the principal and pay off your loan early, you will save good money. It's a matter of simple arithmetic. There's nothing magical about sending in the money biweekly, as opposed to monthly.

Coming Up

Once you select the right loan for your situation, you're ready to request three Good Faith Estimates from the three loan officers on your short list. In Chapter 4, I'll explain how to compare these three estimates so you can get your best deal.

Step 4:
Request Three Good Faith Estimates and Compare the Costs

The high-priced loan officer whispered to me, "The people we get frustrated with are the ones who actually know something about loans."

In this chapter, I introduce a plan these shady pros don't want you to know about. Why? It makes *you* the captain of your financing ship and them the work hands. You get the best deal, and no one takes advantage of you. But, first, I'll alert you to the common pitfalls—the bad ideas.

Bad Ideas

It's a bad idea to:

- Shop for the best interest rate.
- Compare annual percentage rates.
- Compare ads.

Details to prevent you from each of these pitfalls follow.

Shopping for the Best Interest Rate Is a Bad Idea

Most people looking for financing make a big mistake: They call a list of lenders and ask, "What's your interest rate?" But that's not what you want to do, for two reasons. First, the quote you'll get is meaningless; and, second, you reveal that you don't know what you're doing.

However, if your goal is simply to drive mortgage people crazy, then go right ahead, make a long list of lenders, call them, and as soon as they pick up the phone and say, "How may I help you?" reply with, "What's your interest rate?" It's a fantastic way to waste everybody's time, especially your own.

During the refinance boom of 2001, all day long I got such calls, as did everyone else in the mortgage business. I tried my best to educate all of these callers as to how they could guarantee getting the lowest interest rate and why calling a list with this question would not help them. Unfortunately, the vast majority were on a roll with their plan and could not be persuaded to listen to reason.

After awhile, these calls took up so much of my time, with no benefit to me, that I became annoyed. It wasn't just me, either. There was a lot of talk among loan officers about how to handle these consumers, and the question was posed in mortgage forums all over the Internet. Those of us who answered honestly as to "today's rate" could not compete with the liars who were quoting lower rates.

Why Rate Quotes over the Phone Are Worthless. When the refinance boom was over in 2004, plenty of loan officers just kept up this approach. Quote low, get the application, take money for the appraisal as fast as you can to obligate the person to you, and then say, "Sorry, but rates took an upturn. You'll have to lock in at this higher rate." It was their plan all along, but there's no way you can prove it.

The point is, in a rising rate environment, you're sure to be a victim of such tactics if you insist on calling around asking the "What is your rate?" question. It just doesn't work as a strategy for getting the cheapest loan.

 Every lender makes up its own formula for calculating the APR. It's tantamount to saying, "This is how we interpret it."

A Joke That Paid Off

One day during the refinance boom, I'd had enough. The next caller was a single woman who owned a nice condominium, and she asked this same question. Why spend the time trying to educate her? I knew she'd just hang up and take her business to a liar. Fine, I thought, let the liars compete with this! So I quoted her an impossibly low rate— one that would cause a company to actually lose money.

She said, "Thanks," and hung up, no doubt, scribbling on her pad and moving on to call the next victim on her list.

Two days later she called back and left me a message saying she wanted more information. I didn't take her seriously, so I didn't return her call. I was busy with my real clients, and I was sick and tired of rate shoppers who had no clue. The next day she left another message, and once again I pressed the Message Delete button on my answering machine.

Several days later, she called a third time and said, "I've left you several messages, and you haven't returned my call yet. I want to refinance with you, and I need to know how to proceed." Ha! Clearly, my lowball quote had worked.

The funny thing was, rates *had* dropped, so I could make good on my quote. It was no longer a joke. I called her back, did her refinance, and she was very happy.

Managers and owners of mortgage companies were advising their loan officers to use this very approach for handling "rate quote" callers. We couldn't compete with the liars by giving an accurate quote on "today's rate," so we were told to quote low and hope the market kept falling.

Mortgage gurus, so called, teach loan officers how to handle rate callers. They have scripts loan officers can follow to divert the attention away from the rate and onto more important things, such as the overall picture of their loan, their financial goals, and their superior service.

Comparing APR Is a Bad Idea

It's a bad idea to put too much stock in the annual percentage rate (APR). Why? It was originally created as a way for consumers to compare loan pricing, but the system failed from the get-go. This is because different lenders use different methods of calculating the APR.

Once lenders got wind that consumers were using APR as their measuring rod, out came the magicians. Even the biggest national lenders have their own "creative" ways of calculating their annual percentage rates so their loans look cheaper when they're actually more expensive.

I almost lost a loan to a famous bank doing sleight-of-hand tricks. A client came into my office to say he was switching to "Big Bank," because its APR was lower. Luckily, he had the Good Faith Estimate with him, so we went over it together line by line, and we found that the Big Bank loan was actually more expensive by a couple hundred dollars. It's just that Big Bank chose not to count some of the fees in its APR calculation. Once I pointed out these fees, and the absence of a prorated finance charge (PFC) next to them (which tells you the fee is included in the APR calculation), my client chose to stick with the cheaper loan I was getting for him. (Figure 4.1 shows a Good Faith Estimate with PFCs clearly identified.)

Comparing Ads Is a Bad Idea

It's a bad idea to try to find the best loan by comparing advertisements. For example, you can spot a newspaper ad that looks attractive; but when you call, the loan officer is likely to say, "Sorry, you can't get that rate any more."

You suppress a deep sigh, then ask, "Why not? I have your ad right in front of me."

He replies, "Rates change daily. We had to submit our ad to the paper last week and, meantime, rates went up. However . . ." [and then he goes into a sales pitch].

If Rates Change Daily, How Do You Comparison Shop?   What can you do? Rates do change daily for prime loans, giving all the companies a perfect "out" for not delivering on what they advertise. (For subprime or nonconforming loans, the loans designed for people with risky credit, rates do not change daily.) The mortgage industry is one of the few that has the luxury of advertising one price and selling at another. Your grocer would never do that. If it advertises watermelon for 10 cents a pound, it will honor the price, even if it was a misprint, and should have been advertised at 50 cents a pound. Everyone knows the price of watermelons doesn't change daily. But the price of borrowing money does.

GOOD FAITH ESTIMATE

Applicants: **CAROLYN WARREN**	Application No: **WARREN INT ONLY**
Property Addr:	Date Prepared: **05/09/2006**
Prepared By:	Loan Program: **30 YEAR FIXED IO**

The information provided below reflects estimates of the charges which you are likely to incur at the settlement of your loan. The fees listed are estimates-actual charges may be more or less. Your transaction may not involve a fee for every item listed. The numbers listed beside the estimates generally correspond to the numbered lines contained in the HUD-1 settlement statement which you will be receiving at settlement. The HUD-1 settlement statement will show you the actual cost for items paid at settlement

Total Loan Amount $ **320,000**   Interest Rate: **7.000** %   Term: **360 / 360** mths

800	ITEMS PAYABLE IN CONNECTION WITH LOAN:			PFC S F POC
801	Loan Origination Fee		$	
802	Loan Discount			✓
803	Appraisal Fee			400.00
804	Credit Report			18.00
805	Lender's Inspection Fee			
808	Mortgage Broker Fee	1.000%		3,200.00 ✓
809	Tax Related Service Fee			94.00 ✓
810	Processing Fee			500.00 ✓
811	Underwriting Fee			550.00 ✓
812	Wire Transfer Fee			15.00 ✓

(handwritten notes: "Lines with ✓ are included in APR." / "Does not include credit report in APR calculations. But some do." / "Loan offers can alter it as they wish.")

1100	TITLE CHARGES:		PFC S F POC
1101	Closing or Escrow Fee: **ANY ESCROW**	$	575.00 ✓
1105	Document Preparation Fee		✓
1106	Notary Fees		
1107	Attorney Fees		
1108	Title Insurance: **ANY TITLE**		525.00
	1109. ESCROW COURIER AND WIRE		94.00 ✓

1200	GOVERNMENT RECORDING & TRANSFER CHARGES:		PFC S F POC
1201	Recording Fees:	$	70.00
1202	City/County Tax/Stamps:		
1203	State Tax/Stamps:		

1300	ADDITIONAL SETTLEMENT CHARGES:		PFC S F POC
1302	Pest Inspection	$	

		Estimated Closing Costs	6,041.00
900	ITEMS REQUIRED BY LENDER TO BE PAID IN ADVANCE:		PFC S F POC
901	Interest for **15** days @ $ **62.2222** per day	$	933.33 ✓
902	Mortgage Insurance Premium		✓
903	Hazard Insurance Premium		480.00
904			
905	VA Funding Fee		✓

1000	RESERVES DEPOSITED WITH LENDER:			PFC S F POC
1001	Hazard Insurance Premium	3 months @ $ 40.00 per month	$	120.00
1002	Mortgage Ins. Premium Reserves	months @ $ per month		✓
1003	School Tax	months @ $ per month		
1004	Taxes and Assessment Reserves	6 months @ $ 350.00 per month		2,100.00
1005	Flood Insurance Reserves	months @ $ per month		
		months @ $ per month		
		months @ $ per month		

	Estimated Prepaid Items/Reserves	3,633.33
TOTAL ESTIMATED SETTLEMENT CHARGES		9,674.33

COMPENSATION TO BROKER (Not Paid Out of Loan Proceeds):

1303. ysp 1	$

TOTAL ESTIMATED FUNDS NEEDED TO CLOSE:			TOTAL ESTIMATED MONTHLY PAYMENT:	
Purchase Price/Payoff (+)	400,000.00	New First Mortgage(-)	Principal & Interest	1,866.67
Loan Amount (-)	320,000.00	Sub Financing(-)	Other Financing (P & I)	
Est. Closing Costs (+)	6,041.00	New 2nd Mtg Closing Costs(+)	Hazard Insurance	40.00
Est. Prepaid Items/Reserves (+)	3,633.33		Real Estate Taxes	350.00
Amount Paid by Seller (-)			Mortgage Insurance	
			Homeowner Assn. Dues	
			Other	
Total Est. Funds needed to close		89,674.33	Total Monthly Payment	2,256.67

☑ This Good Faith Estimate is being provided by _____, a mortgage broker, and no lender has been obtained. These estimates are provided pursuant to the Real Estate Settlement Procedures Act of 1974, as amended (RESPA). Additional information can be found in the HUD Special Information Booklet, which is to be provided to you by your mortgage broker or lender, if your application is to purchase residential real property and the lender will take a first lien on the property. The undersigned acknowledges receipt of the booklet "Settlement Costs," and if applicable the Consumer Handbook on ARM Mortgages.

Applicant **CAROLYN WARREN**	Date	Applicant	Date

Calyx Form gfe.frm 11/01

Figure 4.1

The purpose of an ad is to get you to call in; it's not to disclose an actual rate.

You have to expect rates printed by a mortgage company in the newspaper to be inaccurate. Expect it to be a "lowball number." Or, better yet, ignore newspaper advertised mortgage rates altogether, because they're pretty much meaningless.

Some newspapers print a quarterly list of local lenders, their interest rate, their points, their APR, and so on. Typically, it appears on the front of the real estate section as "spring mortgage rates," or something similar. You should know several things about this. First, they have to submit their numbers to the paper days in advance, so changes in the market are to be expected. Second, each company knows that it is appearing in a list with all its competitors, so it's strategizing on how it can position itself to look better. Doing so is a bit of a crapshoot, because no company knows what its competitors will post.

Here's an example of what four mortgage companies might submit for a 30-year fixed rate:

Company A.   6.25 percent with 1 point

Company B.   6.5 percent with a half point

Company C.   6.0 percent with two points

Company D.   5.625 percent with four points

You cannot hold a bank or mortgage company to the interest rate it quoted you, because rates fluctuate constantly. Your rate is not secure until it is locked in.

Company D is hoping people will see that its interest rate is the lowest and pick it, disregarding the points. Company B is hoping its combination will appeal to more people. Of course, there will be about 50 or more lenders competing, so this example is simplified. How will consumers decide which deal is best, especially since the APR will also be listed, confusing people all the more? But let's say you do study all 50 lenders and select the one that looks the best. Then you call that lender, all ready to move ahead, only to find that rate is no longer available.

The honest mortgage people, the real "stars" in this difficult business, do their best to post accurate rates; however, they're very aware that they're being judged by consumers against sneaky competitors. The loan sharks are out to make megabucks any way and every way possible, and they intend to post the lowest rate they can get away with, without looking like imposters. Mortgage is a highly competitive industry— even more so when the market is tough with rising rates.

Last, you should know that these companies have to pay the newspaper to be on the list. That tells you something, too, including the reason that some mortgage companies choose *not* to be included. They think, why pay money to be a part of a meaningless list? Good point.

How can you tell if an advertised rate was a good, honest quote, and the rates actually went up in the last couple days versus a totally false bait-and-switch ad? You can't. You might have a hunch, but you will never be able to prove it, or make a company hold true to its advertised rate. Companies advertise rates, because it brings in phone calls.

This same principle applies to television, radio, and even the Internet. "I'm sorry, but we had a rate change 30 minutes ago." So you can easily see why it's a bad idea to use advertisements as a way to shop for a mortgage.

 The law says a Good Faith Estimate must be sent out to you within three business days of making an application.

How Should You Shop for a Mortgage?

It's unanimous among mortgage professionals: the absolute best way to shop for a loan is to look at *all* the terms of the loan, and to get it in writing. You must look at the cost of the *entire* loan. Get all your Good Faith Estimates on the *same day* from each company, because rates change daily. That way, you'll have an accurate comparison. This easy plan provides you with three big benefits: you save money, time, and emotional grief.

✐ NOTE: RECEIVING A GOOD FAITH ESTIMATE IS YOUR LEGAL RIGHT
Federal law requires mortgage lenders to provide you (by fax, mail with postage date, by email, or in person) with a

Good Faith Estimate and Truth-in-Lending form within three business days of making a formal loan application. It is your right and your responsibility to receive this. If day four comes, and you don't have it, call and cite the law and complain. ✎

In a year-long study in 2004, it was found that only one in four borrowers received the required Good Faith Estimate. Obviously, the cure to ending nondisclosure practices is not passing a law. A law has already been passed and ignored. The answer is to educate Americans so they become their own self-advocates. Informed Americans are the only ones who can stop the slop.

How to Ask for Your Good Faith Estimates

As I recommended in Chapter 2, you're going to get three Good Faith Estimates, two from mortgage brokers and one from a bank. This will be equivalent to shopping a hundred lenders, because brokers can go to all the wholesale lenders. You're going to throw in one bank just for good measure. Some locales have hometown banks with very good deals.

Then, when you call, use this effective script:

I will be buying a house soon for approximately $_____ . My down payment will be $_____ , so my loan will be $_____ . I would like a 30-year fixed rate with no prepayment penalty.

Or:

I would like a 5/1 ARM and don't mind a prepayment penalty. [State what you want.] I am calling three companies to compare loans, and I will choose one of the three. My credit is excellent, I have all my income and asset information, and I will be easy to work with. Will you please fax or email me a Good Faith Estimate and Truth-in-Lending form by tomorrow? I want to compare the three on the same day, so I get an accurate comparison.

After you get the loan officer's agreement to send you a Good Faith Estimate by fax or email, then say, "By the way, will you be sure to include the Truth-in-Lending form?" The loan officer should automatically include this document, but some do not, so be sure to mention it—not to insult them, but as a confirmation.

When loan officers know they have a one in three chance of getting your business, they'll be happy to provide you with their best quote. Get their verbal commitment to do this; if they say they can't, then select another company to get your three GFEs, so you'll have three to compare and contrast.

✎ WARNING

Notice that you tell the loan officers you have excellent credit, but you do not give out your Social Security number, nor do you give permission to pull your credit. This is very important. You don't want three credit reports pulled. If they insist in asking to pull your credit, tell them you'll let one company pull it once you've made your choice from the three Good Faith Estimates. Because you know your credit (per Chapter 1), you can let them take your word for it until you've made a decision on which company to go with. ✎

What if You Don't Know Your Credit Score?

You'll have to know your credit score to get an accurate Good Faith Estimate. If you don't, you can let the first loan officer on your short list pull your credit, but only if he or she agrees to tell you your score afterward. (If he or she won't, move on to someone who will.) Then you will be able to tell the next two people on your short list your score.

 Review your Good Faith Estimate and Truth-in-Lending form before you make a commitment with your money.

Be aware that the loan officers may tell you that you can have unlimited credit pulls within a 14-day period, and they count as one credit pull, as far as your score goes. This is true for mortgage and auto credit checks. The idea is to allow you to shop without being penalized. If you have three mortgage credit pulls, the bureaus assume you're shopping with three companies for one house—not that you're getting ready to buy three houses and significantly increase your debt loan. Nonetheless, why have your credit report pulled more often than necessary? It's not a good idea.

✐ INSIDER SECRET

Another secret to success is to say you've got all your documentation handy and you'll be easy to work with. (Only say this if it's true, however.) This will tell the loan officer that he or she will spend fewer hours than average processing your loan; therefore, he or she can afford to work for less money. If the officer requires less back-end commission, you'll get a lower interest rate. (This is explained in detail in Chapter 5.) ✎

How to Compare Good Faith Estimates

To begin this important process, compare the three Good Faith Estimates for the following six items:

1. *Loan amount.* Verify that it is correct.

2. *Interest rate.* This is an important consideration that is influenced by other factors, such as points and YSP (below).

3. *Monthly payment (principal and interest payment only).* The taxes and insurance are set and will be the same with any company; or you might choose to pay them separately from the loan. The three companies may estimate differently for your taxes and insurance, or they may not include them at all, so just look at principal and income (P&I). Lenders cannot control your taxes or insurance, and in the end, they'll be the same no matter which one you go with.

4. *Points.* These comprise origination fee, loan discount, and broker fee. Think of these fees as the interest you're paying up front to buy your interest rate.

5. *Loan fees.* These are extremely important and often overlooked. You'll know how to determine which are fair and reasonable after you read about junk fees in the next chapter.

6. *Yield spread premium, YSP (back-end commission).* This is important, because it's a major factor in determining your interest rate. (More about this in Chapter 5.)

In addition, look at the Truth-in-Lending form to verify these four additional items:

For People in a Hurry: Super-Speedy Short-Short List

Are you in a super-rush to get a loan officer and race to closing? If so, here's a two-step plan for you!

1. Call your local bank (preferably the one you already do business with) and ask for a Good Faith Estimate, following the script given previously, but saying you're going to compare just two, rather than three. Tell the loan officer what your closing date is to make sure he or she can close that quickly. This will also demonstrate you're very serious about getting financing.
2. Call your local mortgage broker (preferably a referral from someone you know), and say, "I have a Good Faith Estimate from the bank and a closing date of next Friday (or whenever). Can you get me a better deal?"

That's it: your super-quick plan for getting a good deal with a short-short list.

 Don't shop interest rates. Instead, compare Good Faith Estimates and get a statement in writing saying the fixed costs won't vary by more than 10 percent.

Banks usually have pretty good loans—that is, not as bad as a pricey broker and not as good as a great broker. So you go to them first, and then see if your broker is willing to beat it. Usually they will, especially for a quick turnaround. Just be sure you object to any junk fees that show up. It's highly likely they'll try to sneak in some junk, knowing you're in a hurry and hoping you won't notice. In addition, get your guarantee.

1. *Prepayment penalty.* In the lower half of the form, there is a check box that tells you whether or not the loan has a prepayment penalty. If no box is checked, ask for a new Truth-in-Lending form. If the "May Have" box is checked, you can expect to have some type of prepayment penalty on the loan.

2. *Terms of the adjustments.* If you have an ARM, it tells you these terms:

   - *Index.* What the interest rate is based on.

   - *Margin.* Profit margin between index and your rate.

   - *First adjustment cap.* Maximum it can go up on your first adjustment.

   - *Lifetime cap.* Maximum it can go up, ever.

3. *Balance due date.* If you have a balloon loan, it will show when the balance is due.

4. *Credit life insurance.* Confirms your loan doesn't have this rip-off feature. It will also tell you your loan is *not assumable,* which is normal nowadays.

Getting a Guarantee

Ask your chosen loan officer for a written guarantee that the lender's fees will not vary from the Good Faith Estimate by more than 10 percent. That's very fair, and no honest mortgage professional will object. With this in hand, you are safe from being victim to last-minute surprises such as trumped-up charges and added "garbage" fees. But please understand that this guarantee does not include property taxes and homeowner's insurance. The mortgage company has no control over what the county charges for taxes, and taxes can vary greatly with the price of the house and the neighborhood. And you pick your own insurance coverage, so the loan officer can't possibly guarantee that either.

You cannot expect a Good Faith Estimate to be exact; after all, it is called an estimate. A 10 percent variance is reasonable, so you plan for that. If a loan officer refuses to agree to the guarantee, then you have to wonder if he or she plans on pulling a bait and switch later or throwing in a junk fee later.

Finding an Honest Pro

With the GFE and guarantee letter, officially in writing, in front of you, you will be able to select your best loan option. Now ask yourself some questions to double-check your impression of the loan officer's honesty. I call it using your "integrity detector."

- *How will the loan officer keep me updated during the loan process?* He or she should have a system in place so you don't have to stress out from worry and wonder. Any method that's to your own satisfaction is good. Some prefer email; others prefer phone messages. The important thing is that you know what's happening so you can relax and look forward to your new home (or your new loan, if it's a refinance).

- *Did I have good communication with the loan officer?* This is personal, so you need to trust your inner voice. There are many excellent loan officers who take extra time explaining mortgages and how the process will work at their company. They don't dodge questions. They desire and value your business, and they will work hard to give you a good experience, so they can earn your recommendation in the future.

- *Did I get a straightforward answer when I asked, "What's par rate?"* If the loan officer won't tell you, move on without wasting your time. If he or she does a verbal dance, explain that you'd like to work with someone who gives direct answers. Don't bother getting into a lengthy argument, because there's no point; if he or she is not of "star" quality, you don't want to give him or her your business anyway.

- *Do my instincts say the loan officer is trustworthy?* If the answer is yes, go ahead and make the commitment.

If you're the type who likes to bargain, call back the company that offered you the second-best deal, tell the loan officer there what your best deal is, and ask if he or she would like to do better. If the is yes, you've got yourself a bargain. Take it with no further ado. Don't be iniquitous by going back and forth multiple times.

A softer approach would be to call back number two and say, "Thank you for your GFE; however, I had one that was a little better." Then see if he or she offers to beat it.

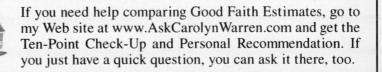 If you need help comparing Good Faith Estimates, go to my Web site at www.AskCarolynWarren.com and get the Ten-Point Check-Up and Personal Recommendation. If you just have a quick question, you can ask it there, too.

Once you've determined that you have a fair deal and an honest mortgage professional, do not "shoplift" that person's time by scuttling off to another company. I've seen homebuyers go from company to company to company, leaving a wake of destruction in their path—loan officers who put in hours of work and will not get paid a penny for their time—and that's not right. Remember, loan officers only get their commission *after* your loan funds.

Also be aware that it's normal to pay for the appraisal in advance. Once you've signed off on the Good Faith Estimate, go ahead and write your check for the appraisal. It'll be that much less you have to bring in at closing; or, if the seller is paying all your closing costs, you can be reimbursed for the appraisal at closing.

The Key to a Good Borrowing Experience

The most important key to a good loan experience is to have a knowledgeable, ethical loan officer who looks out for your best interests. I recommend working with someone who has a minimum of two years' experience doing mortgages, especially if you have subprime credit. Once you've accomplished that, you can stop worrying about being cheated and concentrate on the loan process. A "mortgage star" will never rip you off, regardless of whether you choose a fixed rate or an adjustable rate, and regardless of whether your credit is A+ or subprime.

One final piece of advice: After you've selected your loan officer, stop shopping around. Treat this professional with respect. Don't, in order to save a pittance, dump him or her after many hours of work have been put into your loan. You'll have a better experience if you relax and trust your loan advocate to work for you.

Coming Up

The next chapter is about the best-kept and most controversial secret in the mortgage industry. I urge every homebuyer and homeowner to read it and refer to it in the future. Also, do your friends and associates a great favor by telling them about it. Armed with this knowledge, consumers possess the power to reform the home loan business.

CHAPTER 5

Step 5:
Uncover the Best-Kept Secret of the Mortgage Industry

How do loan officers make more than doctors? How can they make $20,000 (or more) off of you—*without you having the slightest clue?*

Prepare to be outraged. In this chapter I reveal the mortgage industry's best-kept secret—the secret that funnels tens of thousands of dollars right out of your pocket and into their coffers. I'm talking about the back-end commission you never saw on your paperwork. It's money the wholesale lender passes under the table to the loan officer after your deal closes.

Why should you care? Because you're paying for it!

If you don't mind being taken advantage of, skip this section. On the other hand, if you are determined to protect yourself financially, and save tens of thousands of dollars, read on.

Buried deep in the Good Faith Estimate is a little number I'm going to point out to you that reads "1" (see Figure 5.1). That's it—just a tiny "1." What does it mean? Does it stand $1.00, or what? Moreover, who would even notice it or pay any attention to it?

That's exactly the point. The loan officer is hoping (and expecting) you will ignore that little number 1. But it means you're going to pay an extra $59,760 over the 30 years of your loan, all so the loan officer can

GOOD FAITH ESTIMATE

Applicants: **CAROLYN WARREN**
Property Addr:
Prepared By:

Application No: **WARREN 30 YR FX**
Date Prepared: **05/09/2006**
Loan Program: **30 YEAR FIXED IO**

The information provided below reflects estimates of the charges which you are likely to incur at the settlement of your loan. The fees listed are estimates-actual charges may be more or less. Your transaction may not involve a fee for every item listed. The numbers listed beside the estimates generally correspond to the numbered lines contained in the HUD-1 settlement statement which you will be receiving at settlement. The HUD-1 settlement statement will show you the actual cost for items paid at settlement.

Total Loan Amount $ **320,000**   Interest Rate: **6.750** %   Term: **360 / 360** mths

800	ITEMS PAYABLE IN CONNECTION WITH LOAN:				PFC S F POC
801	Loan Origination Fee			$	
802	Loan Discount				
803	Appraisal Fee				400.00
804	Credit Report				18.00
805	Lender's Inspection Fee				
808	Mortgage Broker Fee	1.000%			3,200.00 ✓
809	Tax Related Service Fee				94.00 ✓
810	Processing Fee				500.00 ✓
811	Underwriting Fee				550.00 ✓
812	Wire Transfer Fee				15.00 ✓

1100	TITLE CHARGES:			PFC S F POC
1101	Closing or Escrow Fee: **ANY ESCROW**	$		575.00 ✓
1105	Document Preparation Fee			✓
1106	Notary Fees			
1107	Attorney Fees			
1108	Title Insurance: **ANY TITLE**			525.00
	1109. ESCROW COURIER AND WIRE			94.00 ✓

1200	GOVERNMENT RECORDING & TRANSFER CHARGES:			PFC S F POC
1201	Recording Fees:	$		70.00
1202	City/County Tax/Stamps:			
1203	State Tax/Stamps:			

1300	ADDITIONAL SETTLEMENT CHARGES:			PFC S F POC
1302	Pest Inspection	$		

				Estimated Closing Costs	6,041.00
900	ITEMS REQUIRED BY LENDER TO BE PAID IN ADVANCE:				PFC S F POC
901	Interest for 15 days @ $	60.0000	per day	$	900.00 ✓
902	Mortgage Insurance Premium				✓
903	Hazard Insurance Premium				480.00
904					
905	VA Funding Fee				✓

1000	RESERVES DEPOSITED WITH LENDER:				PFC S F POC
1001	Hazard Insurance Premium	3 months @ $	40.00 per month	$	120.00
1002	Mortgage Ins. Premium Reserves	months @ $	per month		✓
1003	School Tax	months @ $	per month		
1004	Taxes and Assessment Reserves	6 months @ $	350.00 per month		2,100.00
1005	Flood Insurance Reserves	months @ $	per month		
		months @ $	per month		
		months @ $	per month		

		Estimated Prepaid Items/Reserves	3,600.00
	TOTAL ESTIMATED SETTLEMENT CHARGES		9,641.00

COMPENSATION TO BROKER (Not Paid Out of Loan Proceeds):

1303. ysp 1	$

(handwritten) ✱ what does this mean? Turns out, it was 1%. — ($) Dollar figure missing

TOTAL ESTIMATED FUNDS NEEDED TO CLOSE:				TOTAL ESTIMATED MONTHLY PAYMENT:	
Purchase Price/Payoff (+)	400,000.00	New First Mortgage(-)		Principal & Interest	2,075.51
Loan Amount (-)	320,000.00	Sub Financing(-)		Other Financing (P & I)	
Est. Closing Costs (+)	6,041.00	New 2nd Mtg Closing Costs(+)		Hazard Insurance	40.00
Est. Prepaid Items/Reserves (+)	3,600.00			Real Estate Taxes	350.00
Amount Paid by Seller (-)				Mortgage Insurance	
				Homeowner Assn. Dues	
				Other	

Total Est. Funds needed to close		89,641.00	Total Monthly Payment	2,465.51

☑ This Good Faith Estimate is being provided by _____ , a mortgage broker, and no lender has been obtained   These estimates are provided pursuant to the Real Estate Settlement Procedures Act of 1974, as amended (RESPA). Additional information can be found in the HUD Special Information Booklet, which is to be provided to you by your mortgage broker or lender, if your application is to purchase residential real property and the lender will take a first lien on the property. The undersigned acknowledges receipt of the booklet "Settlement Costs," and if applicable the Consumer Handbook on ARM Mortgages.

Applicant **CAROLYN WARREN** _____ Date _____   Applicant _____ Date _____

Calyx Form gfe.frm 11/01

Figure 5.1

If Only You Knew . . .

If only you knew that little 1 stood for 1 percent of the loan amount. If only you knew that you were paying for it each and every month with a higher interest rate. If only you knew that your monthly payment is $166 higher because of it.

 It's easy to get a better deal if you know the right question to ask.

If only you knew, you could have negotiated. Because truth be told, the loan officer already made $10,000 in up front commissions, so he didn't really have to make an extra five grand on the back end, too. But he did. And he was smiling all the way to his Mercedes as he hopped in to drive to his bank after I handed him his $15,000 check. You see, I was his account executive at the wholesale lending company he did his loan with, so I witnessed the whole thing. But as his wholesale account rep, it's none of my business what he charges his clients, so I'm not allowed to say anything. In fact, he could have charged them 2 percent extra and pocketed an extra $10,000, making a cool 20 grand for himself for just three weeks' work.

collect an *extra* $5,000 commission "on the back end." (That's what they call it: "Getting one back.")

Or, if you keep that $500,000 loan for only five years, you'll pay an extra $9,990. Does that make you feel better? You pay almost 10 grand extra so the loan officer can pocket an additional $5,000 to what he or she already made in up-front commissions; and the lending company gets to keep the rest.

I hope I've caught your attention, because you need to understand how this works if you want good financing. If you're like most people, you're paying too much for your home loan.

Stop Paying Too Much!

That was the bad news. The good news is that it's not hard to understand, and there most certainly is something you can do about it.

If the client in the scenario just described hadn't been clueless, he would have known that loan officers are not supposed to put "1" for 1 percent back-end commission. They're supposed to write out the dollar amount. The client could have asked about it, like this:

"What is this 1 for?"

"That's the yield spread," the loan officer might have said.

"So that's the money you make by charging me a higher interest rate than par?" asks the client.

Surprised, the loan officer can't lie, so he says, "Yes."

"So this 1 means I'm paying a 1 percent yield spread premium?" confirms the client.

"Yes; and things are going very smoothly with your loan. We got the approval back already," says the loan officer, trying to change the subject.

"What would my interest rate be at par?" asks the client, refusing to be distracted.

"Six and a half percent," says the loan officer.

"So I'm paying 7 percent in order to give you the 1 percent yield spread premium. I don't want to pay an extra half percent and jack up my monthly payment. I'd like to have par rate, please. Either that, or I'll keep shopping around."

"Um, no. No problem. That shouldn't have been there anyway. Heh-heh," the loan officer chuckles nervously. "Here, let me fix this for you right away. I want to keep your business."

 Outrageous conversations are taking place behind closed doors. They're scheming on ways to make more money off of you.

That's how easily this client could have saved himself almost 60 grand—if he'd only known.

Conversations They Don't Want You to Hear

If you were a fly on the wall during one conversation that took place between mortgage loan officers last December, this is what you would have heard. (The numbers are real; only the names have been changed.)

Ben said, "I've got a $760,000 loan. I'm doing an Option ARM with a 1 percent start rate. The X wholesale lender will give me 3 on the back end. Who can top that?"

(He's getting a 3 percent commission on the back end for a loan with an interest rate of just 1 percent. On $760,000, that would be a cool $22,800 commission. But Ben was hoping for more.)

"Y wholesale lender will give you 3.75," said Peggy.

"Z wholesale lender will give you 4, but there's a three-year prepayment penalty," said Robert.

"Great. Thanks a lot," said Ben smiling. He'd make $30,400 on this loan. Looks like he'd have a nice income for December. Perhaps a thought of the holidays crossed his mind.

But then one spoilsport spoke up and said:

"What's best for the client? Nice to make a profit, but why not provide the best financial solution to your client? All too often I see, What's best for *me*? No one minds someone making a buck, but a ton of loan officers today are abusing this. You're burning your client with a margin of 3.25 percent."

After that display of conscience, a rowdy argument ensued.

Peggy defended Ben saying:

"You're going down the right path. It's a screamin' deal."

To which the spoilsport angrily responded:

"Greed, baby, plain and simple, to the broker's benefit, not the client's. You can't tell me that the interest-carrying cost of 6.25 percent on that loan is better than the 5/1 ARM."

Did the homeowner who was refinancing into the 1 percent loan know his real cost was 6.25 percent? Did he know the margin was jacked up so his loan officer could make a bigger commission? Did he know it had a prepayment penalty that would guarantee the lender a bigger profit, and his loan officer a bigger commission? Valid questions, all.

How Do Commissions Work?

Loan officers are paid on commission, and they can receive commissions in two ways: (1) the origination fee and (2) yield spread premium

(YSP). The origination fee is the front-end commission that's clearly visible; the YSP is the back-end commission.

> Some loan officers, with only a high school education, are making more money than people with a doctorate degree.

Let's say you're buying a house, and you apply for a loan. You make your short list and get three Good Faith Estimates.

Near the top on the left side, you'll see the Origination Fee (sometimes it is under Broker's Fee) on your Good Faith Estimate. It's Line 801 on the standard GFE form (see Figure 5.2). (Line 800 is the top heading that reads: "Items Payable in Connection with Loan.") If it's listed under Mortgage Broker Fee instead, it will be Line 808. It may be a percentage point or a dollar amount, but usually it's a percentage point.

The most common Origination Fee is 1 percent, meaning 1 percent of the loan amount. On a $300,000 loan, for example, 1 percent = $3,000. You would be paying one point, or 1 percent.

How Do Loan Officers' Commissions Work?

Loan officers get commission based on this point. If their commission split is 50/50 with their employer, then they make $1,500 on the $3,000 Origination Fee. If they work for a more generous employer, and their commission split is 70/30, they make $2,100.

✐ NOTE
Commission splits between employers and loan officers can vary. More about this in Chapter 15. ✎

It's easy enough to see the Origination Fee you're paying: just look at your Good Faith Estimate.

But wait, there's more.

Your loan officer might not be happy making a measly $1,500 in commission on your loan. He or she may want to make more—make that, he or she *undoubtedly* wants to make more. Even if your loan officer were getting 100 percent commission, he or she still would want to make more. Why make $3,000 on a $300,000 loan when it's so easy to make double? Of course. The loan officer doubles his or her income, at your expense.

GOOD FAITH ESTIMATE

Applicants: **CAROLYN WARREN**	Application No. **WARREN 40 YEAR**
Property Addr:	Date Prepared: **05/09/2006**
Prepared By:	Loan Program: **40 YEAR FIXED**

The information provided below reflects estimates of the charges which you are likely to incur at the settlement of your loan. The fees listed are estimates-actual charges may be more or less. Your transaction may not involve a fee for every item listed. The numbers listed beside the estimates generally correspond to the numbered lines contained in the HUD-1 settlement statement which you will be receiving at settlement. The HUD-1 settlement statement will show you the actual cost for items paid at settlement.

Total Loan Amount $ **320,000**   Interest Rate: **7.000** %   Term: **480 / 480** mths.

800	ITEMS PAYABLE IN CONNECTION WITH LOAN:			PFC S F POC
801	Loan Origination Fee	*The 1 Point could be here*	$	
802	Loan Discount	*or on Line 808 below.*		✓
803	Appraisal Fee			400.00
804	Credit Report			18.00
805	Lender's Inspection Fee			
808	Mortgage Broker Fee	1.000%		3,200.00 ✓
809	Tax Related Service Fee			94.00 ✓
810	Processing Fee			500.00 ✓
811	Underwriting Fee			550.00 ✓
812	Wire Transfer Fee			15.00 ✓

1100	TITLE CHARGES:			PFC S F POC
1101	Closing or Escrow Fee	ANY ESCROW	$	575.00 ✓
1105	Document Preparation Fee			✓
1106	Notary Fees			
1107	Attorney Fees			
1108	Title Insurance	ANY TITLE		525.00
	1109. ESCROW COURIER AND WIRE			94.00 ✓

1200	GOVERNMENT RECORDING & TRANSFER CHARGES:		PFC S F POC
1201	Recording Fees	$	70.00
1202	City/County Tax/Stamps:		
1203	State Tax/Stamps:		

1300	ADDITIONAL SETTLEMENT CHARGES:		PFC S F POC
1302	Pest Inspection	$	

	Estimated Closing Costs		6,041.00

900	ITEMS REQUIRED BY LENDER TO BE PAID IN ADVANCE:			PFC S F POC
901	Interest for	15 days @ $	62.2222 per day	$	933.33 ✓
902	Mortgage Insurance Premium			✓
903	Hazard Insurance Premium			480.00
904				
905	VA Funding Fee			✓

1000	RESERVES DEPOSITED WITH LENDER:				PFC S F POC
1001	Hazard Insurance Premium	3 months @ $	40.00 per month	$	120.00
1002	Mortgage Ins. Premium Reserves	months @ $	per month		✓
1003	School Tax	months @ $	per month		
1004	Taxes and Assessment Reserves	6 months @ $	350.00 per month		2,100.00
1005	Flood Insurance Reserves	months @ $	per month		
		months @ $	per month		
		months @ $	per month		

	Estimated Prepaid Items/Reserves	3,633.33
TOTAL ESTIMATED SETTLEMENT CHARGES		9,674.33

COMPENSATION TO BROKER (Not Paid Out of Loan Proceeds):

1303. ysp 1	$

TOTAL ESTIMATED FUNDS NEEDED TO CLOSE:				TOTAL ESTIMATED MONTHLY PAYMENT:	
Purchase Price/Payoff (+)	400,000.00	New First Mortgage(-)		Principal & Interest	1,988.58
Loan Amount (-)	320,000.00	Sub Financing(-)		Other Financing (P & I)	
Est. Closing Costs (+)	6,041.00	New 2nd Mtg Closing Costs(+)		Hazard Insurance	40.00
Est. Prepaid Items/Reserves (+)	3,633.33			Real Estate Taxes	350.00
Amount Paid by Seller (-)				Mortgage Insurance	
				Homeowner Assn. Dues	
				Other	

Total Est. Funds needed to close	89,674.33	Total Monthly Payment	2,578.58

☑ This Good Faith Estimate is being provided by _____ a mortgage broker, and no lender has been obtained. These estimates are provided pursuant to the Real Estate Settlement Procedures Act of 1974, as amended (RESPA). Additional information can be found in the HUD Special Information Booklet, which is to be provided to you by your mortgage broker or lender, if your application is to purchase residential real property and the lender will take a first lien on the property. The undersigned acknowledges receipt of the booklet "Settlement Costs." and if applicable the Consumer Handbook on ARM Mortgages.

Applicant **CAROLYN WARREN**	Date	Applicant	Date

Calyx Form gfe.frm 11/01

Figure 5.2

So your loan officer structures your loan so that he or she will make a 1 percent commission "on the back," in addition to the 1 percent "on the front." The front-end commission is what you see—the Origination Fee or the Broker Fee. The back-end commission is the Big Secret. Now the officer gets $6,000 instead of $3,000. Much better, he or she thinks, with a smile.

Who's Getting Par Rate?

Par rate is the interest rate for which there would be zero rebate to the loan officer. It is possible to get par rate. That would be the lowest possible interest rate for the day. At par, your loan officer would make no back-end commission, because there would be no yield spread premium. In that case, you would pay an Origination Fee or a Broker Fee.

 You have the right to know what par rate is on your loan. Always ask that simple question.

But chances are, you're not getting par. According to several studies, 85 percent to 90 percent of loans have a YSP. Your loan officer is getting a little richer with a back-end commission, and you're paying for it every month for the rest of your life, until the loan is paid off, because you have a higher interest rate than you would have had if it had been the par rate. Clearly, you have a right to know about the back-end commissions.

 Loan officers do loans for themselves at par rate, unless they want to use the YSP to cover their closing costs.

Consider the following example:

$300,000 @ 6.5% = $1,896 per month, with 0 going to the broker (YSP)
$300,000 @ 7% = $1,996 per month, with $6,000 going to the broker

If you have a $300,000 loan and your interest rate is half a percent higher than par, you'll end up paying considerably more on a 30-year fixed rate. If your rate is 7 percent when par was 6.5 percent, then you're paying $1,996 each month instead of $1,896 (principal and interest payment; we don't need to factor in property taxes and insurance here, as they are separate from your loan). That's $100 more a month, which comes out to $36,000 more over the life of your loan. Does it annoy you that you could have had $100 more each month for yourself?

What could you have done with the $36,000 if you hadn't paid it out in extra interest payments? How much richer would you be if you'd invested that money for yourself instead of forking it over to fat-cat lenders?

"How can he (or she) live with himself?" you might wonder. "He knows he's making me shell out an extra hundred bucks every month, so how does he sleep at night?"

I'll tell you. He sleeps just fine, because he thinks he's worth it. He gave you good service at a price *you agreed to*. Besides, the underwriters approved your debt ratio with the higher payment, so there's nothing to worry about. That's what he thinks. His conscience is just fine. So what about the law?

There Should Be a Law

"There should be a law!" you cry, and you're right. And, in fact, there is a law. Federal regulations require mortgage brokers to disclose the yield spread premium, both on your Good Faith Estimate and on your HUD-1 Settlement Statement you sign at closing. On your GFE, you'll find it near the bottom. Under the list of "Total Estimated Settlement Charges," there is a line, in gray, that reads: "Compensation to Broker." It is there that they are supposed to state the estimated yield spread premium; although, most people don't notice it. It might read: "P.O.C. $6,000." If you don't know what that is, you might ask. Here's a typical explanation:

> P.O.C. stands for paid out of closing. It's what the bank pays us when we sell the loan to them.

That's true and accurate, but did you know that it is *you* who will be paying for that $6,000? Did you know you'll be paying for it every single month over the next 30 years? Did you know you'll be paying much more than $6,000 over 30 years, because 30 years is a long time to collect? Like I said before, you could pay an extra $36,000 so your loan officer can put an extra six grand in his or her own pocket.

Sidestepping the Law. Some mortgage brokers claim they don't have to disclose the YSP until you're at the signing table reviewing your Final

HUD-1 Settlement Statement. But how could that be fair? By that time, it's too late to negotiate your pricing. Besides, a Statement of Policy (Statement of Policy, 2001-1, October 18, 2001) from the department of Housing and Urban Development (HUD) says this:

> HUD currently requires the disclosure of yield spread premiums on the Good Faith Estimate and the HUD-1.

Recall from the first example in this chapter that the loan officer just put a "1" for the yield spread premium. That is illegal. According to the 1999 HUD Statement of Policy, it is to be "clearly disclosed so that the consumer can understand the nature and recipient of the payment"; and "at a minimum, all fees to the mortgage broker are to be clearly labeled and properly estimated on the GFE." (You can read the entire 27-page policy at www.hud.gov. Use the Search feature to locate it.)

In spite of the fact that inserting a "1" violates HUD policy, some loan officers do it anyway, and no one has ever objected. Of course, how can anyone object if they don't understand it? Even if, instead, it was written "1 percent," making it easier to understand, it would still be wrong. They're supposed to state it in dollars, to make it clear.

Some companies put a range, such as $0 to $6,000. They're saying they could make zero at par, or they could make up to $6,000. That's also wrong. They're supposed to give you an actual estimate for your own loan. (It is an estimate until your rate is locked in, because rates and YSPs vary daily.)

You should know how much over par rate you are paying. By law, they have to tell you if they broker out the loan to a wholesale lender.

The loan officer might downplay the issue by saying something like, "Naturally, that money doesn't go to me personally" (followed by cheerful laughter). But some of it does. And it doesn't matter to you how much does or doesn't; the loan officer's commission split is irrelevant. You still pay for it.

It's your right and your responsibility to know what the YSP is; therefore, don't be shy or reticent about asking. Simply say, "What is the yield spread premium on my loan?"

By law, the loan officer has to tell you. He or she will probably be surprised that you're savvy enough to know what YSP is—and will respect you more. You will be sending a silent yet very loud message that says, "I know what I'm doing here, so don't try any funny stuff. I'm onto loan shark tactics, and I'll notice. If you want my business, treat me with honesty." That's a very good message to send, by the way, and it's all done by asking one simple little question: "What is the YSP on this loan?"

When you get the dollar amount for the YSP, you will know if it's an additional 1 percent or more, because if your loan is $200,000 and the YSP is $2,000, you will see that it equals 1 percent. You'll have an idea of how much higher your interest rate is over par. But don't guess, ask. Just say, "What is par rate?" Again, the loan officer is required by law to tell you.

Understanding back-end commissions is the first step to getting a low rate, and everyone wants a low interest rate. I can recall only one person asking me up front what the YSP was on my rate quote. It was a man calling around, looking for the best refinance. I told him par rate and 1 percent YSP, to give him a choice. His next words, essentially, accused me of lying. Since I wasn't lying, I invited him to come in and see the rate sheets for himself. He refused.

> ✐ **NOTE**
> To be fair, I must say there are many mortgage stars who regularly disclose and explain the YSP. These are the people you want to do business with and recommend to your friends and associates. ✎

Deciding between Broker and Banker

Bankers are snickering, and the mortgage brokers are screaming, "Unfair!" What's all the furor about? It's the banker's best-kept secret, or as some would say, their dirty little secret.

Here it is: Bankers and direct lenders do not have to disclose their yield spread premium. Unlike mortgage brokers, they get to keep their back-end commissions private. They don't have to put it on your Good Faith Estimate; and when you ask, they don't have to tell you. When I did my loan mystery shopping, every single one I asked told me a fib.

"I don't see a yield spread premium on this Good Faith Estimate," I said. "What is the YSP on this loan?" Of course, I knew it was 1 percent, or $4,000 on my requested loan amount, but I wanted to test them.

"We're a bank, so we don't have that," they'd say proudly. What a lie! They received commissions for rates over par all right, they just didn't have to tell me—because they were lending their "own money" rather than getting paid by another wholesaler.

High Score, But Also High Maintenance

One time I had a woman call me for a loan on a house she was purchasing. She was a single woman, a first-time homebuyer. I knew she was shopping around for the best deal, because she told me. But here's the thing: she had a credit score of 820. Wow! It was the highest score I'd seen up to that point. She had my instant and utmost respect, because of her stellar score. I really wanted the honor of having her business. So I told her about back-end commissions, and that she could come into my office and I would show her the wholesale rate sheets, with the yield spread premiums on them.

 If your credit score is over 800, you have rock star status.

There would be no mysteries. We would shop together for the very cheapest loan for her. I told her my company needed to make 1 percent. (I got a fifty-fifty split, but that was irrelevant, so I didn't need to mention it.) She could have her choice of paying 1 percent Origination Fee or getting par, with the company getting 1 percent yield spread premium. (Or she could take a compromise with 5 percent Origination Fee and .5 percent YSP.)

She told me that of all the calls she had made I was the only loan officer who offered to bare it all. She came into my office; I showed her the rate sheets from various wholesale lenders, and we easily found the cheapest one. She chose to pay 1 percent Origination Fee and take the par rate, because she wanted the cheapest rate she could get for the long haul. I locked in her interest rate and gave her a Lock Confirmation form.

"Keep this. It is your guarantee of your interest rate," I explained.

She got a beautiful loan and was very happy. Her brother, an Internet millionaire, scrutinized her loan and agreed. His sister was getting a good deal.

Several years later, interest rates plummeted to an all-time low. It was news in all the papers and on television. So she called me up and asked if I would do her refinance. I said no thanks and let her go elsewhere. Surprised? It turned out that she was a very high-maintenance woman. She called me nearly every day for updates and asked more and more picayune questions about irrelevant details. What's more, her loan was time-consuming, because she had a complicated income that required tons of paperwork to go over in meticulous detail. She was a lot of work, so much so that I didn't make much per hour with my fifty-fifty split on 1 percent. I knew she'd expect to get par rate with 1 percent again, and I wasn't willing to work for that cheap a second time. Had she been easier to work with, however, I'd have happily said yes.

Brokers Acting like Bankers

Some mortgage brokers have the ability to do loans either "in house" or "brokered out." "In house" means they have their own money to lend on a very short-term basis. (Remember from the Introduction, where I told you about my lunch date with the loan officer who made 40 grand?)

They do the loan in the name of their own broker shop, funding with their own money, but then sell it to a larger lender within 3 to 21 days. When the law passed requiring them to disclose YSP, it made doing loans in house a more attractive option, because it put them on a level playing field with the bankers and direct lenders. Some loan officers always give their clients an "in house" loan, even though the interest rate may be higher by .25 to .5 percent, just because they don't want to reveal their back-end commission.

Why Does the Law Treat Brokers and Bankers Differently?

Why do mortgage brokers have to reveal their YSP while the bankers and direct lenders do not? Is it fair? Is it in the consumer's best interest? If you don't think it's right to have the back-end commission hidden from you, then you have an easy solution: choose to go to a mortgage broker for your home loan. This is why I advise having at least two mortgage brokers on your short list when you're shopping around.

You'll be with the majority of Americans if you choose to work with a mortgage broker. According to the National Mortgage Brokers Association, over 60 percent of all mortgages are arranged through mortgage brokers. Having worked for three national direct lenders and one mortgage broker, I'll admit to having a strong bias in favor of the mortgage brokers, because I was able to get cheaper loans for my clients by "going wholesale" as a mortgage broker. However, there are exceptions. In some communities there are independent banks that will undercut everyone else for certain types of loans that they happen to specialize in. I can't be more specific about that, because it will vary from state to state and from month to month.

> Some loan officers are afraid they'll lose your business if you see the YSP. This is your chance to show you value candor.

What's a Fair Price to Pay for Your Loan?

This issue of back-end commissions begs the question, What's fair? How much is too much, and what's a fair commission so the loan officer doesn't feel underpriced and refuses to take your business in the future? The answer to that is highly subjective, but I'll give you some information to base a ballpark figure on. Remember the loan officer who bragged about making 4 percent and $16,000? He told me the minimum he was willing to work for was $1,500—*if* the clients had good credit and were easy to work with. Others want at least $2,000. Most loan officers expect to make more if you have nonprime credit (a score of less than 620), because there's more work that goes into a loan with credit challenges. The same goes for an income-challenged loan. While most loan officers are willing to accept a $2,000 commission, others won't work for less than $5,000, so it's up to you to decide how much you're willing to pay.

> "I hate it that every time I do a loan I have to renegotiate my salary," one mortgage consultant told me.

The loan officer spends considerably more time shopping around for a subprime loan, getting the approval, and getting all the documentation conditions met. Because these loans take more time, loan officers deserve a bigger commission. More about that later, but the point is that greed drives many people, and they feel downright jolly about making obscenely large commissions at their client's expense when, if fact, they are willing to do the same work for less.

A 1 percent Origination Fee is pretty standard for the midsize market (approximately $200,000 to $450,000). If your loan is small (less than $150,000), you might expect to pay more points, especially if it is less than $100,000, because a small loan is just as much work and takes as much time as a larger loan. If you have a jumbo loan, then you can expect to pay less than one point. In some markets where jumbo and super-jumbo loans are the norm, zero origination points is standard, and the loan officer gets paid on back-end commission only. Again, it is your right, under the law, to ask what the YSP is.

A loan for subprime credit costs more, but charging quadruple is taking advantage.

More on YSPs

I want to address two additional questions regarding YSPs before moving on to the next chapter.

What Should You Do if YSP Is a Big Secret?

Mortgage brokers who have the ability to broker out loans to wholesale lenders or do loans "in house" with their own money have another trick up their sleeve to keep you in the dark. They can legally avoid disclosing the back-end commission to you by going with in-house lending, but then "change their mind" later and broker out. You'll see the YSP on your Final Settlement Statement at signing, but you didn't get the opportunity to see it earlier, and that's not fair to you.

There are two ways to solve this problem. One is to insist on having the YSP disclosed and only do business with a loan officer who puts it on your GFE. The other is for federal law to change, requiring bankers to reveal their YSPs as they do brokers. (In the meantime, I recommend the first option.)

Results of My Mystery Shopping Experiment

I posed as a homebuyer and applied for a loan with several companies, including an online mortgage company, two local mortgage brokers, a national direct lender, and Lending Tree, an online lead referral service. (Lending Tree can also do its own loans, but I used its referral service, which advertises, "When banks compete, you win." According to its disclosure, Lending Tree charges up to $1,300 to a mortgage company for a referral. So there is an extra middleman charge in your loan when you use a referral service.) The result of this experiment was fascinating.

Sadly, my mystery shopping experience uncovered lies and deception—even among the "reputable" lenders.

All but one kept their yield spread premium top secret. (The Good Faith Estimates are at the end of this chapter on pages 94–97 for you to see, in Figures 5.4 to 5.7. I've blocked out the names to protect their privacy and, in some cases, to spare their embarrassment.)

After reviewing one GFE that I received through a company referred by Lending Tree, I asked the loan officer what the yield spread premium was, because none was stated. Sounding surprised at my question, he said, "I see that you've been doing your homework."

But then he refused to tell me. He gave me a two-minute explanation on how they were their own bank (a mortgage broker that can either broker out to wholesale, or lend their own money temporarily and then sell the loan). As a bank, he said, they didn't have to *have* a yield spread premium, and that was how he could save me money over a mortgage broker. This is a lie. The truth is that they don't have to *disclose* it, but they *still make more money by offering rates over par.*

You can save an average of $1,225 by having unnecessary charges waived.

He wasn't saving me any money; his rate was the same, which is to be expected, because they all get their money from the same sources—such as the Federal National Mortgage Association (FNMA; also called Fannie Mae) chartered by Congress. I suppose he uses this slick speech on many unsuspecting people, but I found his dishonesty to be disappointing.

One GFE had a processing fee of $550. Since the processing fee is a "junk fee," designed to pad the lender's profits, I thought it was too high. I told him I thought the processing fee was a bit high and asked if there was room for negotiation. He was quick to offer to reduce it by a couple hundred dollars. He said that he had to pay his processor something, however. So maybe he hires an independent processor to work on his loans; if that's the case, and if his loan was the cheapest, I would be willing to pay a $300 processing fee. But in my opinion, $550 is too high.

I had the most intriguing experience with a local direct lender that specializes in doing subprime loans, but can also do prime loans. The loan officer there was by far the most "slippery." Get a load of this, because it goes with the territory for people with marginal credit. (I posed as having a 620 credit score on this one since his specialty was subprime lending.)

First, he flat-out refused to give me a Good Faith Estimate without pulling my credit report. He didn't want to believe what I told him about my credit and score. He said it was company policy not to provide a GFE without looking at credit. I told him to write in big red letters, "Based on information provided. Not a guarantee," but he still said it couldn't be done.

 Be wary of Good Faith Estimates that are formatted "creatively." What is it they don't want you to notice?

After his lengthy speech, I politely said, "If that's your company policy, I understand. Have a nice day."

Five hours later, I got a phone call from him. He said he'd spoken to his manager about my loan, and he really wanted my business. I stood firm on not giving my Social Security number for a credit check and told him I'd received a couple of Good Faith

(continued)

Estimates from other companies. After 10 more minutes of trying to persuade me to give out my Social Security number, he said he'd mail me a couple of his business cards.

I replied, "Since you're spending a stamp on me, why don't you go ahead and throw in a Good Faith Estimate with it?"

"Okay," he said, "but I have to write 'No Guarantee' on it."

The GFE arrived. It wasn't on the standard form. It stated ".75 Point" at the top of the page in bold but didn't state the dollar figure associated with the point. At the bottom, in smaller print, it showed an additional point of approximately 1.38, expressed as "Discount Pt. $3,328." Thus, he was charging $1,800 (.75 on $240,000) + $3,328 for a total of $5,128. Wow! No wonder he was splitting it up and hiding part of it—that's high for a $300,000 purchase. Then there were the junk fees: $100 for document preparation and a super-high processing fee of $675. In addition, his reconveyance fee, a fee charged by the county, and which is typically about $85, was $240, so it looked like an "up-charge" (a topic you'll read about in Chapter 6 on junk fees). However, on a purchase loan, there is no reconveyance fee, so it shouldn't have been on there at all. Instead, there should have been a recording fee of about $85.

Two more amazing things about this GFE, which was getting more laughable by the moment: First, he gave me an Interest-Only loan, even though I did not ask for that. I guess he was trying to entice me with the lower payment, but an Interest-Only loan was not in my best financial interest. Why put someone with a low debt ratio of 19 percent into that loan? Not smart. Second, he had my interest rate at 5.5 percent, but the APR was stated as 2.59 percent, which is an impossibility. The APR must be equal to or greater than the interest rate.

All-in-all, this was a sloppy, overpriced, sleazy estimate (see Figure 5.3); a real disappointment coming from one of the largest, most well-known, national home loan lenders in the United States. But never mind that, because according to this loan officer, I was going to get my best deal from them, because they had two people, including an underwriter, check over my loan—*as if that were unique.*

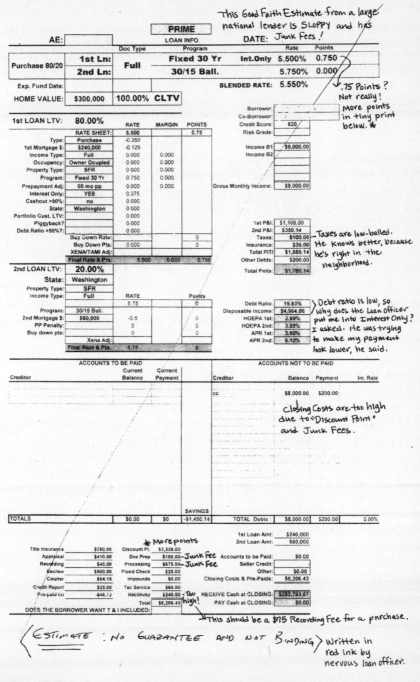

Figure 5.3

When I was posing as a loan mystery shopper, I got a follow-up email from one of the mortgage brokers who failed to reveal the YSP.

"I don't see a yield spread premium on your Good Faith Estimate," I replied. Here is his email response:

Carolyn,

I wanted you to know that YSP in not disclosed in GFEs, or I at least have not seen one. I also want you to know that there is no YSP on this transaction with us. YSP is also the first thing that I would look at if I was buying a house. My wife and I had a broker take advantage of us the first time we bought a house; he charged us 1 percent on the front and then we found out later he made 3 percent on the back of the loan.

This loan officer doesn't think YSP should be or ever is disclosed. Interesting. That told me a lot about the mortgage company he works for and how its employees are trained. Furthermore, the rate was not a par rate.

Sadly, this company received an award from their local Better Business Bureau. But then again, that's not so surprising—the BBB doesn't specialize in knowledge about fair lending, and it doesn't analyze Good Faith Estimates.

What if the YSP on Your Loan Goes Up?

One more thing: What if your Good Faith Estimate says the YSP is $3,000 but then at the signing table you see on the HUD Settlement Statement that the YSP is $4,000? What's the story?

It's highly likely that the YSP changed between the time the GFE was printed and the time you sign your final loan documents, especially since federal regulations require your loan officer to send you a GFE within three business days of making a formal application. There could be three reasons for this happening:

1. Your loan officer kept shopping and found a lender that paid more for the same interest rate.

2. Rates went down and your loan officer didn't tell you; he or she locked in your rate at the original agreed-upon rate.

3. Your loan officer chose not to lock in your rate because he or she wanted to gamble on making a bigger commission. Your loan was actually locked right before docs were drawn, and the officer's gamble paid off (rates went down).

Let's take the first scenario. If your loan officer spends an extra three hours loan shopping, should he or she get to keep the extra commission? If you insist the answer is no, then why should the loan officer bother? He or she will just go with the original wholesale lender he or she found and save time. When this happened to me, as a loan officer, I chose to split the windfall with my clients. I felt I deserved to make more because I took the extra trouble; but I also wanted to pass on the good fortune, so I'd make a call and let the clients know the good news. This was one way I earned their referral business.

In the second instance, when rates go down in the days between the original Good Faith Estimate and locking in the rate, who should benefit? The client, or the loan officer, or both? This would be a sophisticated question for you to ask your loan officer right up front. His or her answer will reveal a lot about what kind of person you are dealing with, and you'll position yourself as an intelligent, savvy consumer. You might think, "What's the point of asking this question?" If your loan officer is a liar, he or she will say you'll get the benefit of the lower rate, but then claim that rates didn't change and pocket extra back-end commission instead.

 Asking intelligent questions is one way you communicate that you are a savvy consumer.

That could happen, of course, but I think that by asking the question, "If rates go down, will you lock me in at a lower rate or will you keep the extra YSP?" you will accomplish two things:

1. You'll let your loan officer know you're not naive.
2. The dialogue will give you a sense of the loan officer's level of honesty, especially if you are an intuitive person and listen as much to *how* the loan officer answers as you do to *what* he or she says.

The third instance (loan officers not locking in loans because they want to gamble on rates) is a real bombshell, and I have a couple great stories you'll want to hear, especially since *most* loan officers play this game of chance. But I'll save them for Chapter 7, which addresses rate locks and rate lock scams (see Figures 5.4–5.7).

GOOD FAITH ESTIMATE

Applicants: **Carolyn Warren**	Application No: **Warren , C**
Property Addr: **TBD**	Date Prepared: **01/11/2006**
Prepared By:	Loan Program: **30 YRS FIXED**

The information provided below reflects estimates of the charges which you are likely to incur at the settlement of your loan. The fees listed are estimates-actual charges may be more or less. Your transaction may not involve a fee for every item listed. The numbers listed beside the estimates generally correspond to the numbered lines contained in the HUD-1 settlement statement which you will be receiving at settlement. The HUD-1 settlement statement will show you the actual cost for items paid at settlement.

Total Loan Amount $ **400,000**   Interest Rate: **6.125** %   Term: **360 / 360** mths

800	ITEMS PAYABLE IN CONNECTION WITH LOAN:			PFC S F POC
801	Loan Origination Fee		$	✓
802	Loan Discount			
803	Appraisal Fee			400.00
804	Credit Report			25.00
805	Lender's Inspection Fee			
808	Mortgage Broker Fee	2.000%	*Expensive. 2% upfront plus 1% YSP below*	8,000.00
809	Tax Related Service Fee		*TOTAL:*	✓
810	Processing Fee		*$12,000 commissions*	500.00 ✓ *Junk Fee*
811	Underwriting Fee			
812	Wire Transfer Fee			
	813 Application Fee			
	814 Lender's Fee		*WOW! A giant Junk Fee*	1,200.00 *Junk Fee*
				$1,700 Junk Fees!

1100	TITLE CHARGES:			PFC S F POC
1101	Closing or Escrow Fee:		$	600.00 ✓
1105	Document Preparation Fee			
1106	Notary Fees			
1107	Attorney Fees			
1108	Title Insurance:	**Title-Purchase**		600.00

1200	GOVERNMENT RECORDING & TRANSFER CHARGES:			PFC S F POC
1201	Recording Fees:		$	65.00
1202	City/County Tax/Stamps:			
1203	State Tax/Stamps:			

1300	ADDITIONAL SETTLEMENT CHARGES:			PFC S F POC
1302	Pest Inspection		$	

		Estimated Closing Costs	11,390.00

900	ITEMS REQUIRED BY LENDER TO BE PAID IN ADVANCE:			PFC S F POC
901	Interest for	15	days @ $	68.0556	per day	$	1,020.83
902	Mortgage Insurance Premium			
903	Hazard Insurance Premium			1,599.96 ✓
904				
905	VA Funding Fee			

1000	RESERVES DEPOSITED WITH LENDER:				PFC S F POC
1001	Hazard Insurance Premium	months @ $	133.33	per month	$
1002	Mortgage Ins. Premium Reserves	months @ $		per month	
1003	School Tax	months @ $		per month	
1004	Taxes and Assessment Reserves	months @ $	500.00	per month	✓
1005	Flood Insurance Reserves	months @ $		per month	
		months @ $		per month	
		months @ $		per month	

	Estimated Prepaid Items/Reserves	2,620.79

TOTAL ESTIMATED SETTLEMENT CHARGES   14,010.79

COMPENSATION TO BROKER (Not Paid Out of Loan Proceeds):

✱ 820 Yield Spread Premium (1%) *In addition to 2% up front, he's making 1% back end commission.* ⓢ *Not filled in $4,000.*

TOTAL ESTIMATED FUNDS NEEDED TO CLOSE:		TOTAL ESTIMATED MONTHLY PAYMENT:	
Purchase Price/Payoff (+)	600,000.00	New First Mortgage(-)	Principal & Interest	2,430.44
Loan Amount (-)	400,000.00	Sub Financing (-)	Other: Financing (P & I)	
Est. Closing Costs (+)	11,390.00	New 2nd Mtg Closing Costs(+)	Hazard Insurance	133.33
Est. Prepaid Items/Reserves (+)	2,620.79		Real Estate Taxes	500.00
Amount Paid by Seller (-)	15,000.00		Mortgage Insurance	
Down Payment	-200,000.00		Homeowner Assn. Dues	
			Other	

Total Est. Funds to you		989.21	Total Monthly Payment	3,063.77

☑ This Good Faith Estimate is being provided by _____ , a mortgage broker, and no lender has been obtained. These estimates are provided ... ement Procedures Act of 1974, as amended (RESPA). Additional information can be found in the HUD Special Information Booklet, which is to be provided to you by your mortgage broker or lender, if your application is to purchase residential real property and the lender will take a first lien on the property. The undersigned acknowledges receipt of the booklet "Settlement Costs." and if applicable the Consumer Handbook on ARM Mortgages.

Applicant **Carolyn Warren** _____ Date _____   Applicant _____ Date _____

Calyx Form gfe.frm 11/01

Figure 5.4

94

GOOD FAITH ESTIMATE

Applicants: CAROLYN N WARREN
Property Addr: TBD
Prepared By:

Application No: WARREN
Date Prepared: 01/06/2006
Loan Program: 30 YEAR FIXED

The information provided below reflects estimates of the charges which you are likely to incur at the settlement of your loan. The fees listed are estimates-actual charges may be more or less. Your transaction may not involve a fee for every item listed. The numbers listed beside the estimates generally correspond to the numbered lines contained in the HUD-1 settlement statement which you will be receiving at settlement. The HUD-1 settlement statement will show you the actual cost for items paid at settlement.

Total Loan Amount $ 400,000   Interest Rate: 5.875 %   Term: 360 / 360 mths

800	ITEMS PAYABLE IN CONNECTION WITH LOAN:				PFC S F POC
801	Loan Origination Fee	0.500%		$	2,000.00 ✓
802	Loan Discount				
803	Appraisal Fee				400.00 ✓
804	Credit Report				25.00 ✓
805	Lender's Inspection Fee				
808	Mortgage Broker Fee				
809	Tax Related Service Fee				
810	Processing Fee		*He quickly agreed to lower the Processing Fee*		350.00 ✓ Junk Fee
811	Underwriting Fee				600.00 ✓
812	Wire Transfer Fee				
	ADMINISTRATION FEE		*Agreed to delete this*		100.00 ✓ Junk Fee

1100	TITLE CHARGES:				PFC S F POC
1101	Closing or Escrow Fee:			$	550.00 ✓
1105	Document Preparation Fee				
1106	Notary Fees				
1107	Attorney Fees				
1108	Title Insurance:				637.00 ✓
	misc. third party fees, not under the control of Kiel Mortgage, may occur at the time of closing.				

1200	GOVERNMENT RECORDING & TRANSFER CHARGES:				PFC S F POC
1201	Recording Fees:			$	70.00 ✓
1202	City/County Tax/Stamps				
1203	State Tax/Stamps:				

1300	ADDITIONAL SETTLEMENT CHARGES:				PFC S F POC
1302	Pest Inspection			$	
	Interest rate and discount (if applicable) float at market, unless locked, and may be higher or lower at the time of settlement.				

			Estimated Closing Costs	4,732.00	

900	ITEMS REQUIRED BY LENDER TO BE PAID IN ADVANCE:				PFC S F POC
901	Interest for 10 days @ $ 65.2778 per day			$	652.78 ✓
902	Mortgage Insurance Premium				
903	Hazard Insurance Premium				1,440.00
904					
905	VA Funding Fee				

1000	RESERVES DEPOSITED WITH LENDER:				PFC S F POC
1001	Hazard Insurance Premium	3 months @ $	120.00 per month	$	360.00
1002	Mortgage Ins. Premium Reserves	months @ $	per month		
1003	School Tax	months @ $	per month		
1004	Taxes and Assessment Reserves	3 months @ $	500.00 per month		1,500.00
1005	Flood Insurance Reserves	months @ $	per month		
		months @ $	per month		
		months @ $	per month		

			Estimated Prepaid Items/Reserves	3,952.78	
				8,684.78	

TOTAL ESTIMATED SETTLEMENT CHARGES

COMPENSATION TO BROKER (Not Paid Out of Loan Proceeds): $

No YSP disclosed. He said it was never put on the GFE.

TOTAL ESTIMATED FUNDS NEEDED TO CLOSE:			TOTAL ESTIMATED MONTHLY PAYMENT:	
Purchase Price/Payoff (+)	600,000.00	New First Mortgage(-)	Principal & Interest	2,366.15
Loan Amount (-)	400,000.00	Sub Financing(-)	Other Financing (P & I)	
Est. Closing Costs (+)	4,732.00	New 2nd Mtg Closing Costs(+)	Hazard Insurance	120.00
Est. Prepaid Items/Reserves (+)	3,952.78		Real Estate Taxes	500.00
Amount Paid by Seller (-)			Mortgage Insurance	
			Homeowner Assn. Dues	
			Other	

Total Est. Funds needed to close		208,684.78	Total Monthly Payment	2,986.15

☑ This Good Faith Estimate is being provided by _____ a mortgage broker, and no lender has been obtained. These estimates are provided _____ Settlement Procedure Act of 1974, as amended (RESPA). Additional information can be found in the HUD Special Information Booklet, which is to be provided to you by your mortgage broker or lender, if your application is to purchase residential real property and the lender will take a first lien on the property. The undersigned acknowledges receipt of the booklet "Settlement Costs." and if applicable the Consumer Handbook on ARM Mortgages.

Applicant CAROLYN N WARREN   Date   Applicant   Date

Calyx Form gfe frm 11/01

Figure 5.5

GOOD FAITH ESTIMATE

Applicants: Carolyn Warren

Property Addr:

Prepared By:

I like this loan, but I don't like it that he fails to disclose the YSP. It was approx. 1% or $4,000 that day.

Application No:

Date Prepared: 01/03/2006

Loan Program: 30 Year Fixed

The information provided below reflects estimates of the charges which you are likely to incur at the settlement of your loan. The fees listed are estimates-actual charges may be more or less. Your transaction may not involve a fee for every item listed. The numbers listed beside the estimates generally correspond to the numbered lines contained in the HUD-1 settlement statement which you will be receiving at settlement. The HUD-1 settlement statement will show you the actual cost for items paid at settlement.

Total Loan Amount $ 400,000   Interest Rate 6.000 %   Term: 360 / 360 mths

800	ITEMS PAYABLE IN CONNECTION WITH LOAN:			PFC S F POC
801	Loan Origination Fee		$	✓
802	Loan Discount	*No Points.*		
803	Appraisal Fee	*this was the cheapest loan*	350.00	
804	Credit Report	*and it came from a local broker*		✓
805	Lender's Inspection Fee			✓
808	Mortgage Broker Fee			✓
809	Tax Related Service Fee			✓
810	Processing Fee	*Junk fee I'd try to cut in half* →	495.00	✓
811	Underwriting Fee		595.00	✓
812	Wire Transfer Fee			✓
	Admin			✓

1100	TITLE CHARGES:		PFC S F POC
1101	Closing or Escrow Fee:	$ 500.00	✓
1105	Document Preparation Fee	50.00	✓
1106	Notary Fees		
1107	Attorney Fees		
1108	Title Insurance:	500.00	

1200	GOVERNMENT RECORDING & TRANSFER CHARGES:		PFC S F POC
1201	Recording Fees:	$ 35.00	
1202	City/County Tax/Stamps:		
1203	State Tax/Stamps:		

1300	ADDITIONAL SETTLEMENT CHARGES:		PFC S F POC
1302	Pest Inspection	$	

		Estimated Closing Costs	2,525.00	

900	ITEMS REQUIRED BY LENDER TO BE PAID IN ADVANCE:			PFC S F POC
901	Interest for 15 days @ $ 65.7634 per day		$ 986.30	✓
902	Mortgage Insurance Premium			✓
903	Hazard Insurance Premium			
904				
905	VA Funding Fee			✓

1000	RESERVES DEPOSITED WITH LENDER:			PFC S F POC
1001	Hazard Insurance Premium	2 months @ $	per month	$
1002	Mortgage Ins. Premium Reserves	months @ $	per month	✓
1003	School Tax	months @ $	per month	
1004	Taxes and Assessment Reserves	6 months @ $	per month	
1005	Flood Insurance Reserves	months @ $	per month	
		months @ $	per month	
		months @ $	per month	

	Estimated Prepaid Items/Reserves	986.30
TOTAL ESTIMATED SETTLEMENT CHARGES		3,511.30

COMPENSATION TO BROKER (Not Paid Out of Loan Proceeds):

☆ *YSP is not disclosed. There MUST be one, because there are no points up front. They don't work for free.* $

TOTAL ESTIMATED FUNDS NEEDED TO CLOSE:			TOTAL ESTIMATED MONTHLY PAYMENT:	
Purchase Price/Payoff (+)	600,000.00	New First Mortgage(-)	Principal & Interest	2,398.20
Loan Amount (-)	400,000.00	Sub Financing (-)	Other Financing (P & I)	
Est. Closing Costs (+)	2,525.00	New 2nd Mtg Closing Costs(+)	Hazard Insurance	
Est. Prepaid Items/Reserves (+)	986.30		Real Estate Taxes	
Amount Paid by Seller (-)			Mortgage Insurance	
			Homeowner Assn. Dues	
			Other	

Total Est. Funds needed to close	203,511.30	Total Monthly Payment	2,398.20

☑ This Good Faith Estimate is being provided by _____ , a mortgage broker, and no lender has been obtained. These estimates are provided _____ e Settlement Procedures Act of 1974, as amended (RESPA). Additional information can be found in the HUD Special Information Booklet, which is to be provided to you by your mortgage broker or lender. If your application is to purchase residential real property and the lender will take a first lien on the property. The undersigned acknowledges receipt of the booklet "Settlement Costs," and if applicable the Consumer Handbook on ARM Mortgages.

Applicant Carolyn Warren   Date   Applicant   Date

Calyx Form gfe.frm 11/01

Figure 5.6

GOOD FAITH ESTIMATE

Applicants: Carolyn Warren
Property Addr:
Prepared By:

Application No:
Date Prepared: 01/03/2006
Loan Program: 30 Year Fixed

The information provided below reflects estimates of the charges which you are likely to incur at the settlement of your loan. The fees listed are estimates–actual charges may be more or less. Your transaction may not involve a fee for every item listed. The numbers listed beside the estimates generally correspond to the numbered lines contained in the HUD-1 settlement statement which you will be receiving at settlement. The HUD-1 settlement statement will show you the actual cost for items paid at settlement.

Total Loan Amount $ 400,000   Interest Rate: 6.000 %   Term: 360 / 360 mths

800	ITEMS PAYABLE IN CONNECTION WITH LOAN:		$	PFC S F POC
801	Loan Origination Fee			✓
802	Loan Discount			
803	Appraisal Fee		350.00	
804	Credit Report			
805	Lender's Inspection Fee			✓
808	Mortgage Broker Fee			✓
809	Tax Related Service Fee			✓
810	Processing Fee		495.00	✓
811	Underwriting Fee		595.00	✓
812	Wire Transfer Fee			✓
	Admin			✓

Handwritten: No Origination Fee or Broker Fee, so we know there must be a YSP. (see below.)

1100	TITLE CHARGES:			PFC S F POC
1101	Closing or Escrow Fee:		500.00	✓
1105	Document Preparation Fee		50.00	✓
1106	Notary Fees			
1107	Attorney Fees			
1108	Title Insurance:		500.00	

Handwritten: >Doc Prep Junk Fee $50.<

1200	GOVERNMENT RECORDING & TRANSFER CHARGES:			PFC S F POC
1201	Recording Fees:		35.00	
1202	City/County Tax/Stamps:			
1203	State Tax/Stamps:			

1300	ADDITIONAL SETTLEMENT CHARGES:			PFC S F POC
1302	Pest Inspection	$		

		Estimated Closing Costs	2,525.00	

900	ITEMS REQUIRED BY LENDER TO BE PAID IN ADVANCE:			PFC S F POC
901	Interest for 15 days @ $ 65.7534 per day	$	986.30	✓
902	Mortgage Insurance Premium			
903	Hazard Insurance Premium			
904				
905	VA Funding Fee			✓

1000	RESERVES DEPOSITED WITH LENDER:			PFC S F POC
1001	Hazard Insurance Premium	2 months @ $	per month $	
1002	Mortgage Ins. Premium Reserves	months @ $	per month	✓
1003	School Tax	months @ $	per month	
1004	Taxes and Assessment Reserves	6 months @ $	per month	
1005	Flood Insurance Reserves	months @ $	per month	
		months @ $	per month	
		months @ $	per month	

		Estimated Prepaid Items/Reserves	986.30

TOTAL ESTIMATED SETTLEMENT CHARGES	3,511.30

COMPENSATION TO BROKER (Not Paid Out of Loan Proceeds):

Handwritten: ✱ No YSP Disclosed! Violates Federal law. ($4,000 should be shown) left blank.

TOTAL ESTIMATED FUNDS NEEDED TO CLOSE:		TOTAL ESTIMATED MONTHLY PAYMENT:	
Purchase Price/Payoff (+)	600,000.00	New First Mortgage(-)	Principal & Interest	2,398.20
Loan Amount (-)	400,000.00	Sub Financing(-)	Other Financing (P & I)	
Est. Closing Costs (+)	2,525.00	New 2nd Mtg Closing Costs(+)	Hazard Insurance	
Est. Prepaid Items/Reserves (+)	986.30		Real Estate Taxes	
Amount Paid by Seller (-)			Mortgage Insurance	
			Homeowner Assn. Dues	
			Other	

Total Est. Funds needed to close	203,511.30	Total Monthly Payment	2,398.20

☑ This Good Faith Estimate is being provided by _____, a mortgage broker, and no lender has been obtained. These estimates are provided pursuant to the Real Estate Settlement Procedures Act of 1974, as amended (RESPA). Additional information can be found in the HUD Special Information Booklet, which is to be provided to you by your mortgage broker or lender, if your application is to purchase residential real property and the lender will take a first lien on the property. The undersigned acknowledges receipt of the booklet "Settlement Costs," and if applicable the Consumer Handbook on ARM Mortgages.

Applicant Carolyn Warren _____ Date _____ Applicant _____ Date _____

Calyx Form gfe.frm 11/01

Figure 5.7

Coming Up

Would you like the straight scoop on fair fees versus rip-offs that cost consumers thousands of dollars? The next chapter demystifies loan costs, answers sticky questions, and lets you be a "fly on the wall" to some outrageous conversations.

CHAPTER 6

Step 6:
Negotiate Lower
Fees and Rates

Will someone please empty the garbage? The pile of junk fees is stinking up the place! It's a disgrace to the mortgage industry, and it's an outrage to the American public. What's more, it's getting worse. I've never seen so many junk fees as on new loans written in the last 12 months.

If you go bumbling into dangerous avenues in the dark without protection, you've got to expect to get hurt. The metaphor applies. Extreme corporate greed has made the streets of Mortgage Land perilous. If you don't watch where you step, they'll rob you blind. They've been practicing what to say, and how to say it fluidly, and how to move on to the next topic before you can protest. For instance, one mentor to a new loan officer had this advice about explaining closing costs to clients: "Be confident when you tell them what the charges are. If you blink or stutter, the customer will pick up on that."

> Your only defense against being overcharged is knowledge.

That's why, in this chapter, I blow the cover off the book of tricks used by smooth-talking sharks to fatten their own wallets at your expense. I'll explain how to negotiate for lower fees and rates—and, specifically, tell you what to say and what to ask for.

I place the blame for unnecessary fees and exorbitant charges on the fat cats sitting high in their fancy corporate offices. It's not the individual loan officers who invent stupid fees like the Document Preparation Fee and the Administration Fee. As employees of the companies they work for, they're required, for the most part, to charge the fees dictated by their companies. Loan officers do not get paid commission based on fees; they are pure profit for the corporations and banks. They're also negotiable.

You are not required to pay these insane, extra fees. You can negotiate to have them waived, and you should. The time to do that is *before* you sign your Good Faith Estimate. And because it's law that you be provided with a GFE within three business days of making an application, that's early on in the game.

Keep in mind that if you sign and return the GFE with all kinds of bogus charges, then you have agreed to pay them. If you try to object when you go to sign your final loan documents, they'll just pull out a copy of your signed GFE and say, "Sorry, you agreed." Therefore, the time to negotiate your fees is when you're choosing your loan officer off of your short list.

Here's a sample scenario. Let's say you've narrowed your list down from three to two:

1. The first GFE has an interest rate of 6.25 percent, a 1 percent origination fee, a $600 processing fee, and a $250 document preparation fee.

2. The second GFE has an interest rate of 6.5 percent, a 1 percent origination fee, and a $250 processing fee.

You want the lower rate of 6.25 percent, but you don't want to waste $850 in bogus processing and document preparation fees, so you call loan officer number one. Here is a script you can follow or adapt to fit your own situation:

Homebuyer: "This is Carolyn, and I'm calling back to thank you for your Good Faith Estimate."

Loan Officer: "Great! Are you ready to get started?"

Homebuyer: "To be frank, I'm trying to decide between your company and one other. I'd like to work with you, but the two junk fees are holding me back from making a commitment. Do you have any flexibility?"

Loan Officer: "Certainly, I can be flexible. Which fees are holding you back?"

Homebuyer: "Two—the processing fee and the document preparation fee. I don't want to waste $850 on nonessential junk fees that other companies don't charge."

Now the ball is in the loan officer's court. He or she wants your business and is going to negotiate.

There are two important takeaway points here:

1. You should protest every nonessential fee.
2. If a particular company is loaded with four or more junk fees, cross them off your short list.

Categorizing Fees

For your convenience and ease, I'm going to divide fees into three categories:

1. Fees you should never pay
2. Fees you may or may not wish to negotiate
3. Fees that are required

More often than not, people misinterpret which fees they are obligated to pay and which fees are bogus. Here are my suggestions.

Junk Fees: The Dirty Dozen

There are 12 fees you should *not* pay. In alphabetical order, they are:

> ✐ **NOTE**
> This list is my professional opinion, based on more than a decade in the mortgage business, on both the retail and wholesale sides of lending. ✎

1. *Administrative (Admin Fee).* Does nothing more than add profit to the corporate office.
2. *Application Fee.* Some companies collect money from you up front so you won't jump ship. Most companies take the risk, so you never have to pay this fee. Jump before getting onboard if they try to obligate you early.

3. *Appraisal Review Fee.* On zero-down loans, lenders often get a second opinion from another appraiser. This shouldn't be an issue on purchase loans, because the market value is where buyer and seller meet on price. If lenders feel they want another opinion, let them pay for it.

4. *Ancillary Fee.* I couldn't believe my eyes when I saw this one. They ran out of names for their junk fees. The mortgage company that charged an Ancillary Fee advertised "No Points!" It would be better to pay a point than an Ancillary Fee, because points are up-front interest payments, and usually income tax deductible.

5. *Courier Fee.* Some mortgage brokers hire a courier to transport your signed docs back to the wholesale lender. Others use a free transbox service or overnight courier such as FedEx. At times, the wholesale rep may pick them up. I've seen companies charge for a courier even though they simply walked across the street to hand over the loan docs. A courier fee may be charged by the mortgage company or by the escrow company—or by both. When people object to paying a courier fee(s), they'll delete it. Passing the documents from one office to another is part of the cost of doing business. If they choose to hire a courier, let them pay for it. That is in my opinion, although some argue that the $35 to $75 fee is too small to bother to object.

6. *Document Preparation (Doc Prep Fee).* This fee is a relatively new invention. You don't have to pay extra for lenders to print up your loan documents. Loan docs are about 50 pages, and lenders get their paper for less than a penny a page, so you do the math—the cost for paper and ink does not warrant the $50 to $150 fee they want to charge you. If they say it costs them money to print out the docs, offer them a couple quarters—that should cover their so-called extra expense. Preparing loan documents is a part of the loan business; charging an extra fee for doc prep is like a restaurant charging you for napkins.

7. *Document Review (Doc Review Fee).* The loan funder reviews the documents after they come back from signing to make sure all pages were signed properly and that all conditions (required paperwork such as current pay stubs) are in the file before she funds the loan. It takes 10 to 30 minutes, depending on the loan. No extra cost is warranted.

8. *Email Fee.* Huh? A ridiculous fee some escrow companies add to pad their profits. They claim that it costs them to receive loan docs from the lender via email, because they have to print them out,

using their own paper and ink. I say that's what their big escrow fee is for, and I would refuse to pay it. (See Doc Prep Fee, above.)

9. *Processing Fee.* Charging a processing fee has become increasingly common. Some lenders use it to pay for their advertising and direct mail. If you don't like the idea of supporting junk mail from mortgage lenders, you may not wish to pay for it. Occasionally, a loan officer may hire an independent processor and charge you separately for that assistance. I think that's fair, as long as it's not over $400.

10. *Title Review Fee.* You pay for title insurance, yes, but you don't pay for the underwriter to read it. The money doesn't go to the underwriter anyway, who is on salary. It's just another one of those official-sounding fees to pad company profits.

11. *Settlement Fee.* No, you don't pay for lenders to close the loan. Believe me, they want to close it and get paid. They won't fail to close and let all their hard work go to waste, because you're too smart to pay this extra, meaningless fee. Don't be shy; most companies don't charge a settlement fee.

12. *Survey Fee.* Unnecessary. Plenty of people have had it waived, so why shouldn't you?

Additional "Creative" Fees. You also need to be on the lookout for newly invented nonsense fees, and reject them. Here's a doozey that one company tried to get away with: Photo Review Fee, $15. Ha! As if they couldn't look at the photos on the appraisal report without collecting an extra $15. One bank has a meaningless fee called a $125 Satisfaction Fee.

The Lender's Second Opinion. When I worked for a wholesale lender that specialized in zero-down loans, more times than not the underwriters would order a second opinion on the appraisal. At the time, three out of the four underwriters in our office had less than two years' experience and were wary of signing off on the value of the appraisal. This was understandable: the company was lending hundreds of thousands of dollars with no collateral, and they didn't want to make a mistake. The fourth underwriter was seasoned, so she didn't call for this extra charge, except in the rare instance where something truly was doubtful about the value.

For a second opinion, they would call an appraiser on their list and ask him or her to read over the original appraisal just to assure them the value was valid. As two of the newbies gained experience, they stopped

Follow Through with Your Signed GFE

Be sure to take your signed Good Faith Estimate with you to your final loan signing, as proof that you have refused to sign for any of the "dirty dozen" junk fees just described, as well as any other "creative" ones you noticed. With your GFE in hand, they can't tack these fees on at closing. And they may try, hoping you're too distracted to notice; but don't let them get away with this bait and switch. In fact, feel free to use that term as "mace" against this crime. Bait and switch is illegal, and no one wants to be found guilty.

As noted at the beginning of this discussion, whatever fees you agreed to pay with your signature on the GFE the lender has the right to hold onto; therefore, you must review your GFE carefully. Then at closing, you simply pull out your GFE and compare it to the HUD Settlement Statement. It's quick and easy to compare, because you were smart from the get-go, and that makes you feel confident at closing. As added armor, you've also asked for a written guarantee that the Settlement Statement will be within 10 percent of the Good Faith Estimate.

calling for so many appraisal reviews, but one appeared to be lazy. He called for them all the time, simply because he didn't want to make a decision. Now I ask you this: Is it fair that you have to pay a $400 Appraisal Review Fee if you happen to get Mr. Lazy or Ms. Newbie as an underwriter rather than Ms. Seasoned? (It's all luck of the draw as to which underwriter picks your loan file.) I think not. The company itself should absorb its own training costs.

The poor loan officers were affected by this luck of the draw, too. They could never predict ahead of time whether or not an Appraisal Review Fee would be charged, so they never knew to put it on the GFE ahead of time.

I applaud all the loan officers who called me or my office complaining about the tacked on Appraisal Review Fee, and I applaud all the loan officers who review the HUD Settlement Statement before their clients get to the signing table. These stars in Mortgage Land are truly your advocates, working behind your back to get you the best deal they can and to save you money.

As a wholesale account executive, I objected to the Appraisal Review Fee every chance I got, but there was only so much influence I had, as I'll explain in the minute. The loan officers were our clients, so we wanted to make them happy. Sometimes a loan officer called, steaming mad, exclaiming, "What's this $400 fee I see here? I'm not charging my client that! I want you to waive it before my clients go in to sign." Then the company responded by waiving the fee.

> Some loan officers say a second opinion on an appraisal of a purchase loan is unwarranted, because the market dictates the value.

I told my loan account manager that whenever any of my loan officers called to object about a junk fee, just delete it without further ado. Don't bother asking the sales manager or the branch manager—just delete it. This usually worked, although occasionally she had to get permission over my head (if I had already waived a lot for the month).

Every single month, tens of thousands of dollars worth of junk fees were waived, because someone objected. Conversely, every single month, tens of thousands of dollars of junk fees were paid by homebuyers and homeowners refinancing, because no one bothered to object. In all, far more were paid than waived.

We all hate unnecessary and unfair junk fees. Honorable employees of companies fight them as best we can. But, ultimately, we need you, the client—the homebuyer or the homeowner refinancing—to back us up. If you object and refuse to sign, we'll have better success in getting the fat cats up in their fancy corporate offices, who never have to face a consumer, to stop padding their bottom line.

Questionable Fees

Three fees fall into this, the second, category:

1. *Discount Fee.* Just make sure you truly got a discount on your interest rate, and that there is no yield spread premium, service release premiums, yield differential, rate participation fee, or service release fee. (All various names for the YSP.)

Behind the Scenes

I heard someone say she wished she could be a fly on the wall, overhearing what goes on behind the scenes at mortgage offices. I grant that wish here, with a discussion that went on between loan officers of various companies:

Lady Loan Officer: "Who has creative junk fees? I'm searching for some ideas. Our company would like to switch from using a single large broker fee to using multiple smaller junk fees in order to reduce a client's temptation to negotiate our fees down. So, what are you calling your junk fees? Do you have some ideas for names? I'd really appreciate any help you can provide."

Respondent 1: "We do the PITA fee. People think it has something to do with PITI (principal, interest, taxes, insurance), because they're somewhat familiar with that. But to us it stands for Pain in the Ass, an extra $395 for those annoying borrowers. (I apologize if the term offends you, but that is what they call it.) It's like, sign and get out of here. Next borrower, please."

Respondent 2: "As to creative junk fee names, call them what they are. And don't pad them."

Respondent 3: "Instead of trying to mislead your clients, why not merely explain the process and your profit? It is very simple, easy, and honest. No one can argue with a business making a profit. If they do, they are more than welcome to seek out a charity mortgage firm."

Respondent 4: "This discussion is repulsive. You denigrate our profession. The aspersions cast by your chosen sobriquet junk fee sadden me. How many fees do you need to make? Points and processing. The need to hide your fees, to disperse them throughout a HUD under different names, is revolting. I denounce you in the name of all decent, honest dealers in Notes secured by Deeds of Trust."

Did you see some mortgage professionals here you'd be happy to give your business to? These are what I call the true stars in the mortgage industry.

2. *Underwriting Fee.* Typically, this charge comes from wholesale lenders, and they will not waive it, so if you don't pay it, the loan officer must. If your loan officer is forced to pay this fee out of his or her commission, he or she is going to make sure the commission is large enough to cover it *and* his or her fair take. Even mortgage brokers have to pay this fee when they do their own loans. Personally, I don't object to it, as long as it's not over $600.

3. *Warehouse Fee.* Many mortgage firms must borrow funds on a short-term basis in order to originate loans that are to be sold later in the secondary mortgage market (or to investors). When the prime rate is higher on short-term loans than on mortgage loans, the mortgage firm has an economic loss. They may offset this by charging a warehouse fee.

Legitimate Fees and Third-Party Costs

Eight fees fall under the "legit" category:

1. *Appraisal.* Federal regulations say you have a right to receive a copy of your appraisal report at closing, although it does belong to the mortgage company that ordered it. The appraisal assures you and the lender that the property value warrants the size of the loan. This is a good thing.

2. *Attorney Fee or Escrow Fee.* An independent, impartial party must handle closing and dispersing funds. Just make sure this third party doesn't jump on the bandwagon with its own junk fee, such as an email fee. The regular fee should cover it all.

2. *Credit Report.* Lenders will not approve a loan without reviewing the credit report. Ask for a copy at closing, because it will show your true credit score.

4. *Flood Certification.* Your property may be on the top of Queen Anne Hill, but you still must have it certified as not being in a flood zone. Or, if it is, then you need flood insurance. Pay this small fee; don't make your loan officer pay it, because then he will increase his commission to cover it and you'll be paying for it anyway.

5. *Tax Service Fee.* Lenders require this service to protect their own money; and, remember, they have invested more into your home

than you have. The service makes sure the property taxes are paid, because if they aren't, the state can foreclose, taking ownership of the property. I say, don't make a fuss over this small fee.

6. *Title Insurance.* This one-time cost protects you for the life of the loan. It insures your title against false liens and judgments, which happens frequently, especially if you have a common last name. It also protects you from fraud, false affidavits, forged deeds, unknown heirs, impersonations, and mistakes. It's so important you'd want it even if it weren't required. If you want to check to see if the cost is fair, you can call a couple local title companies for a verbal quote over the phone, but they'll need an address and purchase price to give you a quote.

7. *Recording Fee or Reconveyance Fee.* The county recorder's office or local authority charges for recording the Deed of Trust. The cost depends on the number of pages involved. It's less than $100.

8. *State Tax or State Stamps.* Some states have this as a source of state revenue. If so, it's unavoidable.

Beware Third-Party Padding.   Another thing to be aware of is the reasonable cost for a third-party fee. Some unscrupulous companies add their own profit on top of third-party costs. Here's an example. It was the holiday season, and one major mortgage company threw a Christmas party for its employees. Awards were passed out, honoring the top producers. So far, so good. But then came an award for the loan officer who ripped off the most clients via the *credit report up-charge.*

It works like this: Credit reports cost the company $15, but whenever he could get away with it, the loan officer charged the homebuyer $60, generating an extra $45 profit for the company.

You read that right. A smooth-talker was given an award for lying about how much the credit report actually cost, and for overcharging the client. He had the gall to quadruple the fee, and then got an award for being dishonest more often than the others in his company.

If a third-party fee seems unreasonably high, you can ask to see the original invoice.

Good Client/Bad Client

If a person causes a loan officer extreme aggravation, thereby making his or her loan far more time-consuming, then the loan officer is likely to add a fee to help compensate for the extra grief. As one of my friends says about certain difficult clients, "I see an irritation fee in these people's future."

If a client is obstinate, difficult, throws tantrums, shouts and pouts, refuses to provide paperwork until he or she gets a dozen reminders, falsely represents his or income and assets, then why shouldn't that client pay more for the extra work hours he or she caused?

On the other hand, if a client has all his or her paperwork ready and is a joy to work with, why shouldn't that person get a price break? Often he or she does. I've heard many loan officers say that they were going to waive a fee or lower their YSP because a particular client was so great. I've done it myself when a loan turned out to be easier and quicker than expected. That's why I said earlier, when you're shopping three lenders for your short list, be sure to say you have all your documentation handy, and say that you'll be easy to work with.

Don't make a pest of yourself by calling every day. Your loan isn't the only one in the pipeline.

One time I had a homeowner who was doing a small ($40,000) loan to get cash for a remodeling project. He said he was in a hurry, and I told him closing would take approximately two to three weeks, because that was the way the market was at that time. Every day, without fail, he called the underwriter and asked her if his loan was done yet and whined about what a hurry he was in to get the cash. After about 10 days of this, the underwriter stomped into my office and said she was going to turn down his loan, because she was sick and tired of his daily tirades. She was serious. She was printing out a denial to send him. Knowing how desperate this guy was for the cash, I persuaded her to keep the loan open by saying I'd add a grief fee to the closing costs. I don't remember what we called it on the Settlement Statement, but his fussing cost him $400.

Help on My Web Site, AskCarolynWarren.com

I'd like to share with you an email letter I received from a woman whom I helped save money on her refinance. I've never met her, because she and her husband live states away, but I advised her on how she could (and should) save money via my Web site. Her letter follows.

> Hi Carolyn,
>
> I have good news to report! First, I want to thank you for your advice on challenging the lender on the unnecessary charges on my GFE.
>
> I must admit, my husband took over the negotiations, and he got them to waive the Doc Draw Fee of $200. Not only that, but they waived the $300 Survey Fee; the $250 Settlement of Closing Fee; the Title Insurance of $1,714.20 was reduced to $967.80 (because of a discount owed to us); the Tax Certificate of $100 was reduced to $65.92; and a Home Equity charge of $161.10 (associated with home equity loans, which this is not) was also waived!
>
> The good news is, our closing costs were $2,892.17 instead of the original estimate of $4,358.86.
>
> Thank you for bringing to our awareness how junk fees appear as legitimate charges, and once questioned, the lenders come clean. Our lender didn't give my husband any trouble at all! By the time he was finished with them, they had his respect. Our closing went without a hitch, in the comfort of our living room!
>
> Judy

And in Figure 6.1 take a look at a Good Faith Estimate of another homebuyer I coached. The crossed-off fees saved her a total of $3,825. Her loan officer was more than happy to remove six unnecessary fees to keep her business.

My Web sites are www.AskCarolynWarren.com and www.Mortgage-Helper.com.

GOOD FAITH ESTIMATE
(Not a Loan Commitment)

The information provided below reflects estimates of the charges which you are likely to incur at the settlement of your loan. The fees listed are estimates - actual charges may be more or less. Your transaction may not involve a fee for every item listed. The numbers listed beside the estimates generally correspond to the numbered lines contained in the HUD-1 or HUD-1A settlement statement which you will be receiving at settlement. The HUD-1 or HUD-1A settlement statement will show you the actual cost for items paid at settlement.

HUD-1	DESCRIPTION OF CHARGES	AMOUNT
801	Loan Origination Fee @ 1.000%	3,150.00 A
802	Loan Discount Fee @ 1.000%	3,150.00 A *deleted
803	Appraisal Fee	450.00
804	Credit Report	40.00
805	Inspection Fee	0.00
806	Mortgage Insurance Application Fee	0.00
807	Assumption Fee	0.00
808	Mortgage Broker Fee	109.00 A
809	Tax Related Service Fee	195.00 A *deleted
810	Processing Fee	325.00
811	Underwriting Fee	0.00
812	Wire Transfer Fee	295.00 *deleted
813	Application Fee	375.00 A
814	Commitment Fee	0.00
815	Lender's Rate Lock-In Fee	0.00
901	Interest @ $86.3014/day for 15 days	1,294.52 A
902	Mortgage Insurance Premium for 0 months	0.00
903	Hazard Insurance Premium	1,260.00
904	County Property Taxes	0.00
905	Flood Insurance	0.00
1001	Hazard Ins. @ $105.0000/mo. for 3 months	315.00
1002	Mortgage Ins.	0.00
1004	Tax & Assmt. @ $120.0000/mo. for 6 months	720.00
1006	Flood Insurance	0.00
1008	Aggregate Escrow Adjustment	0.00
1101	Settlement or Closing/Escrow Fee	215.00
1102	Abstract or Title Search	100.00
1103	Title Examination	0.00
1105	Document Preparation Fee	0.00
1106	Notary Fee	650.00
1107	Attorney's Fee	1,979.10
1108	Title Insurance	130.00
1201	Recording Fee	3,150.00
1202	City/County Tax/Stamps	2,362.50
1203	State Tax/Stamps	0.00
1204	Intangible Tax	0.00
1301	Survey existing $450	50.00 *deleted
1302	Pest Inspection	80.00 deleted
1303	LENDER PD.PREM.TO BKR (0-4%)	0.00
1304	Flood Certification	20.00
1305	Post Closing Review	55.00 deleted

Bank Fees

*Look at the 6 fees the Loan Officer crossed off after my client objected!

Title Fees

"S"/"L" designates those costs to be paid by Seller/Lender "A" designates those costs affecting APR. "F" designates financed costs

Total Estimated Settlement Charges   20,480.12

Prepaid Items / Reserves	3,589.52	- Total Charges to Borrower 20,480.12
Total Charges Affecting APR	8,273.52	
Items Paid by Borrower	0.00	

What is PMI %

These estimates are provided pursuant to the Real Estate Settlement Procedures Act of 1974, as amended (RESPA). Additional information can be found in the HUD Special Information Booklet, which is to be provided to you by your mortgage broker or lender, if your application is to purchase residential property and the Lender will take a first lien on the property.

Mailing Address

Property Address   9.50/975

Proposed Loan Amount	315,000	Loan Type	Estimated Interest Rate 10.000 %
Preparation Date	05/03/	☐ FHA ☐ VA ☐ Conventional	Loan Number

_____ Date   _____ Date

_____ Date   _____ Date

GENESIS 2000, INC. * W16.0 * (800) 882-0504   Page 1 of 1   Form GFE (03/95)

Figure 6.1

The practice of padding a third-party fee is an outrage. And the credit report is just one example. The appraisal is another. If you had a drive-by appraisal, you should not be paying for the traditional Uniform Residential Appraisal Report (URAR) that includes a thorough interior inspection. I've seen borrowers who had the $250 drive-by appraisal be charged $400 for the traditional URAR. Sometimes it's an honest mistake, because people do get busy. Not all loan officers are detail-oriented, and they may rely on an assistant who is new and didn't think to double-check. Either way, you have to look out for your own pocketbook.

Some states have made padding the true cost illegal, as it should be. Unfortunately, the *naked up-charge* is still a reality.

Coming Up

The information I provide in Chapter 8 could save you more than a thousand dollars in up-front cash and tens of thousands of dollars over the life of your loan. But before we move on, review these handy lists summarizing bogus and legitimate fees.

Unnecessary and Negotiable Loan Fees

- Administration Fee
- Application Fee
- Appraisal Review Fee
- Ancillary Fee
- Courier Fee (especially if there are two different courier fees)
- Document Preparation Fee
- Document Review Fee
- Email Fee
- Processing Fee
- Title Review Fee
- Settlement Fee
- Survey Fee

Questionable Loan Fees

- Discount Fee (It's legitimate if you're getting a discount on your interest rate.)
- Underwriting Fee (I don't object to this fee, but some people do.)
- Warehouse Fee

Legitimate, Unavoidable Loan Fees

- Appraisal Fee
- Attorney Fee or Escrow Fee
- Credit Report
- Flood Certification
- Tax Service Fee
- Title Insurance Fee
- Recording Fee (purchase loan) or Reconveyance Fee (refinance)
- State Tax or State Stamps

Other

- *"Creative" fees (photo review, PITA, etc.).* Refuse them and have them waived.
- *Duplicate fees.* Don't pay twice for the same thing, such as two courier fees.
- *Up-charges.* When an appraisal or credit report seems too high, check it out.

CHAPTER 7

Step 7:
Decide Whether It
Makes Sense to Pay
Points, and Lock In
Your Rate—Carefully

Would you pay an extra $2,000 to join a resort club if that joining fee meant you could golf, swim, and dine at a discount for the next 30 years? Let's say you love the club and it looks like you'll save money, so you go ahead and shell out the two grand. But then a week later, you discover that other members are playing and dining for the same price as you—only without having paid the additional $2,000 joining fee. You'd be hopping mad, right? You'd call foul play.

That's exactly what it's like when you pay a discount point on a $200,000 loan but don't get a discount on your interest rate.

The Truth about Par Rate
and Discount Points

Your loan officer tells you you're getting a better rate by paying the extra percentage point, but you're not. You're getting *par*, the same interest rate as your neighbor who didn't pay the extra fee—only your loan officer just doubled his or her commission by lying to you. That's what I call a "fake discount point" (as opposed to a real discount point where you do get a lower rate). For example, if par is 6 percent, you may get 5.75 percent by paying a 1 percent Discount Fee.

1% Discount fee = 1% of your loan amount
($2,000 on a $200,000 loan)

The buy-down rate will vary lender to lender.

On Line 802 on your GFE, right below Loan Origination Fee is a spot for a Loan Discount (see Figure 7.1). The Discount Fee is supposed to offer you a choice of getting an interest rate below par by "buying down your rate."

Perhaps a lower payment is vital to your debt ratio, you plan to stay in the house for more than five years, and you have plenty of cash on hand to buy down the rate. You could pay an additional 1 percent (that's 1 percent of your loan amount) to get a lower interest rate. Technically, you're paying the lender additional interest up front in exchange for paying less interest on a monthly basis.

Charging a discount point without giving a discount is deceitful; but never mind that—it's done all the time. But wait, it gets worse. Some sleazy loan officers charge an Origination Fee, a Loan Discount, and get extra YSP, as well. It's an outrage! How could you be buying down your interest rate and then taking a rate higher than par to yield extra back-

GOOD FAITH ESTIMATE

Applicants:				Application No:		
Property Addr:				Date Prepared:		
Prepared By:				Loan Program: **2/28 ARM**		

The information provided below reflects estimates of the charges which you are likely to incur at the settlement of your loan. The fees listed are estimates-actual charges may be more or less. Your transaction may not involve a fee for every item listed. The numbers listed beside the estimates generally correspond to the numbered lines contained in the HUD-1 settlement statement which you will be receiving at settlement. The HUD-1 settlement statement will show you the actual cost for items paid at settlement.

Total Loan Amount $ **218,405**   Interest Rate: **7.500** %   Term **360 / 360** mths

800	ITEMS PAYABLE IN CONNECTION WITH LOAN:				PFC	S	F	POC
801	Loan Origination Fee			$				
802	Loan Discount	**1.500%**	The loan officer wanted to	3,276.08				
803	Appraisal Fee		charge 3%, so she split it	(600.00)				✓
804	Credit Report		up, over Lines 802, 808.	(18.00)				✓
805	Lender's Inspection Fee							
808	Mortgage Broker Fee	**1.500%**	There was no Discount on the	3,276.08	✓			
809	Tax Related Service Fee		interest rate! BOGUS FEE.	64.00	✓			
810	Processing Fee			500.00	✓			— Junk Fee
811	Underwriting Fee		In addition, there was 1% YSP, $2,184.	795.00	✓			
812	Wire Transfer Fee			30.00	✓			
	813. Broker Courier			30.00	✓			— Junk Fee
	814. Flood Certification			18.00	✓			

1100	TITLE CHARGES:				PFC	S	F	POC
1101	Closing or Escrow Fee	**Chicago**		$	800.00	✓		

Figure 7.1

Sneaking Past the Real Estate Agents

When I decided to quit working for a direct lender and go to work for a mortgage broker, I interviewed with five mortgage brokerages. I favored one particular company, because it was located only eight blocks from my home and situated next to a beautiful waterfront park.

During the interview, I asked the manager if I could see a typical GFE, and he said sure. I noticed that there was a 1 percent Origination Fee and a 1 percent Loan Discount, so I asked about it. Here's what he told me.

"We like to charge 2 percent up front, but we divide it between the two lines so the real estate agents don't freak out." How interesting.

He knew they could charge two points without having the homebuyers balk, but if their real estate agents saw it, they'd object. So by splitting it up between Origination and Discount Fees, they flew under the radar of even the real estate professionals. There was no true discount being given for the extra cost.

Sadly, I passed on the offer to work in an office next to the park.

end commission at the same time? Like double-talk, it makes no sense. For this reason, some lenders don't allow the loan officers to make a YSP if they charge a discount point. But others do.

If you do choose to pay a discount fee, never pay more than 1 percent. And make sure you're getting a rate lower than par; otherwise, your loan officer is pocketing extra commission at your expense.

Are You Protected with a Government Loan?

You'd think a person would be safe with a government loan from the Veterans Administration (VA) or Federal Housing Administration (FHA), but you can't take anything for granted nowadays.

A Bogus Fee on a Veteran's Loan

A Hispanic woman contacted me about a Good Faith Estimate she'd received from her local mortgage broker. Her husband served in the army, qualifying them for a zero-down VA loan. She didn't read English well, but she was a smart woman and she questioned whether she was being overcharged.

I offered to review the GFE for her, although I doubted that she was being cheated, because the VA loan is a wonderful program designed to help men and women who have served our country further the American dream of home ownership.

But I was in for a surprise. Her clever loan officer found a way to cheat her out of $1,780. This particular loan shark was charging the couple a 1 percent Origination Fee and a 1 percent Loan Discount without giving them a lower interest rate. Since their loan was for $178,000, they were getting ripped off by $1,780. It was a scam. They decided to switch to a mortgage broker who gave them the same interest rate without the bogus Discount Fee.

In 2006, the government loans changed their guidelines to allow loan officers to charge an Origination Fee, a Discount Fee, and still make a YSP back-end commission. Clearly, this revision from the former rule of "no YSP when a discount is charged" was not in the best interests of the homebuyer. It was a competitive move. Loan volume for government loans had declined severely in recent years, so the guidelines were relaxed and documentation was simplified in a move to increase business. It was a strategy to compete with the popular zero-down programs being offered by conventional lenders.

When Does It Make Sense to Pay a Loan Discount?

Most often, it is *not* in your best interest to pay a discount fee to get a lower interest rate. The cost can vary from lender to lender, but on a conventional fixed-rate loan, paying 1 percent could lower your interest rate by .25 percent. Let's say you're buying a house that's $400,000 and you're putting 3 percent down; thus, your loan is $388,000. A 1 percent discount point is going to cost you $3,880.

Now assume par is 6.25 percent, but now you're getting 6.0 percent. How much will you save?

$388,000 @ 6.25% = $2,389 per month principal and interest
$388,000 @ 6.0% = $2,326 per month principal and interest

Savings of $63 per month

You paid $3,880 to save $63 per month. How long will it take you to break even?

$$\frac{\$3,880}{63} = 61.5 \text{ months (a little more than five years)}$$

In this example, it will take you about five years before you will recover the cost of the loan discount fee and start coming out ahead.

What if it takes five to eight years just to break even: is it worth it to you? You will have to keep this loan for five years before you'll start coming out ahead. I would not advise paying the discount point in a case like this. Furthermore, you will have the burden of bringing in the extra $3,880 on a purchase loan. If it's a refinance, you'll roll it into your loan, making your loan go up to $391,880 and lowering your savings to just $40 a month (because your payment will be $2,349 on the higher loan amount). On the refinance, it will take you eight years to break even. Now you can see it's clearly *not* a good deal; and yet, people pay discount points and roll it into their refinance all the time, because they don't understand how to do the math.

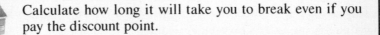 Calculate how long it will take you to break even if you pay the discount point.

You can follow the model here and do the math for your own loan. If you don't have an amortization calculator, just use the free instant calculator at www.mortgage-helper.com to get the two payments. Then subtract to get your savings. Divide the savings by the dollar amount of the loan discount (or 1 percent of your loan). It's very easy to do the basic arithmetic, and you'll feel confident about the decision you've made.

Most people come out better *without a discount fee*. Most homebuyers, especially first-timers, do not keep their homes long enough to pay a discount fee.

When It Might Make Sense to Buy Down Your Rate

Buying down your rate might make sense if:

- You will absolutely, positively keep your house for 10, 20, or 30 years.
- You are forced to buy the lower rate, because your debt ratio cannot qualify otherwise.
- Your seller has agreed to pay all your closing costs, up to a certain amount, and you're going to have to waste a good chunk of that money if you don't buy down your rate.

In the last case, it makes good sense and would be foolish to pass up the opportunity to get a lower interest rate for free. If your seller has agreed to pay a sizeable sum, be on the lookout for this. You can also "compromise" with a .5 percent loan discount and a rate of one-eighth better. Just don't waste the seller's contribution. An experienced loan officer should be on the lookout for you, but be sure to mention it anyway, because he or she might get busy and forget.

One last reminder: If you're paying a discount point out of your own pocket or out of your own home equity (in a refinance), be on the lookout that there's not also a YSP.

Summary Guidelines for Getting the Cheapest Loan.   To sum it up, follow these three guidelines (and use the provided Insider's Worksheet for Calculating Loan Discount Advantage):

1. Don't compare interest rates, compare Good Faith Estimates. You want to look at all the terms and costs of the loan, not just the interest rate. That way you won't get duped into thinking one company has the cheapest deal when, in fact, it's charging 4 percent in Origination and Discount Fees and throwing in $1,000 in junk fees to boot. By stating up front that you'll compare three and then make a

selection, you show yourself to be intelligent and fair. This will go a long way to getting you an honest quote and the best deal they have to offer. You're comparing on the same day, so you're comparing "apples to apples," so to speak.

2. Look at the Truth-in-Lending form also, to make sure you've got the loan you want and the absence of prepayment penalty. If you're comparing an Adjustable Rate Mortgage (ARM), then you'll also be looking at the start rate, the margin, and the first adjustment cap, and the lifetime cap.

3. Because federal law does not require mortgage companies to be consistent with their estimates, ask for a statement (or guarantee) in writing that says the mortgage company's final costs will not vary from the Good Faith Estimate by more than 10 percent.

Now you can go ahead and sign the Good Faith Estimate, Truth-in-Lending form, loan application, and the other disclosures. You're ready to make a commitment and proceed with confidence.

Insider's Worksheet for Calculating Loan Discount Advantage

Your loan amount: $_____   1% of your loan amount: $_____

Loan amount (from above) $_____ @ par _____ % = $_____ per month

Loan amount $_____ @ discount rate _____ % = $_____ per month

(Note: Go to www.mortgagehelper.com and click on Mortgage Calculator to get these numbers.)

First payment minus second payment = Savings of $_____

Divide your savings by the number in the top right corner, 1% of your loan amount:

_____ months to break even

Divide by 12: _____ years to break even.

Should you buy down the rate: Yes _____ No _____

Lock In Your Rate

Your next step is to make sure your interest rate is locked in. This is extremely important, so please read this section carefully.

If you're not aware of "rate lock gambling," this next story may surprise you. Newspaper headlines were announcing interest rates at a 40-year low. It was midmorning, and a wind of change was in the air. I had one loan in my pipeline that didn't have a secure, locked-in interest rate yet, because the homeowner had a good feeling and wanted to "float." ("Float" here means you're waiting to lock, because you think the market may improve and you may be able to get a lower interest rate.) I worked in an office with about 30 loan officers, so when one person got news, word spread fast. We had two loan officers who were considered to be the gurus of the market. On that particular morning, one of them started a buzz that we should lock in *now*.

I called my client and told him what was going on, and that I recommended he lock in, or his rate could be in jeopardy. (I always let the client make the decision when to lock in.) He said, "Go ahead and lock," and then asked some questions, beginning a lengthy conversation.

I said, "I can call you back so we can talk, but I'd better hang up and get your rate locked in immediately." He said okay.

I filled out the lock form as fast as I could, then I literally sprinted down the long office hallway in my high heels and business suit to get to the closest fax machine to send in his lock form. Chug, chug, chug . . . I stood there waiting nervously for the page to go through our rather old machine until I had the fax confirmation in my hand.

Tom, the loan officer who started the buzz about locking in rates, was trying to fax in a lock form on another fax machine. He stood there for 45 minutes, sending and resending.

"Damn! I can't get my lock to fax!" he shouted.

I thought I'd help him out, so I called our wholesale account executive. She told me the lock desk closed up, because rates were changing. They were accepting no more locks.

"What time did that happen?" I asked.

She told me, and I looked at my fax confirmation for my client's rate lock. I had made it by 14 seconds! What if I'd dallied on the phone with him? What if I'd strolled down the hall rather than ran? Whew, that was close. Poor Tom. His client wasn't so lucky.

Rates increased by .75 percent that day. That means a $300,000 loan that would have locked at 5.25 percent was now at 6 percent; and the monthly payment would go up by $136—a pretty penny. A loan officer across the hall from me had a client crying in her office the next day, because she didn't get her rate locked before it went up. People were heartbroken and furious. It was awful, and there was nothing any of us could do about it.

Interest rates may change several times during the course of a day.

People get very upset about losing an interest rate. It happens. You think you're getting a good rate, and you have a signed Good Faith Estimate to show it. But that's no guarantee against what the market might do.

Interest rates change daily in the conforming market, and sometimes midday as well. Anytime you are in a rising rate environment, this topic is of utmost important. You have no guarantee of getting your interest rate until it is "locked" and you have a *written confirmation* of the lock.

✏ **NOTE**
The critical points of this chapter are that, one, your rate must be locked in, and, two, you must have it in writing. ✏

Loan officers do not get advance notice of rate increases. In fact, when the market goes through a major change, the lenders will "close their lock desks" so no more loans can be locked while they figure out how much rates are going to increase. The only way loan officers can anticipate this is by watching the market, just as you, the consumer, can. On an "iffy" day when a loan officer has a jumbo loan or an "important" loan or several loans floating, he or she may check the market every 30 minutes for changes, so he or she can lock in at the optimal time. They do this by watching the bond market online. Still, don't expect your loan officer to accurately predict if rates will go up or down. Clairvoyance is not a requirement for being a mortgage professional, and not even the experts can be right all the time.

 If you ask your loan officer what rates will be next week, he or she may tell you a joke that involves a crystal ball.

What Is a Rate Lock and How Does It Work?

A rate lock is a commitment, a legal contract, between you and a lender that includes four elements:

1. The interest rate you have agreed upon
2. The loan product (30-year fixed rate, 5/1 ARM, etc.)
3. The points you will be charged (includes Origination Fee, Broker Fee, Discount Fee)
4. The rate lock period and expiration date (such as a 30-day lock)

This commitment confirms the terms of your loan, and it confirms what you've been quoted is what you're going to get. You must keep handy your rate lock letter and take it with you to your loan signing.

 A promise made on the telephone is not a legal commitment to your rate. When your rate is locked in, get a written confirmation.

With that definition in mind, it's important to answer four related questions:

1. When can you lock in your rate?
2. What if your loan doesn't close on time?
3. What if rates go down after you lock?
4. Do mortgage brokers have an advantage over bankers?

When Can You Lock In Your Rate?

Some lenders allow you to lock in as soon as you have an address to tie the loan terms to. Most don't allow you to "lock and shop," although there are exceptions. Some lenders require that you get your loan approved before you can lock in your rate. You'll need to discuss this important question with your loan officer to find out which guidelines apply to you.

Rate Locks Are for a Limited Time. It is important to point out that your rate is not guaranteed indefinitely. Your rate may be locked in for 15 days, 21 days, 30 days, 40 days, or 60 days. The shorter guarantee your lender gives you, the less risk there is to the lender of rates increasing; therefore, a shorter rate lock will give you a slightly better rate. Typically, a 15-day lock may be .125 percent better than a 30-day lock, and a 60-day lock may be .25 percent higher than a 30-day lock. This is just an example, because it varies from lender to lender.

What if Your Loan Doesn't Close on Time?

If your loan doesn't close by the expiration date, one of two things will happen. Some lenders allow you to buy an extension, which will increase your closing costs. Other lenders will require that you take the new, current, higher rate. Your loan officer can advise you of your lender's policy.

What if Rates Go Down after You Lock?

If interest rates go down after you lock in your rate, you will not get a lower rate, just as when rates go up after you lock in your rate you will not have to take the higher rate. That's why it's called a "lock." It works both ways. My philosophy is that if you were happy with your rate when you locked it in, then don't drive yourself crazy by following the daily dips and swells of the market. It was a good rate when you locked in, and it's still a good rate, even if the market changes.

Recently, I read a book in which a loan officer tells his client, "If rates go down after you lock in, I'll get the lender to lower your rate." Either this was a hypothetical story, and a gross error by the author, or the loan officer was a liar. No wholesale lender or bank will let you "break the lock" and get a lower rate. The loan officer would have to switch to another lender—in essence, start over with another company.

Do Mortgage Brokers Have an Advantage over Bankers?

If your loan officer works for a mortgage broker, as opposed to a direct lender or a bank, you have an advantage concerning changing interest

Subprime Loans Are Locked Differently

If you have credit or income challenges and you're taking a subprime (also called nonprime or nonconforming) loan, then rates do not change daily. Those lenders have a different set of criteria for their rates, including the short-term investment market, what their own investors are requiring, what their own loan portfolio consists of, and other factors.

Some subprime lenders don't lock in your rate until after the loan is approved; some don't lock until you're ready to draw docs. Meanwhile, rates could go up! It's painful when people get blindsided. Such as when you were quoted 7.75 percent by your loan officer, and you're waiting for final approval, then suddenly you get a call saying your rate's gone up to 8.25 percent. What do you do?

First, prevent this by asking up front when you can lock in, and request a written lock confirmation. They probably won't offer it to you in writing without your request, and you *must* have this as security. Remember, verbal quotes cannot be enforced. You're vulnerable until you have a Lock Confirmation in hand.

Second, if your rate went up and you're sure the loan officer is lying and taking advantage, ask your loan officer to have the wholesale lender send you an email confirming how much rates increased. When I was a wholesale account rep, I was more than happy to send email confirmations when asked. (Wholesale account reps will not risk their job by lying about this.)

rates. Let's say you lock in your rate for 60 days, but to everyone's surprise, rates decline significantly. (A quarter percent change is not significant; I'm referring to a change that would affect your monthly payment by $150 or more.) Because your rate is locked, the wholesale lender will not lower your rate, no matter how much the market declined; however, your loan officer could switch to another wholesale lender in order to take advantage of the market decline for you. Wholesale lenders hate this, because they get "burned" by losing out on a loan they've been working on; nonetheless, it is done when rates decline significantly.

Listen to the Pros

The wholesale company I worked for rolled out a special deal one month. It offered a 30-year fixed rate at 4.99 percent par, well below the rates the banks and other lenders were offering, simply because its portfolio was shy of loans with borrowers having 700-plus credit scores. So to attract people with excellent credit, it had a special deal for a short time, offered to borrowers with the high scores.

One of my brokers offered his client who was buying a house the 4.99 percent with one point up front, so he could get paid. It was a killer deal. People with credit scores over 700 were eagerly snatching it up. But this client was skeptical, so he talked to a friend of his at his church. His friend told him it was too good to be true, the rates weren't that low, and that he should walk away from this scam. So he went to a bank and took a higher interest rate. It really annoyed me that this borrower would take a friend's word over the rate lock confirmation, a written contract. The 4.99 percent at par was genuine and legitimate, and he lost out, because of he listened to his buddy rather than his broker.

Beware Rate Gambling!

You've been misled. You think your interest rate is locked in when it's still floating, subject to the winds of change. This happens when loan officers decide to take a gamble with their clients' rate lock. Sure, they give the clients a written lock confirmation, but don't actually lock in their rate with the lender. They have a hunch the rates are going to decline, resulting in a bigger yield spread premium.

On a $300,000 loan, even an extra one-eighth of 1 percent (.125 percent) could put another $375 in the loan officer's pocket. An extra quarter would give them $750. They might gamble to try for that $750. It happens a lot, especially since waiting just one more day, or two . . . or if not today, maybe just one more day would give them additional money. It's the rare loan officer who hasn't played this game.

Of course, the wind could blow the other way too. The market could get worse, and the loan officers could lose $375 or $750 of their commission. It hurts when that happens.

One morning I was called upon to notarize a loan signing for a real estate attorney. (When I wear my notary public hat, I have nothing to do with the loan officer or with the loan itself.) All went well, for the first five minutes. As soon as the attorney saw the Loan Note, he said, "That's not the correct interest rate."

"We'd better call your loan officer and have him correct the mistake then," I said.

The loan officer said, sorry, but rates had gone up suddenly, and he'd missed out on that rate he was expecting. Oops. That was the wrong answer to give to an attorney. He quickly pulled out his Rate Lock Confirmation form. Still, the loan officer stuck to his story. He was sorry that he wasn't able to get it locked in time before the increase.

That was no consolation to the attorney, who demanded to have the manager put on the phone at once. He was using speakerphone, so I could hear both sides of this interesting conversation. The manager apologized profusely, but said there was nothing he could do. The market is what it is, and no one can control interest rates, he explained.

I interrupt this story to ask you a question. What would you have done at this point? Would you have signed anyway? Or would you have walked away?

The attorney calmly told the manager he didn't care what the rates were today, and he didn't care how much of a loss his mortgage company took; he wanted a new Loan Note drawn up that would reflect the interest rate he was promised. He reminded him that he was a real estate attorney and that he wouldn't hesitate to sue him if he didn't make good on his rate lock.

That was that. I went home as my notary services were no longer needed that day.

The next morning I received another notary request: same address, same borrower's name. When I arrived at the attorney's office, new loan documents were waiting, with the desired interest rate—the one originally promised in the Lock Confirmation letter. No doubt that mortgage company took a big loss in order to avoid a possible complaint filed with the attorney general's office against them and a lawsuit.

Should this happen to you, stick to your guns, and collect on the loan terms that are due you. Just make sure you keep your Rate Lock Confirmation form.

If your loan officer gambles with your rate lock, he or she assumes the risk. Don't be a victim of rate switching.

If the company makes an honest mistake on your documents, it will usually correct it immediately and email or fax the corrected pages while you wait. It only takes about 15 minutes, and you can go ahead and sign the other standard pages while you wait. It's no big deal, and mistakes do happen every now and then. But if the company is pulling a shenanigan, it may take a day to settle the fight. Either way, stick to your guns, because *you will win*.

Losing on a Rate Lock Gamble

Even worse than working for nothing is paying to work. This happened to a friend of mine who took a chance and lost. She was gambling with a rate lock, and rates went up. She couldn't tell the client, and she had to make good on her written commitment. She waited to see if the market would come back down, but instead it went up further. My poor friend. Not only did she lose all her YSP, but the market changed so drastically, it actually cost money to get the rate she'd confirmed to her client. She ended up paying about $2,500 out of her own pocket to buy down the rate and close the loan.

Insider's Guide to Protecting Yourself from Rate Lock Scams

I'll end this discussion with some important guidelines regarding rate scams:

- When you sign your Good Faith Estimate and other disclosures, ask your loan officer about locking in your interest rate. You should be the one who decides on when to lock; after all, it is your loan.

- When your rate is locked, get a written confirmation. Assume you do not have a locked-in rate until your written confirmation letter or confirmation form is in your hands.

The Day Thousands of People Lost Their Loans

In July 2003, Capitol Commerce Mortgage Services, a wholesale lender with 15 offices in eight states, closed $3.7 billion in loans. Its amazing success was due to the fabulously low interest rates it offered, especially for 15-year fixed rates. By mid-August, I had nine loans in progress with the firm. On Friday, August 15, I eagerly went into work expecting to sign with one client and fund with another. Instead, I got hit with a nasty surprise: Capitol Commerce, suddenly and without warning, shut its doors forever. Not even its own employees knew what was coming. That fateful day, they went to work, as usual. Then, much to their shock and horror, they were told they had one hour to pack up and get out. Suddenly, they were all unemployed.

What a disaster! Thousands of clients nationwide lost their loans, and there was nothing anyone could do. I had to call nine clients and break the news that their loans no longer existed with Capitol Commerce. I cancelled my vacation, because I had to find new lenders and start over. It was awful.

According to my wholesale account executive, one man took down the whole company. He was a high-level employee who failed to lock in billions of dollars worth of loans; thus, the company could not make good on them when rates took a sudden upturn. His hedging put the company out of business.

- Check the wording on your rate lock confirmation, to ensure it includes:
  —The interest rate you have agreed upon
  —The loan type (fixed rate or adjustable)
  —Total points (Origination Fee, Broker Fee, Discount Fee)
  —The rate lock period and expiration date
- Take your lock confirmation to closing, just in case you need it. If there is a mistake on your loan documents, you can call your loan officer, and he or she can have new docs printed and emailed over

while you wait. Errors do happen, and they can usually be fixed in 10 to 15 minutes.

- If you are subject to a rate-switch shenanigan, do not sign the loan documents. Walk away. More on this in Chapter 8.

Coming Up

Worrying about what might go wrong causes people stress and gives them sleepless nights, and that's no fun. In Chapter 8, the last in Part I of this book, I offer insight and advice, to help you avoid unpleasant surprises and have a smooth closing.

Step 8: Avoid the Five Most Common Unpleasant Closing Surprises

No one likes to be blindsided by a last-minute unpleasant surprise. To prevent that happening to you, in this chapter, I identify the five most common predicaments you might face, along with my suggestions for handling each of them. They are:

- Denial of Appraisal
- Bait and Switch
- Mistakes
- Tricks at Signing
- Surprise Prepayment Penalty

Denial of Appraisal

The best way to avoid having your appraisal denied is to work with a local lender who understands your neighborhood and your market. And the best way to turn around an already-denied appraisal is to offer a bigger down payment.

Some lenders don't like "unique properties," because if they have to foreclose, they fear they won't be able to unload it quickly and at a good price. (More on these types of properties in the upcoming subsection, "Seven Reasons a Lender Might Reject Your Appraisal.") The last thing they want is to have some oddball property on their hands they can't get rid of. The surprise pops up when the underwriter interprets your appraisal as being odd when you (and your real estate agent) know it's perfectly normal.

For example, I know one lender based in California who thinks metal roofs are unique and undesirable; therefore, the underwriters are very hard on those appraisals and turn down lovely houses with quality metal roofs. Whereas a local lender sees no problem with metal roofs, because they understand they're not a negative for the area they're in.

If you're working with an experienced mortgage broker, he or she will know which lenders have certain quirky guidelines about appraisals. They can switch wholesale lenders if they need to. If you're working with a bank and it denies your appraisal, you have to hit the streets looking for a new lender. This is another advantage of having a broker over a bank or a direct lender: a broker can shop the wholesalers faster and more efficiently than you can shop retail lenders.

If five lenders reject your dream home, I strongly advise you to reconsider. If a majority of investors think the property is risky, then you need to understand that if you go ahead with the purchase, you'll have a tough time selling it in the future. How will another buyer find a lender if you had to pull teeth to get one?

But maybe you don't care about any of that. This is your one and only dream home, and you really must have it. Then the way to get a lender to accept the appraisal is to lessen the risk for them by making a larger down payment.

Seven Reasons a Lender Might Reject Your Appraisal

It helps to know in advance why some lenders don't like certain appraisals. Every lender has its own guidelines, so do not regard this information as hard-and-fast determining factors. For example, one lender in California might turn down acreage with horse stables, but your local lender may think it's desirable for your area and have no problem with it. Rather, the purpose of this list is to give you general background infor-

The Couple Who Wouldn't Give Up

When I was a loan officer at a brokerage, a couple came to me in desperation. They couldn't find anyone to give them a loan on their dream home. It was a little house of just 650 square feet, but it had a covered walkway to a detached studio. These people fell in love with it for two reasons: it was inexpensive, and the detached studio would be perfect for the wife to give piano lessons. But seven lenders thought it was weird and didn't want to touch it.

I used every bit of logic I had to try to convince the couple they should find a different house—it was small; not many people want half their house detached; it would be hard to resell; it was a 45-minute commute from the city. I even cautioned them that it wouldn't be good from an investment standpoint. They didn't care. They had their hearts set on this house with the low price tag. So I persisted and finally found them a wholesale lender who would do the loan. It closed, and the wife sent me a lovely thank-you card.

A year later the wife called me in a panic. Her husband had died, and she could no longer afford the payments. I suggested she get a roommate, and she thanked me profusely for the idea.

Another year went by, and she called me again. This time she was hopping mad. The roommate had moved out and she was two months behind on her payments. She tried to sell the house, but she couldn't get a buyer, and she'd already lowered the price to the point at which she'd walk away with nothing. She was just trying to bail out before it went into foreclosure and ruined her credit. I suggested she call the lender and work out a payment plan. But she'd already done that. The lender graciously lowered her payments for six months, and now she'd used up her grace period. She was stuck. And she was mad—*at me!*

"Why did you get us a loan on this house?" she yelled angrily.

"Because you insisted on it," I said.

"That's fine for you to say up there in that nice neighborhood, but down here it's become more and more of a slum and gangs have moved in. If I'd known you were going to get us into this mess, I never would have done it."

Right. It was all my fault.

The lesson: Think twice if you're buying a house that seven out of eight lenders deny.

mation; it is *not* to encourage you to do your own underwriting. Your *experienced* local loan officer will know which, if any of these, are concerns for your locale.

- Unusual construction, such as a metal roof, built on stilts, or a house that was converted from a church or a train station.
- Too small; lenders have a minimum square-footage requirement. Some require 800 square feet, but others will go lower.
- Unusual floor plan, such as a studio condo with no separate bedroom or a big post in the center of the living room.
- Unusual characteristics, such as a working farm, horse stables, dog kennel, or, for some, a high-rise building.
- Proximity to something undesirable, such as a house bordering on a freeway or a graveyard.
- No comparable homes within the desired range. (The desired range varies, but if your dream house is out in the middle of nowhere, rural, or up in the woods, you'll have to make a larger down payment to compensate for the risk of lending on it. If you've found a half-million-dollar two-story home in a neighborhood full of small track houses, you could have a problem, too.)
- Zoning issues. Guidelines such as these are all about risk. The question the underwriter asks is: "If we were forced to foreclose on this property due to nonpayment, would we be able to resell it easily, quickly, and at a decent price?"

In sum, if the property is too unusual, there won't be many interested buyers, so the lender will have to drop the price. The way you overcome this objection for the lender is to make a bigger down payment.

Bait and Switch

Bait and switch is one form of fraud. It is deliberate misrepresentation that causes another person damage, usually financial.

Since you have your Good Faith Estimate with the guarantee that it won't vary by more than 10 percent, your Truth-in-Lending form, and Rate Lock Confirmation in a nice file or envelope, you have your defense weapons ready. With this arsenal, bait and switch is a battle you will win, and probably without too much hassle.

Determining Whether You've Been Duped

Here's a question posed to me by one homebuyer:

> The morning of my loan signing, I was informed about some charges that had never come up until then: Lender's Attorney Fee, Document Preparation Fee, Endorsement Fee, and Document Review Fee. These fees totaled up to an additional $495.
>
> The loan officer said that these fees merely reimbursed the lender for expenses, and if he hadn't mentioned them before he was very sorry. I was not going to torpedo my home purchase for $495, but I hate to think that I have been duped. Have I?

And here was my answer:

> Yes, you have been duped, but you don't have to take it. These are all unnecessary junk fees designed to add profit to the lender. All you have to do is to say you won't sign until these tacked-on fees are deleted. Since they can do this is a matter of minutes, you won't "torpedo" your home loan. Sit and wait for them to fix it, and refuse to sign until they do. Believe me, they don't want to lose your loan (and tens of thousands of dollars) over $495, especially when they know they're in the wrong.
>
> No doubt, your loan officer uses his "forgetfulness" as a tactic to keep his borrowers from objecting when they read their Good Faith Estimate. He's counting on homebuyers feeling the pressure to sign and not making a big fuss in the end. This is dishonest.

Bait and Switch or Honest Mistake?

If the terms of your loan were changed without your knowledge or consent, as in the incidence just described, first speak with your loan officer, and politely tell him or her of the error, and that you would like it to be corrected immediately.

If the loan officer is uncooperative, I suggest saying something like this:

> My signed Good Faith Estimate and my Rate Lock Confirmation show such and such, but my loan documents say otherwise [be specific]. If you made an error, then you will have to take the loss, because I am

holding you to the terms on my legal commitments from (your company). Let's resolve this quickly between you and me, so I don't have to involve your manager and the attorney general's office.

If your loan officer still won't help you, talk to the manager. If the manager won't help you, talk to the company president or CEO. The higher up you go, the more cooperation you'll receive. You should be able to get the problem fixed by going "up" in the company without having to spend your time and money going through an attorney.

Here's how to get the name and number of the company CEO: Call the receptionist and politely ask, "What is the name of the CEO of your company? Oh, and what is his or her telephone number?" If the receptionist asks you why you want the phone number, just say, "In case I want to call in a compliment later"; that way she won't divert you to someone else. Who knows, you might be calling in a compliment after the CEO helps you resolve the issue.

Once you have the number, make the call. If a "gatekeeper" answers, speak in a firm and confident voice and say, "I'd like to speak with Mr./Ms. X please."

Probably the receptionist will ask, "What is this regarding?" Don't tell her you have a complaint, or she'll switch you over to someone else. Instead say, "I'm returning his/her call." If you don't feel right about saying that, then say, "He/She is expecting my call." (And with loan sharks for employees, he or she should be expecting such calls!) I learned this telephone strategy from a training executive at a job placement service, and it works quite well.

I gave this advice to Elizabeth, a woman who was distraught when she discovered discrepancies after signing and funding. (It's more difficult to get the issue resolved once you've already signed, but not impossible.) She sought my help via my Web site, and by email I coached her on what to do. Later, I received the following email from her:

Carolyn,

I wanted to let you know that your advice worked like a charm. The vice president was very willing to work with me to resolve the issue. . . . He then answered the many questions that I had regarding other charges that we were charged incorrectly and made right by them. Because of you, we were able to get a refund of almost $5,000. I don't know how to thank you, but I will let everyone know.

Elizabeth

I heard from a nurse who was distraught because her complaint about bait and switch had been ignored. Then I found out why. She'd sent a nasty email to the loan officer, using profanity. Always be professional, even when you're upset.

If you haven't signed papers yet, chances are you'll be able to resolve your issue with the loan officer and manager. Just stand firm and refuse to sign until they make it right. I can't stress enough the fact that they do not want to lose a loan in the eleventh hour.

If you're still feeling shy, remember those horrid things I've heard loan officers confess:

- "If they're stupid enough to take it, it's their fault."
- "I bumped up the rate, because he wasn't paying attention."
- "Consumers are in a total daze. They're signing everything you put in front of them."

Usually, all you have to do to get them to come clean is to call them on it. They don't want to lose your loan—not after all the time they've put into it. They want to get paid, and they won't get paid unless your loan funds. If your loan doesn't fund, they've spent all that time working for free, so they're highly motivated to get your deal closed. However, if you do happen to get one of those managers whose code of conduct is to "leave your morals at the door," then don't hesitate to talk to the top individual in the company.

Call on the phone. Don't write a letter first, because it takes too long and because company VIPs have secretaries who open their mail for them. Likewise, don't hide behind an email. Emails are easily lost or deleted. A mortgage company president is likely to receive more than 100 emails daily. Call, for efficiency. When you do, use a polite tone of voice. Don't call screaming or using foul language, as that will surely work against you. Come across as professional if you want a professional response.

✎ **NOTE**
I'd love to hear your success story, so please send me an email at www.AskCarolynWarren.com. ✎

Mistakes

People make mistakes. When they do, get them fixed—pronto! If you go to sign your loan and see that the fees are wrong, the interest rate is wrong, the prepayment penalty is wrong, taxes and insurance aren't included, or anything else, don't freak out. All you have to do is call your lender, politely inform him or her of the error, and ask to have the particular pages with the error fixed and emailed over, immediately. In fact, your signing agent will be happy to make the call for you. Or if your loan officer is attending your signing with you, he or she will handle it.

The person who draws docs can fix the error and have the corrected copy to you within 10 to 15 minutes. No sweat. You can go ahead and sign the other papers while you're waiting.

Tricks at Signing

"When you sign, use a shiny pen." Lenders say that to distract you, in hopes that you won't read the numbers or notice the prepayment penalty or big margin on the adjustable rate. That might sound juvenile but, in practice, the principle of distraction works very well on adults, too.

Here's how you might be a victim and not even know it. You go in to sign your final loan documents. Turns out your loan officer is going to be your signing agent. This happens in states where the loan officer has a notary license or where the loan officer is going to be your signing agent and have someone else do the notarizing. That's legal. It goes something like this.

"Hi, how are you today?" asks your cheery loan officer. He or she should be cheery—she's about to make a month's wages off your one loan. Then comes the diatribe:

> How was the drive here, I hope you didn't get stuck in that bad traffic, this is the first page, please sign here, I heard on the radio there was an accident down on the highway, please sign here too, did you know that last month a semi full of broomsticks lost its load on that highway, ha-ha, can you imagine the real estate convention without its broomsticks? Ha-ha, oh, this is the HUD, you've already seen these numbers, they were on your Good Faith I went over with you already, just sign here, by the way, help yourself to these chocolates, sign here, they're from Godiva, don't you just love really, really good chocolate? Here is the Loan Note, all standard stuff, please

sign here, did you know that in ancient times chocolate beans were used for money? And sign here. It's true, ha-ha, too bad you can't buy a house with chocolates, eh? Sign here, blah, blah, ha-ha.

On and on they go, in one long, nonstop sentence. They use charm and humor to distract you from reading the actual figures on your documents.

One particular mortgage company used to call me in to notarize its loans. I was never allowed to do the signing, as I might actually go over the terms of the loan with the client. Horrors. The employees at this company were experts at keeping a running monologue going, all the while flipping through the pages of the loan documents, pointing with a shiny pen, saying, "Sign here." The clients were so charmed by the good humor they never even read what they were signing. Those were some high-priced loans, too!

The way to avoid tricks at signing is to pay attention. That's it. Read what you sign and ask questions. Have your Good Faith Estimate, Truth-in-Lending form, Letter of Guarantee, and Lock Confirmation with you—they're your weapons against con artists.

Surprise Prepayment Penalty

A young married couple, modestly dressed, came into an office to sign loan papers for a refinance. They looked like nice folks, and they had a baby girl with them. I'd been called in to notarize their signatures. Their loan officer, who was conducting their signing, was a middle-aged woman who wore an expensive suit, gobs of gold jewelry, and a diamond ring on her index finger that must have weighed at least three carats.

They were about 10 minutes into the signing, chatting happily about this and that, when suddenly the husband notices something about a prepayment penalty, so he halts the shiny pen and flying pages to inquire. He says they were not expecting a prepayment penalty; and, in fact, specifically do not want one. Their plan is to use the cash-out from their refinance to fix up the kitchen, and then they're going to put their house on the market so they can buy a larger one for their growing family. In other words, this is to be a short-term loan they don't want to be stuck in.

In response, the loan officer spouts some gobbledygook about the prepayment penalty not being significant and about how people "just don't find it a stopper."

"It's not a stopper," she says over and over again.

So the husband asks how much the penalty is.

She replies, "It's right here," pointing to the legalese. Silence follows while he reads through the verbiage. She doesn't offer to explain it in everyday terms.

Then the husband fishes around in his pockets for a calculator, but can't find one, so he asks the loan officer if he can borrow hers.

"Sure," she says, with a smirk. "But do you know how to use it?" Of course, she's got the "negative polarization calculator" that people in the mortgage industry use, so it doesn't work like a regular one. The husband punches in numbers, and then the sign key, and more numbers, then the equal key; but it doesn't work like that.

Finally he says, "I can't use your calculator," and hands it back to her.

He then asks his wife if she's got one. A hunt ensues as they root around in her handbag, then in the diaper bag, then in his backpack. It's really awkward sitting there watching them struggle, but the loan officer never offers to do the math for them. She just sits there waiting. Finally, they come up with a simple calculator.

The husband does some math and comes up with a couple hundred dollars for the answer—I don't remember exactly what, but it was way off. The actual penalty was closer to $6,000.

So the husband looks at the wife and says, "I guess that's not so bad, huh? A couple hundred dollars."

She says, "No, we can live with that."

Still the loan officer keeps silent.

Finally, I can't stand it any longer. I'm supposed to limit my involvement to verifying their identification and notarizing their signatures. I'm not a part of the transaction in any way; I'm there strictly as an impartial notary public. But I just can't sit idly by while these nice people get robbed blind. So I whip out my own negative polarization calculator and calculate their prepayment penalty, and then I hold out the screen so they can see it.

"This is your prepayment penalty," I say. Oops.

"Is this true?" asks the husband to the loan officer, looking somewhat alarmed.

She nods her head yes. "But your house is going to go up in value much more than that, so it doesn't matter. When you sell, it will be absorbed by the increased value. It's not something you'll pay for out of your pocket. It's really not a stopper."

But of course they *will* be paying for it out of their pockets, because when they sell their house, the loan payoff figure will be that much higher, and they'll net exactly that much less into their pockets. Nevertheless, they went ahead and signed the loan with the high prepayment penalty, even though they asked for no prepayment penalty in the beginning. If only they'd stood their ground, the loan officer could have had those pages reprinted in a matter of 10 minutes, and this couple would have saved themselves six grand.

I can't stress strongly enough to *never* sign documents you're uncomfortable with. Don't ignore your shaky feelings. If you think something is wrong, it probably is. If you're at least 18 years of age, you're responsible for what you sign. Loan documents include a form that says you've had a chance to read the papers and you understand them. Some people gloss over that and sign it without knowing it! Then it's too late to say you didn't know what the ARM was going to be like later.

You also have the right to take the documents to a neutral third party and get counsel before you sign. Never allow yourself to be bullied into a legal contract you don't understand.

> ✐ **NOTE**
> If you have an unusual scenario I haven't covered in this book, I'd like to hear about it. Just go to www.AskCarolynWarren .com. ✎

Insider's Handy Checklist for Avoiding Nasty Surprises

You might want to print out this list and check off all the items, to ensure you go into your signing well armed.

- ✓ *Good Faith Estimate.* Take this to your signing so you can compare the fees you agreed on against those you're being charged on the HUD-1 Settlement Statement.
- ✓ *Truth-in-Lending form.* Take this to your signing so you can prove you shouldn't have a prepayment penalty, if needed. If you have an ARM, check the index, margin, first adjustment cap, and lifetime cap.

✓ *Guarantee Letter*. Take this to your signing so you can insist the fees don't vary by more than 10 percent, if necessary.

✓ *Rate Lock Confirmation*. Take this to your signing in case your interest rate is wrong.

One more point: If possible, have your loan officer attend your loan signing with you. He or she will be able to help out in case anything goes wrong. If that's not possible, take your cell phone and the phone number of your loan officer.

> ✐ **NOTE**
> You must read through the HUD-1 Settlement Statement, the Loan Note, and the Addendum to the Loan Note (if there is one). Review your costs and your loan terms. Ask questions if you don't understand, and don't sign documents that are incorrect. They can be fixed within the hour, often within 10 minutes. ✑

All that said, don't become paranoid. There are about 50 pages of loan documents to sign, many of them repetitious and standard forms that are boilerplate for every loan. You don't have to scrutinize every word on those papers. You should be able to sign your loan documents within 45 to 60 minutes. If it's taking more than an hour, probably you should take the papers home to review on your own first. Don't make the signer sit through three hours with you, because that's an inconsiderate waste of his or her time.

Coming Up

If you or someone you know is considering a refinance, don't go a step further until you read Part II, because what you don't know could cost you dearly and cause many regrets! The second part begins with Chapter 9, where I provide tips for homeowners who are refinancing.

TIPS FOR HOMEOWNERS WHO ARE REFINANCING

What You Must Know before You Refinance

The most skillful and deadly hunters in the animal kingdom are the lion, the wolf, the crocodile, the great white shark—and the unscrupulous loan officer. If you own a home, watch out. Predators are out to snatch a piece of your home equity, and you need to defend your territory like a mama cat.

You are especially vulnerable if any of the following apply to you:

- You carry high credit card balances.
- You're late on a credit card payment.
- You have a collector calling you on a large debt.
- You're in need of a lower payment.
- You want to make home improvements you don't have the cash for, and you don't have patience to wait.

 When interest rates are moving up, the mortgage business slows down, and loan officers desperate for business will write up any loan they can find—even when it's not in your best interest.

Being in any one of these situations puts you at risk for giving up some (or all) of your precious equity. You're vulnerable to either a deceptively expensive loan, such as the Option ARM, Interest Only, or 40-year mortgage; or to an equity-gobbling second mortgage, like the home equity line of credit. By taking those loans, you risk putting yourself financially behind.

There are exceptions, and I'll discuss savvy refinancing strategies in a moment. But for now, realize that too often consumers overspend their budgets and use their house as a "bank" to fund their desire for nonessentials.

How the Smooth-Talkers Work

One mortgage manager told her loan officers, "Always ask about their children. Find out their ages. Kids are equity spenders." What did she mean by that? She was instructing her staff on how they could get a larger loan. Here's how it works.

The loan officer is taking the application on the phone, and she gets to the space that asks for number of children. The purpose of this question is so the underwriter can calculate net disposable income, meaning how much money will you have left over after paying all your obligations. It takes more to feed a family of eight than a family of three.

So you say, "I have a stepdaughter in college and a six-year-old."

"College is certainly expensive isn't it?" says your loan officer.

"Oh yes, it really adds up," you say.

"What interest rate do you have on those student loans?" asks your loan officer.

"They're an adjustable rate," you reply.

"Most of them are. With the way the federal reserve board is raising rates, that could turn into a dangerous loan in the future. I suggest you lock it into a fixed rate now. In fact, we could bump up your loan to cover it, and then you'd get the mortgage tax deductible interest as well."

"Good idea," you say, thinking she's looking out for your best interests.

"What about your six-year-old? Would you like a couple grand extra for schooling, private lessons, a computer, anything else?"

Then on to the next idea.

"Are there any home improvements you'd like to do?" she asks, "because I just read an article that says upgrading the kitchen and bathroom are extremely desirable for resale value."

When she gets done spending all your equity she can, she'll likely add an extra two or three grand to your loan, just for good measure.

Smooth-talking loan officers regularly bump up loans by $5,000 to $10,000. If they're on a "tier" pay structure, whereby reaching a certain level gives them a bigger commission percentage on all their loans, it makes sense for them to work for the extra dollars. For instance, I saw a loan officer lose out on several thousand dollars pay for the month, because he was $300 short of making the next tier.

There's nothing illegal about offering you a refinance that make no sense. Just as there's nothing illegal about offering you credit cards and expensive merchandise you don't need. But it's your responsibility to put logic over desire and say no. Being aware of some sales tactics will help you to do just that.

Four Tricks Equity "Strippers" Use

Loan officers are taught to use sales tactics such as these:

- *They showcase your "bottom line" as being a lower monthly outgo.* With this common trick, it's all about how much money you're going to save in your total monthly outgo. They add up your house payment, your auto payment, and all your credit cards. Then they present a new 30- or 40-year loan showing one smaller payment to replace all of the above. But wait. You'll be paying a lot more in the long run. Stretching out a car payment for 30 or 40 years makes no sense, because your automobile won't last that long. Your actual house payment goes up and perhaps the interest rate also. You lose your opportunity to pay off those other bills faster and keep your lower mortgage interest rate. Comparing only "your current monthly outgo" and "your new monthly outgo" without considering the negative factors is foolish and can lead you to a poor decision.

- *They push for you to consolidate all your bills.* The loan officer automatically pays off all your debt in the refinance, even the accounts you could pay off in a year or so. The motive is to get the biggest loan the loan officer can and to try to showcase a lower "monthly outgo."

 You should not spend your home equity on nonessentials such as hot tubs and travel.

- *They have many suggestions for you to spend your home equity.* They offer cash-out for debt consolidation, kids' education, remodeling, a vehicle—even a vacation, of all foolish things!

- *You're coming out of a temporary loan with a prepayment penalty and they want to put you into another temporary loan with a prepayment penalty.* They're seeing you as a lifetime customer—a never-ending source of income.

Dangers of Refinancing Too Often

One loan officer bragged to me that she never ran out of business because she refinanced her clients every two to three years. "How do you do that?" I asked. "I set them up that way," she replied. "Serial refinancing" is not about helping you save money; it is about continued business for the loan officer.

When you make the financially fatal mistake of doing a cash-out refinance every time you gain a bit more equity, it sets you back in two ways:

1. You increase your mortgage debt and decrease your equity.
2. You start over with a 30-year loan (or worse, 40 years).

In the beginning, the largest percentage of your payment goes toward interest and the smallest toward principal. So you're paying the maximum in interest over and over and over again. When you sell your house, you will have less profit, because you've spent more of it with every refinance.

One gentleman called a loan officer I know to inquire about refinancing. "My bills are choking me," he complained. He had a $276,000 mortgage on his house—the very same house he had bought 35 years ago for $25,000.

"It makes me sick," said the loan officer. "He's lived there for 35 years. He shouldn't even have a mortgage anymore. I don't want to refinance him again, but he's begging me. He says he can't afford to make his credit card payments any more."

It would be convenient to blame all the loan officers who refinanced his mortgage over the years, but this man was the one who made the decision to sign papers for more cash-out. Why did he choose to run

Special Alert for Baby Boomers

If you are within a stone's throw of retirement, it is especially important to preserve your equity. That way, you'll be able to pocket a nice profit and downsize or move to the location of your dreams. With significant equity, you can qualify for a good reverse mortgage to help you in your retirement years. I'm a staunch believer that retired people on modest incomes should own their homes free and clear, and I'll tell you why.

I observe retired couples who are debt-free enjoying life to the max. They're out on new adventures, seeing the world. I also observe retired people who are stressed and having no fun at all, because they've got a bigger mortgage than ever due to refinancing over and over, and they're taking low-paying, part-time jobs just to get by.

up credit cards and then consolidate them with a new mortgage every time his home value increased?

All it takes to protect your equity is two words: *No thanks.*

Most experienced loan officers have received requests from homeowners for an equity-spending, bill-paying refinance. They advise against it, but the homeowners insist it's what they need.

"This is a stupid loan, but if I don't give it to them, they'll go down the street and get it from someone else, so what can I do?" I've heard this over and over from loan officers, and I've been there myself. Ultimately, the responsibility falls fair and square on you, the homeowner.

That said, there are times when a debt consolidation refinance makes good sense.

Three Savvy Refinancing Strategies

When does it make sense to refinance? Use these three guidelines to make a savvy decision.

1. *When you're lowering your interest rate enough to make a significant difference in your monthly payment and you're not adding more than five years to your loan.* For example, if you've paid down your mortgage to 12 years remaining, you should not refinance into a 30-year loan, even if you're lowering your interest rate by 1 percent. Instead, you should refinance into a 15-year loan. Otherwise, you'll be going backward beyond the benefit of the lower rate. What is a significant difference in payment? That depends on your income and budget, but $40 is not significant. For most people, $200 a month in savings is.

2. *When you're significantly decreasing your loan term.* The important principle to remember is that, in loans, time is your number-one enemy, not interest rate. If you can afford to take a 20-year or 15-year loan, you'll save yourself tens of thousands of dollars.

3. *When you need a one-time only debt consolidation to lower your interest payments and improve cash flow.* I emphasize *one-time only,* because you don't want to slide into that hellacious equity-stripping trap mentioned earlier. But if you're paying 16 to 24 percent interest on $30,000 worth of credit card debt and are able to make only the minimum payments, you will be paying this high non-tax-deductible rate for nearly 30 years to pay it off. In this case, it would be better to roll it into a 7 percent mortgage. Just take care that you don't get yourself into debt again.

In regard to number 3, you'll want to find out whether your bills are too high. Take this quick test:

1. Add up the monthly payments for all your credit cards, auto loans, and student loans.
2. Divide this number by your take-home pay.
   - Ten percent is in the "good zone." You are living within your means.
   - Over 10 percent is in the "danger zone." You need to scale back your life style to fit your income.

Two Savvy Refinancing Questions to Ask

These are savvy questions to ask, because both have yes and no answers.

Don't Use Credit Cards for Luxuries

One afternoon I got a call from a senior citizen who was paying out so much of her paycheck to credit card companies she could hardly afford to buy food. This is what she told me:

"After I lost my husband, I really didn't know what to do. He had always taken care of our finances. One day I got a beautiful credit card in the mail, so I went on a beautiful cruise. I had a wonderful time! When I got back, I got another credit card in the mail, so I took another beautiful cruise.

"Then when I returned home, I just kept spending on those credit cards. It was so easy. I didn't realize my payments were going to be so high after awhile. Now I'm really stuck, because I'm on a fixed income and I don't have enough money left to live on. I can't even buy milk."

This poor widow felt like she was treading water as fast as she could and was still sinking. Fortunately, she had a lot of equity in her house, so she was able to refinance and lower her monthly payments to a manageable level. And thank goodness she took action before she got behind on her payments and damaged her credit, so she qualified for a good loan.

 Don't use one credit card to pay off another, and then another. This is called "surfing," and it's harmful to your credit.

It doesn't make sense to use credit cards for luxury spending unless you can pay off the balance in one lump sum when the first bill arrives. My client learned this lesson the hard way.

If you have a tendency to overspend your budget with credit cards, don't do a debt consolidation refinance. Why? Because, chances are, you'll do the same thing all over again. You'll end up with no equity and your house will become your burden.

Should You Include Your Vehicle in a Refinance? Should you pay off your auto loan by refinancing? Usually, no. If you have a $20,000 auto loan at 9.5 percent for six years, you will pay $26,280 for your vehicle. But if you roll it into a 30-year fixed rate at 6.25 percent, you will pay $58,336 for the car. That is, if you keep the loan for 30 years. If you refinance again, you'll be paying on that $20,000 for even longer, making it even more expensive. Paying more than double for the car by stretching out the payments is not wise.

However, if you sell the house within a couple years, you'll come out ahead, because you're paying off the loan early, taking a lower interest rate, and gaining a tax deduction on the payment. Therefore, there are times when it makes sense to put the auto in your refinance.

The short answer then is, include the vehicle in your refinance only if you'll be keeping your house for less time than you have left on your original auto loan.

Should You Refinance to Make an Investment? According to the Federal Trade Commission, Americans lose about $1 billion in fraudulent investments *every year*. Don't pay for an investment in stocks or "money-making opportunities" with a home loan—especially if the investment offers "an incredible payout," like 10 percent per month, each and every month. What if the investment doesn't work out as expected? Never take a risk with the place you call home. It's far too precious for that.

On the other hand, if you take out a modest home equity loan to buy an investment property in a good location, you could enjoy a handsome return on your money. Seek the advice of two reputable financial advisors first, because you don't want to make a costly mistake.

Three Refinancing Alerts

At the first mortgage company I worked for, young loan officers wore Rolexes, drove new BMWs, and took exotic vacations, all financed by closing just four to five pricey refinance loans a month. Here are three alerts to help you avoid making a poor refinance decision.

Neophytes Posing as Managers (and Other Callers)

Watch out for newbies passing as pros. Here's a scenario I witnessed. A 22-year-old straight out of college (psychology major) got hired at a finance company. She knew nothing about loans; in fact, she didn't even know how to read a credit report. Three days into her brand-new career, the manager gave her a list of homeowners to call to solicit for refinancing.

"Watch Ashley, everyone!" he announced to all the loan officers in their cubicles. "Let's see how long it takes her to get a loan application."

Ashley started dialing for dollars.

"Hi, my name is Ashley, and I'm the manager for your loan. I'm calling today to see if I can get you a lower monthly payment and save you some money."

Well now, who wouldn't want "the manager of their loan" to save them some money?

In short order, Ashley announced to the group: "I got an application!" holding it up like a schoolgirl, asking "Teacher, teacher, now what do I do?"

The loan officers stood up in their cubicles so they could share a laugh over the partitions. The manager emerged from his office and gave her a high-five. Then he instructed one of the guys to show Ashley how to pull a credit report and put together a loan proposal.

I have seen similar scenarios played out at other companies.

When someone calls you on the phone with this kind of "offer," one thing you can be pretty certain of: he or she is new. The qualified, seasoned mortgage professionals already have business, because they've been doing loans long enough to get referrals. Rarely do they cold-call.

 Sneaky loan officers can be found lurking in every type of lending institution. Choose your individual rep carefully.

Here's another tact newbies take, which you need to be aware of. I worked briefly with a woman I'll call Kendra who was new to the mortgage profession. She succeeded in taking more loan applications on the phone than anyone else, including the more seasoned employees. This endeared her to the manager who had a strict quota for loan applications, which were tracked by the corporate office. I asked Kendra her secret for success.

"Whatever they tell me they want, I say yes," she said, eyes twinkling. "I don't really know if we can do it or not, but I tell them what they want to hear." She laughed.

About nine months later, Kendra accepted a job with a prestigious bank. I'm sure she told them whatever it was that they wanted to hear at her job interview. They set her up with a $5,000 laptop computer so she could take applications from anywhere.

A few months later, she told me she was thinking about moving across the country and taking her laptop with her.

Not long after, collectors were calling the mortgage manager looking for Kendra. No one knew where she had gone. So you see, even a big, safe bank can have an unscrupulous loan officer in the ranks.

The lesson is: You really have to judge individually, not by company or by bank.

✐ NOTE

To stop receiving annoying telephone solicitations for refinancing and second mortgage lines of credit, sign up for the National Do Not Call Registry at www.donotcall.gov; or call toll-free 1-888-382-1222. ✎

Payment Reduction Notices and Other Offers to Save

Just last week, I received a "Payment Reduction Notice." It arrived in an official-looking envelope, the kind you think is from your current lender. It read:

> Dear Carolyn:
>
> I am writing to alert you that your mortgage payment may be reduced to $591.83.* Many customers have taken advantage of this Payment Reduction notice by calling 1-800-XXX-XXXX.

It went on to give hours and a supposed expiration date for the offer, six weeks off.

The asterisk on this so-called notice directed me to some small-print wording at the bottom of the page. It told me the $591.83 payment was based on "an attractive interest rate of 1.25 percent."

All I had to do was call in. And because I wanted to find out if I'd connect with a swindler who would try to wrestle me out of my excellent 15-year fixed-rate mortgage and get me into a loan that would start low and then skyrocket, I posed as someone who was interested in the savings and seeking advice.

"What's your main goal?" the man who answered asked right away. "Is it to pay off your mortgage quickly?" This was a good question, because he knew from public records that I had a 15-year loan.

"Yes," I said.

"This offer is really for a person who would be staying in their house for only three or four years and want lower payments," he said. "It's temporary."

When I asked, he confirmed that this was a negative amortization Option ARM. He was quick to terminate the conversation then, no doubt having lost interest in taking up his time with a call that wouldn't lead to a loan. I was pleased that he hadn't tried to sell me on something that wasn't right for me. He was one of the good guys in the business.

How often do you receive solicitations packaged to look like official notices? Maybe they come in red, white, and blue Priority Mail envelopes, or they look like they're from your current lender. Mortgage lenders hire marketers who know they have but a brief moment to catch your attention and get you to open their letter before you toss it into the rubbish. Some of them use disgustingly dishonest tactics. My advice is to feed them to your shredder, especially if they contain personal information such as your loan balance.

✐ NOTE

If you receive a particularly annoying refinance solicitation, I'd like to see it. You can email it to me at www.AskCarolynWarren .com. ✎

Disputes over Your Home Value

When you refinance based on an overly inflated value of your home, you put yourself in jeopardy of financial loss. Unfortunately, loan sharks push for higher values than they should in order to get bigger loans. But there's another side to this story. Sometimes it's not the loan officer at all, but the homeowner who is insisting the house is worth more.

If you're refinancing and disagree with the appraiser's value of your home, this is for you, because there's a tug-of-war going on between appraisers and homeowners. Loan officers are caught in the middle of the argument; and, in the end, homeowners come out losing. Here's the inside scoop.

Let's assume Mrs. Homeowner desperately needs to consolidate bills, so she seeks a refinance. She says her home is worth $280,000, a value that will allow her to pay off the worst of her debt. But then something goes wrong: the appraiser alerts the loan officer that the value is going to come in at $240,000. With her loan slashed by forty grand, she can't save enough money to make the refinance worthwhile.

"That can't be right," she tells her loan officer. "We put in new carpet and new windows, and painted throughout."

The loan officer calls the appraiser and tells him.

The appraiser says, "Sorry, that's considered normal upkeep and doesn't increase value."

The loan officer reports back to Mrs. Homeowner and explains the value is determined by what similar houses have just sold for.

"But that's ridiculous! There's a house just half a mile away that sold for $290,000, and my house is bigger. I was being conservative when I said it was worth $280,000," she says.

Feeling like a ping-pong ball, the loan officer goes back to the appraiser.

"Sorry again," the appraiser says, "but that house is across a main arterial in a neighborhood with pricier homes. In that neighborhood all the homes are new, and our subject property is 30 years old. It's really not a comparable."

Mrs. Homeowner replies, "My house may be older, but it's just as nice—even nicer, because it's built more solid."

On and on it goes, until the loan officer pleads with the appraiser to strike a compromise.

"I have two more appraisal orders I can give you just as soon as we get this one wrapped up. Can't we find a middle ground?" he asks, desperate to appease his client and keep the loan. He tosses out two more appraisal orders as bait, and a compromise is reached.

Pushing value happens every day in the mortgage business. Here's an abbreviated email an appraiser received from a loan officer:

I was hoping we can make a few changes to the appraisal below. This is far too conservative. We are looking to move the value to 135,000 and change a few of the adjustments:

- Please change the condition from Below Average to Average.
- Please reduce the square footage adjustment on comparable 3 so the dollar amount per square foot is a little less.
- Please reduce the upgrades for comparable 2. Also please reduce the $5,500 for the patio room.
- When reducing the adjustments, please don't forget to take out the extended comments on the addendum section. My under-

writers cannot see the carpet, and it discusses conditions of the property when it was listed in the MLS 1.3 years ago.

In this case, the appraiser refused to make the changes; as a result, she was blacklisted from working for that mortgage company ever again. Here, in part, is her response:

> The ethical and honest appraisers are being "blacklisted" for doing their job correctly. . . . This has fast become a house of cards. . . .
> Appraisers are the ones that must say no to being bribed, or threatened with the loss of business and their income. This situation is now so far out of balance with way too many appraisers that say yes, and way too many (loan officers) that will only use appraisers that say yes, that it can only fall apart.

I overheard a loan officer pleading on the telephone with an appraiser to push up the value for a particular refinance. She said, "I'm not asking you to lie; I'm just asking you to bend the truth."

The appraiser hung up on her. Until more appraisers start hanging up on coercion and bribery, homeowners will ultimately become the losers in this tug-of-war. When you attempt to sell your home, you'll find you can't make a profit, because the value isn't what you thought it was. Or worse, you find you can't break even.

Most often this happens in the subprime lending arena. Values are pushed so that overspending consumers can consolidate their debt. People are not matching their spending to their budgets; rather, they match their spending to their desires. Their debt is way out of whack. Then they take out what they call "a bandage loan" to fix their cash flow and give themselves time to clean up their credit and raise their credit scores. Loan officers are only too happy to help.

These handy bandage loans are 2/28 or 3/27 loans, whereby homeowners get a lower fixed rate for the first two or three years (with two- or three-year prepayment penalties), and then it's time to refinance before the loan turns into an adjustable rate and zooms up into double digits. But when their two years are over and they go to refinance, they discover they don't have the equity they thought they did. Their last loan was based on an inflated value. Now they're stuck with an adjustable rate that's putting their cash flow back into trouble again.

I've seen this happen, and it's not pretty. At first, the homeowners are befuddled and confused. Then after further explanation, they get angry and wonder whether they can sue somebody.

Most lenders are very aware of this problem, so they have systems in place to catch inflated values. But, still, it happens.

Less often, the price on a Purchase and Sale Agreement signed by both buyer and seller is too high for its true value. Perhaps this was the "ideal" property for the buyers, so they're happy with the price; but due to certain factors, it is not ideal for the majority of the population, and the lender will not approve it. This happens most frequently on zero-down loans for which the lender gets no collateral. Lenders may request a second opinion from another appraiser as to value. They have to protect their investment on a no-equity deal, because if the buyers fail to make their payment and let the house default, they're stuck with a piece of real estate they have to try to auction off.

When the verdict is returned that the sales price is too high, everyone goes ballistic. The wholesale account executive gets the unpleasant task of breaking the news to the loan officer, who "can't believe his or her ears." Then the loan officer gets the even more unpleasant task of breaking the news to the homebuyers, who are already feeling stress just because buying a home is a major change to their lives, and this news is the last thing they need. But the worst part of all is breaking the news to the real estate agents, who are trusting the loan officer to close the deal smoothly. It's always the loan officer's "fault" when something goes wrong. The real estate agents don't believe they overpriced and oversold the home, and they have plenty to say in their defense. Then the loan officer passes all this stress back up the line to the wholesale lender. It's a battle you don't want to be caught in the middle of, believe me.

What can you, as a consumer, do about all this? When you're refinancing, don't push the value of your home. You may be tempted to flatter yourself, but it's not in your best interest to do so. And when you're in the market to buy a home, accept the value the appraiser assigns to the property.

Coming Up

If you're considering refinancing, you won't want to miss the next chapter. Get the straight scoop on closing costs and a timely warning about mortgages that rob you of your future security.

CHAPTER 10

Watch Out if You're Rolling Fees into Your Loan!

Refinancing requires no out-of-pocket cash. Unlike a purchase loan, a refinance allows you to roll all the fees into the loan itself. But watch out! This advantage is also exactly where you're vulnerable to be taken advantage of.

The Scoop on Closing Costs

The one question shady loan officers don't want to hear is, "What are your closing costs?" I say, don't even ask it. Verbal quotes mean nothing anyway, so why bother? Instead, get your short list and review your Good Faith Estimate, as explained in Chapters 2 and 4. (And get that written guarantee that says the non-third-party closing costs won't vary by more than 10 percent.)

One day, a new loan officer asked a group of more experienced loan officers, "How do you explain closing costs?"

After several good answers, one quipped, "I lie to them [clients] and tell them that there's no cost at all—zero, zip, nada. Then I let the notary explain the real closing costs at the signing table. This works well, because nobody can argue with *free*. Whatever it takes to get them to the signing table, that's my philosophy. If this still doesn't work, I will usually just change the subject, or act like I didn't hear the question and just move on with the conversation.

"If all else fails," he continued, "I tell them that we're having a fire drill, and I have to evacuate the building; then I never call them back."

Like all good jokes, this one has an element of reality in it. Which is precisely what made it so funny to the loan officers listening, and why a lively discussion ensued about certain people they knew (including themselves) in certain companies who did this sort of thing. But a few of the loan officers responded angrily, insisting it's not funny to joke about the unscrupulous tactics that some loan officers employ.

At the first mortgage company I worked for, my mentor advised me to tell my clients to ignore their Good Faith Estimates. As her protégé, I sat by her desk and listened to what she said.

"In a few days you're going to get a big envelope in the mail with a bunch of paperwork. Don't even open it. Just throw it away. It's something our main office computer spits out when we input a loan application into the system, but it's not accurate for your loan. So don't freak out when you see it. The closing costs will be way too high. But don't worry, that didn't come from me. I'll prepare a more accurate statement for you when you come in to sign."

"Okay, thanks for the heads-up," her unsuspecting clients responded.

By the time the homeowners came in to sign, they were so focused on getting rid of their credit card debt and getting extra cash in their hands, they didn't really care what the closing costs were. In fact, some of them spent their money even before they had it in hand. Like the man who rushed out and signed a deal to buy a new truck when his loan hadn't funded yet. Boy, was he hopping mad when his loan was late to fund! He was shouting about suing for not funding on time—but, of course, he couldn't do that.

The Worst Refinance: Could It Be Yours?

If a prize were given for the most expensive, worst-ever refinance, one of the top contenders would be the loan that has four or five discount points (so-called) *and* a yield spread premium coming back to the loan officer for even more in commissions.

A loan officer may exclaim, "You have no out-of-pocket expenses" as a way to get you to ignore having too many up-front fees rolled into your loan.

Sad to say, homeowners are signing for these loans every day. Just because the points and bogus discount points are rolled into your loan, it doesn't mean you're not paying for them. You are. You're paying these outrageous fees with your precious home equity, and that's every bit as real as paying for it out of your checking account.

I observed one smooth-talking loan officer say to her client, "Most loans for people who have bad credit have five or six points, but I'm only charging you three. When you bought your house, the real estate agent charged 6 percent to the seller, and this is half that, so you're getting a good deal."

"Thank you," said the homeowner who happily signed the Good Faith Estimate in the comfort of her own home for three points up front and three on the back. Plus junk fees, of course.

Pay Attention to the Numbers

My mentor at my first mortgage job told me she always added points to the loan later, so she could bump up her revenue. I was amazed. I asked her how she did this.

"It's easy," she said. "They [Clients] don't pay attention." People taking nonconforming, subprime loans are famous for not paying attention. Their focus is on getting rid of their high-interest credit cards, not on how much it's costing them to do so.

You think your loan officer is being considerate and extra helpful. She suggests ideas for getting cash back on your debt consolidation refinance, such as home improvements. But if there's nothing you need, she'll still bump up the loan to give you four or five grand back.

When you go over your Good Faith Estimate together, she says this is in case your current mortgage pay off comes in higher than expected. But how much higher could it come in? Truth is, you'll start thinking about having that extra five thousand in your hands and get excited about what you're going to spend it on. This "helps" your loan close smoothly, meaning it helps you focus on the advantages of your refinance and overlook the disadvantages—the costs.

Some loan officers reading this will shriek with indignation and say they've never done such a thing, and it's ludicrous. That's true, and they are the mortgage rock stars. But others will chuckle and say, "Yep."

Coming Up

In Chapter 11, which begins Part III, I cover special topics and unique situations. First up: some fantastic bargains for homebuyers.

PART III

SPECIAL TOPICS AND UNIQUE SITUATIONS

Great Deals
on below
Market Rate Loans

Would you like a great loan at a bargain rate? How about a free grant? If so get ready to get excited. These include:

- First-time homebuyer programs available to previous homeowners
- Loans for public servants
- Loans for the community-minded
- Loans for people with a disability

The chapter also gives you the lowdown on free grants, for which you also might be eligible.

First-Time Homebuyer Programs
Open to Anyone

You don't necessarily have to be a first-time homebuyer to qualify for a first-time homebuyer program. Confused? "First time homebuyer program" is a catchy phrase that grabs attention because it makes people think they'll get something special if they've never bought a house before. Good marketing pure and simple.

But these are excellent loans, and the good news is that you may qualify for one of them even if you have previously owned a home. The purpose of the programs is to increase home ownership in America, because it is believed that people who own their homes contribute to a better community. These programs offer advantages such as:

- Down payment assistance
- Lower interest rate for a lower monthly payment (some as low as 3 percent fixed)
- Relaxed approval requirements (previous bankruptcy okay)

✐ **NOTE**
There are many so-called first-time loan programs, and new ones are being created all the time, so regard these guidelines as general. Your loan officer will fill you in on the specifics for your area. ✎

How to Qualify for a "First-Time" Loan

Six common requirements to qualify for a first-time homebuyer program are the following:

1. You have not been a homeowner within the past year (or two or three, depending on the program). Some may not even have this requirement.
2. You do not own other homes, and you will live in the home. (These programs are not for rental properties.)
3. Your income falls within the established limits (usually set by the median income in your area).
4. Your credit qualifies. (May have easier-to-qualify guidelines.)
5. The purchase price of the home falls within the lending limits. (Sorry, no $2 million mansions with these programs.)
6. The home is located within the boundaries allowed by the program. (Some require you to be within the city or within a certain part of a city. Others require you to be in a rural area.)

Here's a small sample listing of the programs available:

- House Key
- First Homes Program (administered by HomeSight)
- First-Time Homebuyer Program (administered by the State Housing Development Authority)
- Low-Interest Mortgage (administered by the local government)

Loans for Public Servants

Both the U.S. Department of Housing and Urban Development (HUD) and the State Housing Finance Commission offer reduced pricing on home loans to professional public servants—teachers, firefighters, police officers, health care workers, and others—the reasoning being that American communities are stronger and safer when people who work in these civic professions move in.

Here are three sample programs:

1. Teachers who are employed full-time by an educational institution may qualify, whether or not they work in the classroom. The Teacher Next Door program offers a purchase price discount of 50 percent of the appraised value in distressed urban areas.

2. Police officers who qualify can buy a house at half the price through the Officer Next Door program.

3. HUD offers emergency medical technicians and other public servants a variety of what are called Good Neighbor Next Door programs.

Inexpensive Loans for the Community-Minded

Are you willing to buy a house in a city neighborhood that's been targeted for improvement? If so, and if you meet the income requirements (based on median income for the county), you may be eligible for assistance for down payment and closing costs.

There are also loans specifically for people who are willing to buy in rural areas and repair their homes. Money provided by the Rural Housing Service may be used for the purchase and renovation of such properties, including supplying water and sewage facilities on the site, if needed.

Loans for People with a Disability

Loans such as Homechoice are for people with disabilities, as defined by the Americans with Disabilities Act (ADA) of 1990, or who have dependent family members with disabilities who live with them. The program may help with a down payment and closing costs. Some offer a lower interest rate and monthly payment. Again, you must meet the income requirements and occupy the home.

Free Grants

The HomeBuyer Funds Web site decribed in the shaded box on page 171 also lists some grant programs that say you must be approved for a loan that allows "gift funds" from a charitable organization. How does this work? I'll explain.

Who Can Get a Grant?

Grant programs make your down payment for you—and sometimes cover closing costs as well. You do *not* have to be low-income, in a hard-ship situation, or in a certain neighborhood to qualify. Neither do you have to be a first-time homebuyer. Anyone who meets the credit and income/asset qualifications can get a grant. (Yes, you can be filthy rich and have owned five homes in the past, and still qualify.) But you must find a seller who is willing to participate in the grant program. And there are limits on the price of the home, based on your county's median home price.

How to Find Below Market Rate Loans You May Qualify For

There are thousands of housing assistance programs offered by the government, nonprofit agencies, and private organizations, so it's not possible to list them all here; but I can tell you how to easily find the ones available in your desired area: use the complimentary Funds Finder Tool offered by HomeBuyer Funds at www.home-buyerfunds.com. In fact, you'll find details on all the programs I mention in this chapter at this Web site.

 HomeBuyer Funds is the nation's largest online funds database. It is a resource for both homebuying and home improvement financing.

One suggestion before you go there, however: Do not click on the bright red Start Here button at the site, which takes you to a mini-application that asks for your personal information. This is a lead generation service that sells your info to several mortgage companies. You don't want that. Instead, click on Funds Finder on the left side. It will take you to an area where you remain anonymous and, on a green map, can select your desired state.

For financing, some of the programs offer a contact and telephone number. If you're getting a 3 percent, 30-year fixed rate via the contact, there is no reason to shop around. If, however, you are referred to a national bank, because you're being offered down payment assistance only (and you're getting the "market rate" financing), then you should proceed with the short list plan explained in Chapter 2.

You can also go to your city's or county's housing department Web site, and the HUD site, at www.hud.gov.

What Are the Grant Programs Called?

There are a number of grant programs. The Nehemiah Program is the largest privately funded down payment assistance program. According to its Web site, since 1997, it has assisted more than 215,000 families get into a home. Other grant programs include:

- Alliance Housing Assistance Gift Funds
- AmeriDream
- AmeriGold
- Futures Home Assistance Program
- Genesis
- God Is King (GIK)
- Home Quest Program
- Neighborhood Gold

Where Can You Get a Grant Program?

I recommend you work with a local mortgage broker on grant programs, because he or she knows your area neighborhood values, title and escrow reps, and so on, as I discussed in Chapter 2. It's best to work with a loan officer who has experience successfully closing these loans, because he or she will already have a relationship with the program representative and know what the pitfalls are.

A word of warning is in order here, however: Some loan officers look on these programs with disfavor and may caution you against them. If, after listening to their reasons, you still want to pursue one, ask for a referral or check your local yellow pages. I'll explain the downside after I explain how they work, so it's clear.

How Do Grant Programs Work?

Some grant programs work through FHA loans, while others allow either FHA or conventional financing. Let's take the aforementioned Nehemiah as an example.

Your local mortgage broker gets you approved for an FHA loan. Approval requires clean credit for the past 12 months (former bankruptcy is okay as long as it has been discharged for 24 months), and an acceptable income and debt ratio.

The down payment requirement is 3 percent of the purchase price, and Nehemiah is going to make that down payment for you. But how does Nehemiah get this money? That's where the catch comes in. As I mentioned previously, you have to find a seller who is willing to participate.

The seller gives Nehemiah 4 percent. Then Nehemiah passes on 3 percent to your lender for the down payment and keeps the other 1 percent for its nonprofit charity. (Lenders do not allow a seller to make the down payment for the buyer. But some of them do allow a nonprofit charity to make the down payment for the buyer.)

In addition to the down payment, there are closing costs. Either you pay the closing costs yourself or you ask the seller to pay them, in addition to the 4 percent he or she is already giving to Nehemiah.

The Controversy

Why should a seller give up 4 percent (or 7 percent to include closing costs)?

Because Nehemiah is a nonprofit, the seller gets to declare the contribution as a tax deduction, true enough. But still, he or she pockets a lot less money.

If it's a slow market and the seller is desperate to sell, he or she may be willing to participate. But more often, the purchase price is bumped up to accommodate the contribution and still allow the seller to net the cash he originally wanted. This is clever, but is there a danger involved?

Some loan officers shout "yes!" They say appraisers are pressured into valuing the property higher than they otherwise would have to accommodate the higher purchase price; thus, in reality, you end up with a loan that is over 100 percent of the true value. What happens if you want to sell in a year or two? You're stuck, because you owe more than what you can get out of it, especially after you factor in selling costs. Detractors of these loans say they're dangerous, putting you at risk for foreclosure.

Another controversy centers around whether these nonprofits are truly charities and should be allowed tax-exempt status. The nonprofits defend their status, perhaps most eloquently by Scott Syphax, President and CEO of the Nehemiah Corporation of America:

May 6, 2006

I am writing to you as President and CEO of Nehemiah to offer perspective and clarification on the IRS Revenue Ruling 2006-27. Nehemiah is currently studying and evaluating this IRS ruling issued yesterday. We are disappointed that a program that has been granted tax-exempt status for more than nine years and has served hundreds of thousands of Americans would have this tax exemption arbitrarily threatened in this fashion. We intend to contest the IRS opinion.

It is important to note that Nehemiah has not been sanctioned by any regulatory agency and that Nehemiah continues to serve homebuyers by delivering world-class down payment assistance through the reputable Nehemiah Program.

The IRS's press release in announcing its administrative ruling, incorrectly gives the impression that by the mere proclamation of the ruling, the tax-exemption held by a charitable organization that operates a down payment assistance program is thereby immediately revoked.

This is wholly inaccurate. The administrative ruling does not have an instantaneous impact on the tax-exempt status of an entity. An administrative ruling sets forth that agency's conclusions as to the issue at hand—the ruling is the beginning, not the end of the discussion.

The Nehemiah Program is operated by the Nehemiah Corporation of America. In January 1998, by written determination, the IRS recognized Nehemiah as a tax-exempt organization as it satisfactorily met the provisions of section 501(c)(3) of the Internal Revenue Code. Nehemiah's ability to operate The Nehemiah Program is not changed in any way by the ruling other than Nehemiah may have to pay appropriate business taxes on the revenues generated by its down payment assistance program. Furthermore, today HUD and FHA have confirmed that any down payment assistance provider whose tax exempt status is in good standing may continue to provide down payment assistance and that those loans will remain insurable under the Federal Housing Administration loan program.

Nehemiah Corporation of America has achieved a great deal in our short history and we remain committed to staying true to our charitable mission through the success of all of Nehemiah's programs: These include:

- The Nehemiah Program has provided in excess of $825 million in gift funds to more than 212,000 families in 8,500 cities, in 50 states.
- Through its tax credit programs, Nehemiah Corporation has provided affordable housing for thousands of individuals and families.
- The Nehemiah Community Reinvestment Fund (NCRF) has generated over $57 million in investment and lending capital (including nearly $30 million of Nehemiah's capital) resulting in the creation of more than 2.6 million square feet of commercial space, nearly 3,000 housing units and almost 10,000 jobs to help revitalize low-income and underserved communities. NCRF-funded projects have a total development cost of over $550 million.
- Since it was launched in 2000, Nehemiah Community Foundation (NCF) has contributed more than $5 million to an annual

average of more than 100 charities across the United States. In Sacramento County, NCF has provided $246,000 in college scholarships to help 66 academically superior, low-income local high school graduates since 2001.

- Since 1999, Nehemiah Urban Ministry Initiatives has provided over $300,000 in college scholarships and funding to send 66 college students to work as volunteer interns with faith-based community service organizations in cities across the nation.

On behalf of Nehemiah Corporation, I thank you for your continued support and the opportunity to work alongside of you in assisting more people to become homeowners.

If you qualify for one of the below market rate programs, I recommend taking it. Follow my advice in Chapter 2 for selecting a good loan officer. If you're considering a grant program, you need to proceed with caution. The wisdom of using a down payment assistance program is tied to the current market for your area. In a city with a fast-moving real estate market, it may be impractical or impossible. But in a small town or slower market, these programs can work out well. Just make sure you understand the true value of the property and the time commitment you need to make in order to achieve enough equity to sell or refinance.

Coming Up

In Chapter 12, I offer savvy advice for buyers of condominiums and two- to four-family homes.

Tips for Loans on Condos and Two- to Four-Family Homes

Are house prices way out of reach in your neighborhood? Welcome to the club I call "the club for singles, first-time buyers, and almost everyone else living in a coastal city." If you can't afford the house you want, please don't give up, because you have options.

How to Get a More Reasonably Priced Home

A condominium (condo) or a townhouse (a condo on two or more levels) can be an excellent choice for affordable housing. Even if it's not your ideal, it is a start in real estate, and that's better than renting.

Buying a Condo

Let's look at the pluses and minuses of condos to help you determine if buying one makes sense for you.

First, the advantages:

- Prices are cheaper than detached family homes.
- There's no yard work (the association takes care of the grounds).

- Garbage disposal is taken care of.
- You have the cozy, secure feeling of having neighbors close by.
- May include a pool, workout facilities, and other amenities.
- May have cheaper heating, especially if the condo is on the top floor.
- If you make a wise selection, you can enjoy a handsome return on your investment when you sell; or you may choose to turn it into rental income later.

Now, the disadvantages:

- Monthly homeowner's dues are not tax deductible.
- There is the possibility of special assessments for major repairs, such as a new roof.
- You have limited or no personal yard space.
- Noisy, annoying neighbors may be close by.
- There may be restrictions on pets.
- Your loan may have a slightly higher interest rate.
- If you make an unwise selection, a condo will take longer to sell and not yield as great a profit as a detached family home.

Some of these considerations, obviously, are personal preference, but indisputably, you must take extra care to select the right condo. Everyone's heard that location is the most important factor in choosing real estate. When you're buying a condo, that goes double. If you buy in a desirable location, and if you buy a condo in a small or midsized community that's well maintained, it can appreciate in value equal to a detached single-family home. In some areas, in fact, luxury condominiums with views have been known to sell for several million dollars.

Financing a Condo. The lender will take several precautions before making a final approval on financing for a condominium. Rather than thinking of this as a hassle, you should regard it as a protection. If the lender is concerned about certain factors, you should be too.

The underwriter will ask to review the bylaws, the budget, and the minutes from previous homeowners' meetings. He or she will look to see if there's enough money in reserves, in case a major repair comes up, and will check what repairs and special assessments have occurred in the past. If there's a pending lawsuit, the lender won't extend financing until it is resolved.

WARNING

If the lender refuses to extend financing on a condo you've fallen in love with, take that as a serious warning. If the lender is not willing to put its money on the line, why would you want to take the risk?

Some lenders have a small increase in the interest rate for condos, such as a quarter of a percent. In my opinion, this is no big deal. It's more important to choose the right loan. If this is your starter home, look at the 3/1 ARM and the 5/1 ARM, because you'll get a lower rate than with a 30-year fixed. And why pay more? (See Chapter 3.)

Investing in a Duplex, Triplex, or Fourplex: The Two- to Four-Family Home

If you buy a duplex, triplex, or fourplex, and live in one of the units, this is considered an *owner-occupied* property. In the right location, this can be a great investment idea. You get a place to live, and your tenants cover the mortgage payment.

 Before investing in a multifamily property, consult with a financial planner and study the landlord/tenant laws.

Because duplexes are less common than condominiums, they're considered by many financial planners to be the better investment. However, they are not nirvana for everyone. For instance, one woman said she'd never own a duplex again, because her tenants placed their piano up against the adjoining wall and "entertained" her with their music. Then there was their pet rodent, which chewed its way into her place.

WARNING

Don't be tempted to pass off an investment property as owner occupied. This is fraud and could land you in a new, special place to live—a jail cell. And don't think no one will ever find out. Lenders have been known to send out an investigator to knock on the door several months later, to check for renters in the property you signed as being owner occupied. They can, and will, recall their loan if that happens, putting you in hot water. And if you already own a single-family house and try to buy a fourplex as owner occupied, the lender won't believe you. "Who would give up their big house and yard to go live in a multifamily unit?" they ask. Then they'll offer to extend financing as an investment property, which will require a larger down payment and higher interest rate. ✎

Financing a Multiunit Property.   You have four basic choices for financing your owner-occupied multiplex, which I describe in a moment. All are available through your local mortgage broker, so follow the short list plan in Chapter 2.

Your first step is to locate a loan officer who:

- Is honest, discloses YSP, and avoids stupid junk fees.
- Communicates well with you.
- Has experience doing multiunit properties.

Once you locate this mortgage professional, he or she will explain loan options and shop a dozen or so wholesale lenders to find you the best deal. Quite a bit of work is involved, so you don't want to "shoplift" anyone's time. Remember, if you don't close a loan with someone, he or she gets paid nothing for their time. Therefore, don't ask a zillion questions about financing options until you've located the loan officer you want to work with. Once you've found someone you like and are committed to, try to meet with him or her in person and get all your questions answered.

Financing Options

- *FHA loan.* Three percent down. Seller may pay closing costs. Both fixed and adjustable rates are available. Loan limits are set according to median home prices in the county. If the loan limit is not too small, this is an excellent choice.

- *VA loan.* Zero down for qualifying veterans. Fixed and adjustable rates are available.

- *Conventional loan.* Ten percent down is typical. The interest rate will be a quarter to a half percent higher than for a single-family home.
- *Nonconforming loan.* Zero-down and Option ARM loans are available, as well as other ARMs and fixed rates.

Again, as I just stated above, all these options are available through your local mortgage broker, who will have the current rates and guidelines.

Financing an Investment Property

It's easier to say *forget it* and walk away from an investment property than it is from your own home that provides you and your family a secure place to sleep. In other words, if a person can't find a renter and can't pay both mortgages, which one is he or she going to give up—the rental or his or her own place?

Because lending on an investment property is riskier, the loan requires a higher interest rate to compensate for the risk. Some lenders will allow zero down for investment properties. Again, the first step is to locate an honest, experienced loan officer, and he or she will search and shop the best deal for you.

Coming Up

"Help! My loan has been denied!" If that's your fear, don't panic, because in the next chapter, I'll tell you how to turn a denial into an approval.

CHAPTER 13

What if You Get Turned Down?

Are there ways of getting a turned-down loan approved? Yes, of course. And in this chapter, I'll reveal the magic of turning a denial into an approval.

Turning a Denied Loan into an Approved Loan

There are three primary ways a denied loan can get turned into an approved loan:

1. The wholesale account executive takes the loan file to the underwriting supervisor or to the branch manager for a second opinion, to override the denial. This is a common approach when the account executive disagrees with the underwriter's decision.

2. If the account executive doesn't have success in getting an override from the underwriting supervisor or branch manager, he or she can send the loan file to the corporate office to request an *exception*. This is most common with subprime loans that fall in the "gray zone." Perhaps the home buyer doesn't qualify for one reason, but there are compensating factors to consider. Someone

with top authority could make a judgment call and approve the loan even though the automated underwriting system says no. When this happens, the loan goes to the corporate office. Note that getting a decision will take extra time, so everyone has to be patient.

3. The underwriter might consider a Letter of Explanation in order to turn a denial into an approval. Some lenders simply don't care how good your reason is for your bad credit, they won't read a Letter of Explanation under any circumstances, but others will. However, you'll need to write the right kind of letter. Read how, below.

The Secret to Writing an Effective Letter of Explanation

The first key to a successful Letter of Explanation is to forget the sob story. Even the most tear-stained letter won't influence an underwriter. I had a client who worked in construction on the streets of New York. A city truck ran over his foot, disabling him from working for many months. I figured I could get an exception for this man by providing a letter from my client, a letter from his doctor, and doctor bills to match. But I was wrong. Loan denied.

The secret is to tell the underwriters *what they want to hear*. And what they want to hear is that the incident that caused your bad credit is a one-time occurrence that is in the past and *will never recur*. You must convince them that you will never again fail to pay on time. Acceptable "one-time occurrences" include:

- Divorce
- Death in the family
- Major illness that required hospitalization

Acceptable is *not* wedding expenses, as one couple stated as their reason for not paying their credit cards. Nor is the fact that you moved and didn't receive your bill, because it is your responsibility to keep

Turning a Denial into an Approval: A Look behind the Scenes

If you're buying a home, what's your worst nightmare? Do you fear that something will go wrong and cause your deal to fall apart?

When this happens, we try to handle it so the client doesn't get stressed out. Here's a look behind the scenes.

When I was working as a wholesale account executive, a loan was overturned a week before closing. It was awful. The homebuyers thought everything was going great; they'd given notice to their landlord, and they had a moving company all lined up. I was driving through town when I got a call on my cell phone from the underwriter saying a problem had just been discovered and the loan was not going to close. This was disastrous, because we were at the point of drawing up the loan documents and the people were expecting to sign papers very soon.

"What happened?" I asked.

The underwriter explained, "On the loan application, it says they've been self-employed for two years. [Two years was required for self-employment.] But guess what? I just got their business license, and it says they've been in business for just 18 months. Sorry, but the loan is denied. There's nothing I can do."

I went straight to my branch manager/VP and asked for an exception. But he said he couldn't grant one, because the homebuyers were putting no money down, and they had low credit scores of 580. With those three layers of risk (short-term self-employment, no down payment, and low credit scores), it couldn't be done.

"Sorry," he said, "but they shouldn't have said they were in business for two years when it was 18 months. It's their fault."

Now I got nervous. Usually I could get an exception. And it wasn't going to make the mortgage broker or the homebuyers feel any better about losing the house because it was "their fault, not ours." Their dream of moving into their own home would be shattered and they'd have no place to live. Furthermore, the loan officer wanted to make a good impression on the real estate agents so they'd refer future clients to him. He was going to be very upset, as well.

(continued)

For all those reasons, I asked my branch manager/VP for permission to send the file to our corporate office requesting an exception.

"Sure, you can send the file down if you want, but I don't give it a good chance," he said. "Corporate doesn't like to make exceptions when the credit score is 580."

Being an optimist, I decided to try anyway. I wrote a cover letter listing the compensating factors and why I felt these borrowers were worthy of an approval. (I pointed out that if the husband's business failed, he could go back to his previous employer, as people his line of work were in great demand. I noted, too, that even though their scores were low, they'd paid off all past collection accounts and had no late payments in the past 24 months. Next, I pointed out that they had good rental payments. And, finally, I noted that their debt-to-income ratio was low.)

Next I called the loan officer to let him know what was going on. And we waited. And waited. Everyone was nervous. The loan officer's processor told me she sprinkled holy water on the loan file. We waited some more. It was one day till closing and these people still had no financing and no idea that their financing had gone south. They expected to be signing papers the next day and moving into their first home over the weekend. But alas, their loan was dead. I needed a loan miracle.

I asked the loan officer why their application said they'd been self-employed for two years when it was only 18 months.

He said, "I rounded up. I didn't think it was a big deal."

Or maybe he didn't think anyone would check. The guidelines are posted clearly. I don't know.

Finally, I got my answer from our corporate office. The loan was approved. Immediately, I called the loan officer with the good news, and we all screamed over the phone and jumped up and down with joy.

When my clients moved in on time, they said, "That went smoothly, didn't it?"

The loan officer just smiled and said, "Yes, it did." Because that's what good loan officers do—they're like shock absorbers, preventing stress from reaching their clients.

track of your financial obligations. And don't even think of blaming your pet!

When writing your letter, at all times, stick to the facts; leave your emotions out of your letter. Don't blame your lousy ex for cheating on you, because it won't help get your loan approved. Instead, state that the collections were due to a divorce, that the accounts in collections were the sole responsibility of your ex, and that your credit has been segregated now. Point out that your credit was perfect before the divorce and has been perfect since, with the exception of these collections that are not yours. (Provide that page of your divorce decree to back your explanation.) This is quite different from saying, for example, "My husband cheated on me and left me with three little children to take care of. He then used our credit cards to finance his affair. Please approve my loan, because I was the victim and I am a good person."

I read one Letter of Explanation where the homeowner said her auto repossession was due to a "scumbag salesman" who "lied through his teeth" and sold her a "lemon." It didn't work. On the contrary, the underwriters concluded the woman was naive, not creditworthy.

✐ **NOTE**
More inside info on this topic in Chapter 16, under "Secrets of the Underwriting Department." ✐

Coming Up

Loan denials aren't the only nail-biting challenge. Even an approved loan may die on the vine. In Chapter 14, you'll learn what to do if your loan doesn't close.

What if Your Loan Doesn't Close?

Just because you've signed all 50-plus pages, and have writer's cramp to prove it, it doesn't mean your loan will fund. The *signing is not the closing*. And a loan isn't officially closed until it funds, meaning it has been recorded with the county; and in the case of a refinance, the money has been wired to and accepted by your present mortgage company. Until then, something could still go wrong.

Reasons Your Loan Might Not Close as Expected

There are many reasons why a loan might fall apart and not fund, even though all the documents have been signed and notarized. This section details eight reasons your loan might close late, or not at all. They are:

1. Something bad popped up on your credit.
2. Your job situation changed.
3. The title wasn't clear.
4. The appraisal was reviewed again and rejected.
5. Fraud was discovered.

6. The funder made an error in wiring.

7. Your file grew legs and walked away.

8. Natural or national disaster struck.

Something Bad Popped Up on Your Credit

This isn't as rare as you might think. For instance, let's say your loan took awhile to process and your credit report is more than 60 days old (or whatever your particular lender's guidelines are). In this case, the lender will pull a new credit report right before your loan funds. Then wham! Up pops that late payment from last week you thought you could let slide. Or up pops an old collection from a cell phone company that someone suddenly decided to pull out of the blue and work on. You had no idea, because you'd forgotten about that pest from three years ago. (This is exactly what happened to one homeowner whose score suddenly plummeted 80 points, causing her to lose her loan and the house she wanted to buy.)

A bad credit report surprise is common when homeowners don't make their mortgage payment because they're in the process of refinancing. No need to pay, they think. Maybe their loan officer told them they shouldn't send in payment because their current company will be paid off by the refinance. But then the process takes longer than expected. When the new month rolls over and a "mortgage late" appears, the loan could be killed.

 Always make your mortgage payment on time, even if you're refinancing. It's better to get a refund than to risk being late.

Your Job Situation Changed

One woman raced back to her office after signing for her refinance and joyfully told her unpleasant boss that she was quitting. The next day, the funder picked up the phone to make the routine call verifying employment.

"She just gave her two weeks' notice."

Oops. Now that she didn't have an income beyond two weeks, how would she pay her mortgage? The loan was killed.

"Why couldn't she have waited until after her loan funded?" wailed the loan officer, who would make no commission for all the work she'd done.

I had a client who got laid off from her job during the three-day recision period.

"How fast can you get new employment?" I asked her. Fortunately, it only took her a couple days, so her funding was delayed by just a little.

The Title Wasn't Clear

Sometimes a bad surprise pops up when your new loan is set to record. On the title report is a judgment or lien that didn't appear on your credit report, and it slipped by unnoticed until now. But alas, your new mortgage cannot record in first position until you pay that lien and your title is clear.

The Appraisal Was Reviewed Again and Rejected

Everything is good to go on your loan. But then the underwriting supervisor decides to have a look-see, and she doesn't like your appraisal. She could reject your loan. Or perhaps the underwriter ordered a second opinion "appraisal review" from an outside company, and that appraiser disagrees with the value. Your loan could be rejected. When this happens, both your loan officer and the wholesale account executive will fight tooth and nail to get the denial overturned, because they'll lose out on their commissions if the loan doesn't fund, and they feel their reputations are at stake. Often, they win. But not always.

> ✐ **NOTE**
> Underwriting may cut the value and offer you a smaller loan if this happens. Again, your two advocates will argue and fight for a compromise, at the least. When the feathers and dust settle, they'll call and tell you you're not going to get as much cash as previously hoped. ✎

You may be tempted to fly into a rage and yell at your loan officer; but please realize it's not his or her fault. He or she wants to get paid on a bigger loan too, and certainly doesn't relish making this unpleasant phone call.

Trust me, your loan officer has already flown into a rage for you, and likely has been pacing up and down the hall moaning, "I'm dreading calling my client with this bad news."

However, if you do have some additional information your loan officer may not have considered, then politely bring that up (information such as your new $9,000 granite counter and your new $15,000 roof, or news that your neighbor's house just sold yesterday for a high price).

Fraud Was Discovered

If either you or your loan officer was tempted to fudge on income or asset figures, it will probably be discovered before funding.

One time a loan officer was doing a loan for a buddy of his. They put their heads together and got someone at his job to provide a phony pay stub showing he made more money than he really did. But the underwriter had taken a class on detecting altered documents, and he busted them. Not only was the loan denied, but the vice president of the wholesale lending company spoke to the mortgage broker and told him he was no longer welcome to submit loans to their company—ever.

The Funder Made an Error in Wiring

I knew a funder who told me that she funds so many loans at the end of the month she accidentally transposes digits on one loan's wiring instructions every month, on average. So each month, there was an upset homeowner wondering why his or her loan didn't fund on time.

"Sorry, I can't be perfect all the time," she said cheerfully.

Your File Grew Legs and Walked Away

"Okay, don't tell anyone, but we can't find the file," whispered the wholesale account executive to the loan officer who was demanding to know why her loan hadn't funded yet. As it turned out, during the night, when no one was around, the rebellious file had slipped down in between a desk and a file cabinet. True story; I was the loan officer.

Natural or National Disaster Strikes

A 6.8 earthquake hit Seattle February 28, 2001, at 10:55 A.M. The courthouse suffered damage and was shut down. As fate would have it, this was the last day of the month—the busiest day to record and fund loans. With the recorder's office closed, the loans that hadn't funded yet that morning could not fund, and there was nothing anyone could do about it. (I did manage to get one loan funded anyway, due to a clever maneuver, but that's a story for Chapter 16.)

 There is no such thing as a guarantee for closing your loan. Verbal guarantees are as reliable as wishes.

And after the sudden terrorist attacks on September 11, 2001, no loans funded for several days.

This is why no one can guarantee you your loan will fund on time.

Coming Up

The next chapter is controversial, and I want to know your opinion, so after you read it, please send me an email to let me know what you think about these issues:

- What do you think of the way loan officers are tricking people into signing exceptions to the legal ceiling on profit?
- Should illegal kickbacks be legalized?
- Should YSP back-end commissions be outlawed?

You can reach me through my website, www.AskCarolynWarren.com.

CHAPTER 15

Controversial Lender Laws

While you're reading about outrageous loan pricing, you might ask, "Isn't there a law that puts a limit on what lenders can make?" The answer is yes.

Maximum Profit Allowed by Law

The Home Ownership and Equity Protection Act (HOEPA) of 1994 puts a ceiling on how high a lender's profit can be for refinances and home equity lines of credit. Sound good?

To simplify, the law allows the points and fees, including YSP back-end commissions (the APR), to total up to 8 percent of your refinance loan amount (unless you sign a special form). So, let's see, on a $200,000 house that would be a $16,000 profit. On an $800,000 house that would be a $64,000 profit. On a home equity line of credit, the APR can go up to 10 percent.

But wait, I mentioned a special form. If lenders want to make more, all they have to do is have you sign a notice at least three days before your loan is finalized. It tells you three things, none of them big news:

1. You don't have to go through with the deal.

2. If you don't make payments, the lender can foreclose on your house.

3. The loan terms have to be stated, such as loan amount, annual percentage rate, payment, credit life insurance, and the rest.

Many people sign a form authorizing their lender to make a higher commission than allowed by law (Section 32, Regulation Z).

If you sign this form and do not rescind for three days, then the super expensive loan is legal. You've granted the lender the right to make an exception to the price ceiling.

When I worked for a finance company, we did Section 32 loans all the time, because a lot of our loans were fairly small and pricey. (They're called Section 32 loans, because the rules are spelled out in Section 32 of Regulation Z that implements the Truth-in-Lending Act.) Never once did a client complain about signing this notification that their loan was so expensive it was an exception to HOEPA.

We would just call up our borrower and say, "Hi, I have a form I'm going to fax over that I need your signature on. The Feds have so many forms mortgage companies are required to have in the file! Sure doesn't help our trees, does it? Ha-ha. So much for a paperless society! Ha-ha. We're not allowed to finalize your loan until three days after you sign and date the form, so will you please get this back to me right away?"

And they would say, "Oh, certainly. No problem."

 To read the details about the law for Section 32 Mortgages, go to www.ftc.gov and use the Search feature.

And that was that. Another high-priced loan was speeding through the pipeline with nary a raised eyebrow.

After three months of this tomfoolery, I washed my hands of this company and never looked back. (It has since closed its doors.)

Illegal Kickbacks

It is illegal, according to federal law, to give or receive money or *anything of value* in exchange for referred business in the mortgage industry. The idea behind the law is that if a loan officer pays someone for a referred client, the client will end up paying for the word of mouth advertising with a higher priced loan. While I understand the spirit of the law and its desire to help the public, I have to say, it's just not working.

Referrals network back and forth between loan officers, real estate agents, collectors, title company reps, escrow agents, appraisers, and anyone else who can pick up a piece of the pie. Since handing over a check is blatantly illegal, instead, tickets, prizes, certificates, lunches, wine, and many other intoxicating delights pass hands. One loan officer handed out flyers at a debt collection company offering a television to the person who referred the most loans for the month. Once a competitor caught sight of the flyer, that little gig was over. Competitors are usually the ones who squeal. Everyone else is happy as a clam at high tide.

And why not? Other industries pay for word-of-mouth advertising and referred business without penalty. Furthermore, if a company doesn't pay for referrals, but advertises on radio or television instead, doesn't that expense get passed on to the consumer?

In some parts of the country, loan officers who try to network with real estate agents say the agents demand gifts in exchange for referred clients. If they inform the agents that it's against the law, the agents say, "Sorry, I have no one to refer to you." These loan officers complain that the only ones who get real estate referrals are the ones who violate the law.

A large Internet lead generation company tells its clients that if they use one of its referred real estate agents, they'll get a $2,000 gift card. The company comes out ahead, because the real estate agents give them an even greater kickback than $2,000. But if a mortgage company gives so much as a stick of gum as a thank you, it's a felony, punishable by a fine of up to $10,000 and/or one-year imprisonment.

Consequently, gifts (and even cash) are passed under the table instead. How can this violation be stopped? Can the government watchdogs keep an eye on what every loan officer says and does, in all locations and at all hours? Can they read all the cards that contain gift certificates and checks? Can they monitor every Saturday afternoon lunch where something of value might exchange hands? Can they watch to see who paid for the tickets to the ballgame and prove it was for referring a loan? Obviously, this law must be run largely on the honor system, and it's failing miserably.

A national bank got slapped with a huge fine, because it threw a party and invited only the loan officers who did at least a million dollars in loans with the bank the previous year. I'm guessing that one loan officer, who was cranky about not receiving an invitation, made a fuss about a "Real Estate Settlement Procedures Act (RESPA) violation." Supposedly, the bank was paying a kickback to certain loan officers in the form of a party.

I doubt that bank will ever throw another party for loan officers. But individuals will continue to be "very, very grateful" for referred business. No law is going to stop what goes on "between friends."

That's why I say this is a law that's not working. And what the mortgage industry needs are not more laws, but better-informed consumers who will monitor their own pricing. Smart consumers don't need the government to tell them when a price is too high.

Should Back-End Commissions Be Illegal?

Since the mid-1990s, there have been more than 150 lawsuits seeking class action certification, some of them claiming that yield spread premiums (YSPs) are an illegal kickback in violation of Section 8 of RESPA.

Prohibiting YSP would prevent many low- and middle-income people from becoming homeowners.

Fortunately, for homebuyers and homeowners alike, yield spread premiums are still legal. It would be a disaster for consumers if their only option was to pay the broker up front. I'll explain why.

Homebuyers need all the flexibility they can get. The more choices you have, the better it will be for you. Here's an illustration.

Emily is a hardworking single mom of three whose husband ran off with another woman. She wants to provide stability for her children, especially since the divorce was a bit unsettling for all. She read on mortgage-helper.com that according to the Home Ownership Alliance, "Children of homeowners are likely to perform higher on academic achievement tests, more likely to finish high school and have fewer behavior problems in school." She doesn't want to throw her money away on rent forever, but she can't save for a down payment as fast as home prices are going up. She feels stuck.

But then she learns that she doesn't need any cash to buy a home. She can get a zero-down loan and have the seller pay her closing costs. Her house payment will be about the same as her rent payment, so, she thinks, why not start building personal wealth through real estate equity and give her children a real home? Why shouldn't she move onward and upward with her life?

Because she has the option of paying no Origination Fee and letting her mortgage broker make his commission on the back end, Emily can qualify without having a lot of cash. She can come up with $500 for *earnest money* and $400 for an appraisal, and that's all the out-of-pocket money she'll need. (Earnest money is a check that accompanies your offer to the seller to show that your offer is sincere. If your offer is accepted, the earnest money is applied to your closing costs; if not, it is refunded.)

> 🖉 **NOTE**
> Sellers will be more impressed if you offer several thousand dollars as earnest money; however, if $500 is all you have, I've seen that amount accepted hundreds of times.) 🖉

Emily sees on her Good Faith Estimate that her mortgage broker is making a commission of $3,000. That's a fair number, and she is fine with it, as she should be. If her loan officer has a fifty-fifty split, he'll pocket $1,500; if he is a 100 percent 1099 employee, he'll pocket $3,000 and pay his own insurance out of that. Either way, it's of no consequence to Emily. She's getting a fair deal, and thanks to the existence of yield spread premiums, she can become a homeowner.

If you don't have the cash to pay all your closing costs, your loan officer may pay some or all of them for you out of his or her YSP. That's a good deal for you.

Emily wouldn't have the $3,000 cash if she had to pay it up front, and her seller has agreed to cover basic closing costs, but not enough to include the 1 percent Origination Fee. Wouldn't it be a shame if a hardworking single mom like Emily were denied the chance to buy a home for her family because some misguided buffoons made YSP illegal? How could having a choice ever be a bad thing?

That said, I should point out that some writers have argued that YSP should be illegal because it is too confusing for consumers to understand. I find that demeaning and insulting. I believe homebuyers and homeowners are intelligent enough to understand what a back-end commission is—when it's explained in clear language. I say let them make their own choice regarding the type of financing they want, and don't deny them any of their options.

Three Ways YSP Is a Benefit to Borrowers

You, the homebuyer, can take advantage of the broker's back-end commission in the following instances:

- You do not have enough cash to pay for an Origination Fee.
- You have the cash for an Origination Fee, but you prefer to keep it in an interest-bearing account as emergency reserve money.
- You don't have cash for either the Origination Fee or your third-party closing costs, such as title and escrow; and the seller will not pay for any of your costs. By taking a higher interest rate, your loan officer can get a good-sized YSP and designate some of that money to pay for your closing costs.

If back-end commissions were illegal, fewer people would have the opportunity to become homeowners. Most of the people who would be denied the chance to realize the American dream of owning their own home would be those with one income in the household and those with lower incomes. Wiping out YSPs would be a strike against the young and the lower middle class—hardworking citizens who are a good credit risk but don't have the means to save fast enough for both a down payment and closing costs. Home values are rising faster than they can save, putting them in an impossible situation.

In a seller's market, it can be difficult or impossible to find a seller to pay the buyer's closing costs, so enabling the loan officer to pay the buyer's closing costs with his or her YSP is extremely useful.

If you see that the YSP is some outrageous amount, simply go to the next lender on your short list. No problem. If there's a loan officer in town who insists on making 20 grand on every deal, so what? As long as every homebuyer in America reads this, no one will be taken advantage of. You'll either decide he or she is a mighty fine loan officer, and worth the 20 grand, or you'll say no thanks and move on to someone else. If everyone says no thanks, the loan officer will have to lower his or her profit margin. That's American commerce at work.

The point is clear: there's nothing wrong with back-end commissions as long as they are properly disclosed, and as long as they're not too high for your own comfort level. By understanding your loan, you make the choice, and that's something you can feel very good about.

Coming Up

I've saved the best for last. In Chapter 16, I reveal secrets never revealed publicly before. When a journalist interviews a mortgage professional, certain goings-on will never be told. Such as? Read on to find out what goes on inside the inner circle.

A Peek
inside the
Mortgage Industry

What is your loan officer saying about you behind your back? What conversations are taking place? What strategies are being devised? What schemes are being implemented? Who's plotting to take advantage, and exactly how are they doing that?

The best defense against mortgage rip-offs is to become an informed consumer. To that end, in this, the last chapter in the book, I offer a peek behind closed doors. For only when there are enough educated, savvy consumers will the shady side of the mortgage industry have to change. The power is in your hands—the hands of the public. When you make a choice, you send a message, because money talks.

If you agree, I ask you to recommend this book to your friends and associates. Help get the word out.

Behind Closed Doors

The public never gets inside the wholesale offices; as a matter of fact, you probably don't even know they're there—those plush offices in tall buildings with no name on the outside. For security reasons, not even the mortgage brokers get past the locked doors between the lobby and the labyrinth of offices, where the important decisions are made. In the Introduction, I said a lot of secrets are told over lunch, and I told you one of those secrets. But that's nothing compared to what goes on behind closed doors.

I hope this exposé will wake up the American public (especially people who don't pay close enough attention to their credit issues) and encourage them to exercise caution and good judgment.

Secrets of the Underwriting Department

The underwriters are the ones who approve and deny loans. Sure, the computer spits out an "accept" or "denied," but a real person follows that up with a final decision before your loan can fund.

Underwriters make sure the information put into the computer is accurate. They recalculate the income and check all the figures. They look over the employment history and ask questions. They read every line on the credit report. They scrutinize every word, every number, and every photo on the appraisal. They check title.

Underwriters also inspect for fraud, and most have been trained specifically on how to do this. They have ways of detecting all types of fraud and falsification for such things as Social Security numbers, income, assets, employment, and signatures.

No one can pay an underwriter to approve a bad loan. That would be committing career suicide, and underwriters aren't foolish. However, payoffs for time do occur. And then there are areas of gray where an underwriter has to make a judgment call.

Bribes

For all they do, underwriters are not magicians. They can't wave a magic wand or approve a loan on a whim. They have manuals with guidelines and rules that they must follow. The underwriters do not create the manuals, but they do interpret them. As people differ, underwriters differ as to their strictness in interpretation. Some underwriters see only black and white, while others see shades of gray, as well, and will make a judgment call based on how gray they see it. Still, even the most lenient underwriter has a limit on what he or she can approve. If an underwriter signs off on a loan that violates the lending company's guidelines too often, he or she can get fired.

Company CEOs will deny that bribes happen in their company. But how can they know what whisperings go on in a cozy bar after hours?

You, as a homebuyer or homeowner, cannot coerce or bribe an underwriter to approve your loan. You may write a Letter of Explanation to help your cause, as described in Chapter 13 and below, but you cannot coerce or bribe. However, the account executive who works for the same company the underwriter works for can coerce or bribe the underwriter—sometimes. Note I didn't say they have permission to do so, nor did I say they should. I'm just saying it happens.

An important loan may be a loan for a friend or family member, or for a special real estate agent who needs to be impressed. A loan that yields a big commission is also a VIP loan.

When I was a loan officer, every now and then I'd have an especially difficult loan or a loan that was a super-rush. I'd call the account executive (AE) for whatever wholesale lender I was using. And more often than not, she would make it happen. What I'm saying is that I got the approval on the "marginal loan" or the super-rush I needed. I used to marvel at how she worked her "magic." All the loan officers in our office raved about what an awesome AE she was.

Then one day I learned the secret behind her magic tricks. She told me that it had cost her a pass to a day spa to get one of my important, super-rush loans closed on time. Evidently, an underwriter was willing to work overtime in exchange for a certificate to the spa; or perhaps she just gave my loan a "cut in line." Whatever happened, everyone involved came out happy, including my homebuyer who had no idea what had transpired behind closed doors.

Speaking of bribes, I have seen an account executive slip $40 to a rate lock gal to buy "cuts in line." She had a big loan ($750,000) and wanted to make sure the interest rate got locked in, because word had come from the corporate office that there would be a rate increase in an hour. The rate lock gal was locking in the loans as fast as she could, in the order they had come in. But the stack of files was so large it was obvious that not all the loans would be able to be locked before the increase. Some people were going to lose out, and the account executive wanted to make sure it wasn't her $750,000 loan.

Paying for "cuts" was against company policy, but as the rate lock gal whispered, "This is our little secret." And it was. Neither the mortgage broker nor the homebuyer knew about this under-the-table financial transaction. All they knew was that their interest rate had been safely locked before the increase that occurred that day. (Forty dollars was a pittance: the account executive saved her $2,400 commission and kept the mortgage broker from getting mad and switching to a different wholesale lender.)

Disappearing Documents

"I'll throw away these papers and pretend I never saw them." That's music straight from an underwriter's mouth to a desperate loan officer's ears—such as when I had a client with a voluntary auto repossession on her credit report. I was trying to turn her loan denial into an approval, so I asked her to write a letter explaining why she returned her car to the dealership.

She wrote, "I decided my payments were too high, so I turned the car in." The underwriter called me and said the loan was still denied.

"We all had a good laugh at her letter," the underwriter confided. She explained: "What if she decides her house payments are too high? Is she going to turn it back to the bank too? We can't have that."

I asked what would be an acceptable reason for a voluntary repossession.

"A one-time occurrence that's in the past, such as divorce or medical," she said.

"Okay, can she write a new letter of explanation?" I asked.

"Sure, I'll rip up this one and pretend I never saw it," said the underwriter.

As it turned out, the reason the woman decided she couldn't afford the payments on her car was that she had to go to the hospital for emergency surgery. This was no lie. We could document this story with medical bills; consequently, I was able to get her loan approved.

Some loan officers and some account executives would have said, "Sorry, we can't approve someone with a voluntary repo." And that would have been the end of it.

Sometimes a bank statement has to be discarded, because it doesn't show a high enough balance to meet the asset requirements. The loan officer may have better luck with a Verification of Deposit (VOD) form that shows the average balance over several months. How does that make sense? Because the client may have $100,000 cash in a black plastic garbage bag hidden in her house (true story). The loan officer counsels them to hurry up and get that money into the bank for verification.

Loan officers appreciate those underwriters who will give their clients a second chance to qualify, and they quickly learn who will and who won't. You take advantage of this knowledge when you work with an experienced mortgage broker.

Playing Favorites

Certain underwriters go strictly by the guidebook and won't allow any grace. They may be afraid to exercise judgment and make an exception, or they may be too lazy to do the extra work, or they may have a quota of loans to get through for the day so they aren't willing to take the extra time, or they may just be the legalistic type who sees only in black and white. Other underwriters operate with more flexibility. Wholesale account executives and retail loan officers get to know who is strict and who is flexible, and they have their favorites. That goes both ways. Underwriters have their favorites, too, and who can say that loan officers who visit and make friends with them and bring them chocolate on their birthday and buy them a martini after work don't get special consideration? I'm sure every underwriter across America would vehemently deny this, but I'm just saying, people are people . . . well, you know.

Which brings me to the secret I mentioned in Chapter 14 about how I got my loan funded after the Seattle earthquake. Recall that the courthouse was shut down due to earthquake damage, so no more loans could record and fund. But due entirely to a relationship I had with a wholesale funder, I got my loan to fund anyway, even without a recording number.

"Please help me out," I said. "My client is a nurse, and we all know how hard nurses work helping sick people. This purchase is her first house, and she absolutely has to be out of her apartment tonight. If she can't move her things into the new home, we're going to have a nurse out on the streets with no place to go. I don't even know if she has a car to sleep in. Please, will you just fund this one loan for me? I wouldn't ask if it wasn't really important."

"Okay, I'll go ahead and send the wire out. We don't want a nurse going homeless," the funder said agreeably.

The moral of this story is, never underestimate the value of your loan officer's relationship with the wholesale company. It wasn't just that my client was a nurse; it was also that I had a good reputation and relationship with the people on the inside.

Secrets in the Sales Office

The competition in the mortgage industry is as fierce as in a dog fight. Especially now. It seems you can't step outside and throw a rock without hitting someone who's into mortgages. With so many contenders for the business, everyone is pulling out all the stops to get clients. Here's a look inside one sales meeting at a wholesale lender.

Phony Specials

"We're going to have a special this month that'll blow all our competition out of the water," announced the sales manager. All the wholesale account executives leaned forward. They were eager to hear about this special that would lure their clients—the loan officers at mortgage broker shops—away from the wholesale competitors.

He continued, "We're going to offer the brokers 1 percent YSP at par rate."

The room erupted into cheers. If their brokers could make 1 percent back-end commission and still offer their homebuyers par rate, that would make them the best-priced lender out there, and they'd rake in the business.

"Do you think they'll like that?" he asked the group eagerly.

An experienced account executive spoke up, "Sure. They'll be able to make 2 percent on the back end at the rate they would have made 1 percent back."

"So you don't think they'll pass on the savings to their borrowers?" asked the sales manager.

Laughter rippled across the room.

"No way," was the consensus.

Well, no matter. Whether the loan officers profited or the public profited from the special, the end result would be the same: more business for the wholesale lender.

The sales manager continued matter-of-factly, "Expect a rate increase then. Of course, we'll have to raise rates to make up for the extra YSP."

Of course. It would be a wash. A "special" that was actually the same.

"How do you think your brokers will react?" asked the sales manager.

"They won't notice," replied a different account executive.

The room of account executives seemed to agree with this insult. Raise rates, offer a YSP special, and rake in the loans. Woo-hoo. Everyone was excited.

"All right then. Everyone go out there and bring in the loans!" he said with the enthusiasm of a yell king on a cheerleading squad.

As you can see, wholesale lending can be cutthroat. Every company watches the rate sheets and specials put on by their rivals. When my sales manager accompanied me on my calls to mortgage brokers, he often stole competitors' flyers out of the loan officers' mailboxes and threw them in the recycle bin.

Three Ways Wholesalers Compete

Pricing loans is a balancing act between keeping company profits at an acceptable level and still beating the other lenders. But interest rates and closing fees are just one component of the game.

We sent our competitors' rate sheets to our corporate office to convince them to lower our rates. But some competitors foiled our efforts by regularly making "rate exceptions" lower than the printed rates. Experienced mortgage brokers will take advantage of these exceptions for you.

Guidelines are another, as mentioned above. If a company is too strict with its approvals, it will earn a bad reputation for issuing too many denials. A loan turned down is worse than a loan high priced. All it takes is one difficult underwriter to ruin a wholesaler's business for an entire area.

A third component is service. If a wholesale lender takes too long getting loans through, mortgage brokers won't use them. On the other hand, if a lender establishes a reputation of being super fast, brokers will send their "rush" loans to them, even if they're priced higher. It's more important to get the loan closed on time than it is to give the borrowers the lowest rate. If a broker closes loans late, word will get around the real estate community, and it's sure to be the death of them. Or so they fear.

If you're a stickler for the absolute cheapest loan, then don't expect to have the fastest service, too. The cheapest lenders are the busiest, and they can't always close a loan in a week. Please understand it's not your loan officer who's being slow. It's the fabulously priced wholesale lender who is five times busier than the others.

The Bank's Bag of Tricks

Retail lenders such as banks and direct lending companies have their own bag of sales tricks.

One mortgage company spies on your credit card payments. If you pay late, the credit card holder alerts them that you might be a candidate for a debt consolidation refinance. Then one of their loan officers calls you to see if you'd like to "pay off some bills and reduce your monthly outgo." This works, because when a consumer is late on one credit card, he or she is usually late on others as well.

Another mortgage company caters to collection agencies. After making friends with the supervisor, the loan officer waltzes in through the side door, circumventing the highly securitized front office, with boxes of chocolates and other sweet treats for the collectors. If a collector encounters a homeowner, he or she refers them to the loan officer for a debt pay-off refinance.

"Refinance and pay off your debt, or I'll sue you," they tell the homeowner.

A loan officer can make a decent living off referrals from collection agencies.

Bankers have another strategy to gain business—one I discovered when I was offered a job at a big national bank. Here's how it works. If the bank's loan officer can convince you to switch your checking and savings accounts to them—in addition to taking the mortgage—they'll make extra bonus money.

The bank's goal is to get your checking account, your savings account, your mortgage, and your line of credit all at that bank. And anything else you have that involves financing, too. Why? Because statistics show that if you have at least three types of transactions going on at a bank, chances are you'll be a customer for life there for all things financial. The next time that loan officer tells you that you can have a fantastic line of credit "only" if you switch your checking account to his or her fine institution, you'll understand why.

Why Minorities Pay More

Charging a homebuyer of a minority race more than a Caucasian home buyer is illegal. Yet some statistical research still shows African Americans and Hispanics pay more. Why? And why can't the government figure this out? They say they're doing more "research."

I say, good luck, because no one is going to admit anything to an outsider.

Here's another lunchtime secret I heard, from an African American loan officer. She obtained the majority of her clients by advertising in a small, local paper published by and for the black community.

When I asked her how she charged more points on her loans than her white coworkers, she confided that it was because of her target audience. She was advertising to the black community and she was black, so there was a natural trust. Therefore, her clients didn't compare her Good Faith Estimate to any others. No one made a short list and compared offers. No one looked for bogus discount points or junk fees. No one asked about YSP. As a result, she was able to make more money off her loans. Since all her clients were black, she wasn't charging her black clients more than her white clients. In fact, she didn't have white clients; she advertised only to the African American community.

Here's another shocking lunchtime confession. I had my first authentic Korean meal when a Korean loan officer took me to lunch and ordered off the Koean menu. Near the end of our lunch, she said to me, "I'm ashamed to tell you this, but Koreans get taken advantage of by other Koreans." Then she showed me a Korean newspaper that contained advertisements by Korean mortgage professionals. I understood her sadness.

I observed the same thing happening in the Hispanic community. Spanish-speaking people naturally feel more comfortable talking with a Spanish-speaking loan officer. It's easy for the Hispanic loan officers to price *all* their loans high, because all their clients are Hispanic and not shopping or comparing.

In these examples, the loan officers can truthfully say, "I don't charge minorities more than whites," because they aren't doing loans for whites (with the rare exception). I have to ask, are these loan officers taking advantage of a same-race trust relationship? Or are they just a higher-priced company? Is their specialized service—communicating in a non-English language or in Ebonics—worthy of their higher price?

Don't misunderstand: I'm not saying you should go only to white loan officers. There are, of course, fine, honest mortgage professionals of all races. What I am saying is that *everyone* should make a short list and compare Good Faith Estimates (as explained in Chapter 2). Simply put, you can't neglect this important step just because your loan officer is of the same race as you—or the same religion, either.

Another—more common—reason minorities pay more, I believe, has nothing to do with race and everything to do with credit. When an individual's credit cannot qualify for a conforming loan, he or she has to take a more lenient subprime loan that carries a higher interest rate to offset the risk to the investors. Unfortunately, many immigrants come into the United States without experience or an understanding of the credit system; consequently, they have subprime credit. The same goes for people pulling themselves up from impoverished backgrounds. They haven't been informed or educated about credit management, and they've had no good role models in their homes to follow. Is it any wonder that they often have to learn the hard way?

When clients have subprime credit, the loan officer qualifies them for a subprime loan, regardless of their race. The solution to this situation is education about finances and credit—which must start in high school or earlier, not in the school of hard knocks. That way, good people won't become targets for greed.

Scenes through a Hidden Camera

What's it really like to work in an industry where you have the potential to make a great six-figure income? Suppose you had a hidden camera: here's what you might see.

Snapshot of the Ugly Side of Wholesale Lending

Corporate pressure rolls down hill like an avalanche picking up force, destined to slay the hardest-working people at the bottom, the soldiers in

Who Pays for Those Lavish Vacations?

"Try to make it to Casino Night. The company flies you to California, and everyone wins really cool prizes," my mentor said (when I was new in the business).

"How do you make it there?" I asked.

"By meeting the quota for loans."

I took her advice, worked hard, and won the trip. Sure enough, all of us who met the quota were flown to San Diego, where we got to play for big prizes—everything from an SUV to a kitchen blender. We were put up in a fancy hotel and wined and dined like celebrities. The free full-service bar was very busy, and the buffet was fit for royalty. I went home with a mountain bike and 14-carat gold earrings.

That trip was just the warm-up. The next one was a lot better.

The prize was for the creme de la creme in the company—those top 100 loan officers (out of about 935) who generated the most *revenue* for the company. Not the most loans closed, not the most in loan volume, but the most in profits. This gave us the incentive to price each and every loan as high as possible.

The winners would score an all-expenses-paid lavish vacation for two at one of the world's most magnificent resorts, the Grand Wailea Resort in Maui.

The race was on! The contest went on for a good part of the year, and at the end of each month, the corporate office faxed out the standings. Eagerly, we crowded around to see if our names were on the list and, if so, to discover where we stood.

The last month was tense. The grading was on a curve, so no one could predict ahead of time exactly what revenue was required to win a top spot. One of my coworkers and I had become close friends, and we both desperately wanted this trip. We knew winning was the only way we'd ever experience such royal extravagance.

Both of us had been pulling out all the stops for months, trying to make it. We worked voluntary overtime. We were on the phone to homeowners, "dialing for dollars," in search of someone who needed to refinance. We called from the file cabinet of past turn-downs. We sent out mail. We networked.

(continued)

For my part, I also regularly called on my local collection agencies for referral business. But still I needed more. I found myself a large collection company in Kansas that was open to having me refinance its debtors to get the past-due accounts paid off. Then I found an attorney's office in Atlanta who handled only debtors with large collection balances. I arranged a business liaison with them, as well. I made friends with a loan officer in New York, and we closed loans cross country together, splitting commissions. (We remain friends to this day.)

My coworker, after signing a loan with one of her clients, a mother-son pair, whispered something to me in confidence. "I really had to work hard for that one," she said. "It wasn't easy convincing them to refinance when they're only saving $40 a month."

"Yeah, it doesn't really make sense, does it?" I said.

"No, but I need every loan I can get for the contest. They almost didn't sign."

"How did you manage it?" I asked.

"I flirted a lot with the man," she said, looking a little guilty. According to law, they had three days to look over the loan and back out if they wanted. My friend said she was worried about them rescinding. It would be really bad if that happened. Our manager did not like rescisions. As it turned out, the loan stuck.

In contrast, my mentor had no problem getting her loans signed. When she met with homeowners, she simply said, "Real estate agents charge 6 percent to sell your house, but I'm only charging 4. And these are just our company junk fees. They add up to about $995, and they're standard. Please sign here."

Our manager pushed us all to succeed. She wanted our branch to have the most winners, because it would be good for her career and help her to win the branch manager's contest, which was for an international trip.

At month-end, she said, "Everyone plan to stay late tomorrow night. Wear comfortable clothes, because you'll all be helping package up files at the end of the day. I'll buy dinner."

"What about beer? Will you buy beer too?" asked one of the guys.

"No, I won't buy beer."

"Then can we bring our own beer?" he asked.

She laughed. That meant she couldn't say yes, but she wasn't saying no, either. So pizza and beer were served at 6:00 the next evening, after a hard day's work. Then we worked until 10 o'clock that night and went home physically and emotionally drained.

One of the challenges we had was getting pay-offs from our clients' current lenders. These companies didn't want to lose their loans to us, so they wouldn't respond in a timely manner. But we were the same way when someone tried to get pay-off figures from us. Whoever happened to walk by the fax machine when the pay-off request came in would simply crumple it up and toss it into the bin. But never mind that. We wanted our clients' pay-off figures so we could get the loans closed ASAP.

Frustrated, one of my coworkers drove over to the finance company that had failed to provide a pay-off. He came back triumphant, pay-off in hand.

"What did you do?" asked our manager, smiling at his success.

"Yelled in the lobby and used the f-word," he said.

That's how it went when a contest was on. People did whatever it took. Another one of my coworkers sat on his clients' porch until 10:00 P.M., when they finally got home, in order to get his loan signed in time for month-end.

Finally, the contest ended. It had been five months of all-out effort. We were exhausted to the core. One of the guys said he couldn't even talk to his wife when he went home from work at the end of each day—he was so burnt out from talking on the phone, selling pricing, finagling deals with collectors, fighting for exceptions, coercing payoffs, and arranging signings.

"All I can do at night is veg out in front of the TV," he said. We all knew how he felt.

When it was all over, we waited on pins and needles for the contest results. At last they came, and our manager called a meeting. My company-assigned mentor had won. My coworker best friend had won. So had my buddy in New York. And so had I. To my utter astonishment, I'd made it into the top tier of winners: and I was awarded $1,000 cash spending money in addition to the trip.

My fiancé and I planned our wedding so that this glorious vacation could double as our honeymoon. It was beyond all expectations. We took a helicopter tour of the island volcanoes and a

(continued)

215

snorkeling trip off Molokai Island, company-paid. We visited coconut-strewn, white-sand beaches. Every morning we were treated to a lavish breakfast buffet overlooking the sapphire-blue Pacific; and we discovered the sweetness of tree-ripened pineapples, guava, and mangoes.

And when the hotel management learned we were on our honeymoon they treated us to a spa and massage as a wedding gift. In the evenings, we dined aboard a romantic sunset cruise or sipped mai tais at an authentic Hawaiian luau. We danced the night away next to the balmy beach. For seven days and seven nights, we lived in paradise.

One evening, I saw my mentor throwing her money around like a wild woman, slipping a $100 tip to the handsome bartender, and such.

"What are you doing?" I asked her.

"Pretending I'm a rock star," she said.

It was certainly the place to do it.

At the end of the year, I found out how much our magnificent vacation cost, because I had to pay taxes on it: $7,000. Simple multiplication says the company paid $700,000 for the extravaganza for the 100 winners.

Homeowners who accepted high-priced refinances paid for this all. And we thank you very much.

the trenches, as it were. The fancy cats up in their floor-to-ceiling window offices with views of the ocean grumble about the profits. "Why aren't they higher? What can be done to increase the profitability of the company?" Their desires are insatiable.

The corporate VPs of sales get rolling. They contact the regional sales managers beneath them and demand projections and business plans to reach new profit goals. The regional managers, in turn, contact the branch managers demanding more sales, bigger profits.

"What's wrong with you down there in your office?" they bark. "Why are your numbers so low? Can't you manage an office? How do you ever expect to be promoted to regional?"

Next down the line the branch managers yell at the sales managers: "What are you, slackers? Why aren't your salespeople doing more? Follow them around. Get to the bottom of it. Bring in a new record this month or else. How do you ever expect to get a branch of your own if you can't manage a sales force?"

Then the sales managers make the salespeople's lives a living hell. "Work harder, work smarter. Sell service. Leave your cell phones on till 9:00 P.M. Take calls on the weekends as well. Return all calls within 10 minutes. Document everything. Write out more goals. I want more lists, more plans, more charts, more databases. Bring in more loans, and don't tell me your brokers don't have another loan to give you. Our goals are not set by their goals. We demand new records, even if the market is down. What others do is of no consequence to us. Kill the competition. Bring in the deals. There are plenty of other people who want your job, if you don't. Do I make myself clear?"

The salespeople don't sleep so well. Sometimes you find one of the females crying in the bathroom. But then something wonderful happens. They have a big month. At the next sales meeting, the sales manager mentions their names and all their peers slap them a high-five. The boss hands them an envelope, and their paychecks are for more money than a lot of people make in six months. They decide to treat themselves to a Rolex or a diamond tennis bracelet. If it happens twice in a row, they'll get a new car. And on it goes.

Snapshot of Direct Lenders

The lucky loan officers work for incredible managers, who are energetic, enthusiastic, and possess a wealth of knowledge about the business. They never say no to a loan. If the borrower has a pulse, they'll find a way to get him or her approved, it seems. If the client has ugly credit and no job, they'll say, "No problem. Just come up with a 35 percent down payment, and you've got yourself a house."

These cheerful managers are ideal mentors for someone brand new to the business. When the corporate office hands down ultimatums, they'll brainstorm with the staff on ways to increase business and generate mini-contests for dinners and such to keep everyone motivated.

For the unlucky loan officers, it's another story. Take the branch manager who called a staff meeting after a disappointing month. He was so infuriated, he cloistered all the loan officers into in a windowless conference room, crammed around one long table, and literally yelled at them for four hours. About three hours into his tirade, nature called, and one young man just had to *go*. He stood up and started to make his way between the wall and the table toward the door.

"*Where* do you *think* you're going?" the manager screamed.

"To the men's room."

"*Sit down!*"

"I really have to go to the men's room."

"You're not going anywhere till I'm done, and I'm *far from done!*"

The desperate young man ignored him and kept walking toward the door. Then the manager, who was as big as a linebacker, stepped around and blocked him with his body. The young man stood trapped between the table, the wall, and the irate manager. But he was desperate. So in his pinstriped suit, white shirt, and silk tie, he stepped up on a chair, stepped up on the conference table, then jumped down to the other side, and escaped out the door, just as the manager hollered after him, "If you leave, don't ever come back!"

Three days later he was back. He was a top producer, and the manager decided that he'd been a little too intense and "invited" him to return to work.

Snapshot of Independent Loan Officers

The loan officers in the mortgage broker shops who are considered "independent" and get paid 100 percent commission via 1099 income are the "truly free" among the employed masses. No one owns their time.

No ringing bell tells them when to wake up—they donated their alarm clocks to charity a long time ago. They roll out of bed when they feel like it and pour themselves a leisurely cup of coffee. Or perhaps they prefer to patronize their local coffee shop for a grande double shot, extra hot, vanilla, no whip. If it's spring, they may spend a pleasant hour in the backyard tending their garden before heading into the office.

They'll saunter in at 9:30 or 10:00 A.M., or whenever. First thing they do is check on interest rates for the day. If they're down, they'll lock in their loans; if not, they'll float. So they check their emails and work for a bit, and then they meander down the hall to one of their colleague's office.

"Hey, where shall we do lunch today?" (Most days, they eat out.)

After lunch, they put their heads down and work like fanatics. They take applications, field phone calls, return phone calls, reassure clients, cajole real estate agents, check up on processing, urge appraisers to speed up the reports, order comps on values for new refinances, go over income and asset documents, and call their clients to remind them, yet again, what's still missing, and plead with them to fax in a copy of their pay stub, because, yes, it really is necessary. That's the afternoon warm-up. Next, they argue with underwriters over conditions in an effort to make the loan process as easy as possible for their clients. They double-check with processing *again*—why is it taking so long to get that insurance binder anyway? They check the bond market in order to foretell where interest rates may be headed tomorrow, because all their clients expect them to have a crystal ball and prophesy on where rates are going. Some days the phone rings constantly, interrupting everything they do, and the phone must *always* be answered cheerfully and eagerly, even if it's that same real estate agent calling to quadruple-check that the loan is still approved and moving along smoothly. Then they input all the new applications into the computer so their processor can submit them for automated underwriting preapproval. Or they'll submit the apps themselves, to speed things up.

How long do they work? However long it takes to get everything done. It might be 5:00 P.M. or 9:30 P.M. They may have appointments to meet with clients after they get off work, so they have to stay late.

If they advertise, network, and build a referral base, they'll work hard and be rewarded a handsome income. But if they kick back and play a round of golf every afternoon, they'll make less, and no one cares. Their business is *their* business.

How do they like their jobs? Let's hear what some of them have to say:

> It's great, except for that wholesale account executive who tells me my loan is good to go when no one's even looked at it yet, and then it gets turned down.

> It's great, except for the real estate agent who stole the client that I referred to him and so he could send them to his friend who slips him tickets to the Super Bowl.

> It's great, except when my borrowers tell me they have good credit and make $5,000 a month—when they actually have a bankruptcy and two collection accounts and make only $2,500 a month . . . and the other client whose Social Security number belongs to a 130-year-old dead woman . . . and my other client who claims he lives in the condo I'm refinancing, but he also has a million-dollar house three miles away.

> It's great, except for the appraisers who won't deliver an appraisal report without me calling a zillion times, and then when they finally

do deliver it, it's got the wrong address and the lender won't take it, because it doesn't match the title report.

It's great, except for the fact that my processor lies to me about what she's really done on my loan files, so then I pass on bad information to my borrowers and agents and look like an idiot.

It's great, except for the clients who cuss and call me names because the interest rates went up. Like it was my fault.

It's great, except for the underwriter at the bank who keeps adding more conditions as the loan progresses so it makes me look like an incompetent fool. Every time we think we're done and ready to draw docs, she asks for some other paperwork, and my clients are like, "Why didn't you tell me you wanted that from the get-go?"

My job was great, but now it's not. My mom referred her friend to me, and now that friend won't talk to my mom anymore. Why? Because at closing, the property taxes were higher than they expected. I tried to explain that property taxes are set by the county and there's nothing I can do to control them, but her real estate agent told her, "Your loan officer messed up," so now she's mad at my mom for referring her to me.

When you hear things like this, you realize how hard loan officers work. That's why I want to give you an opportunity to nominate the stars in this business.

Mortgage Stars Who Rock

The mortgage industry is one of the most stressful businesses there is. If you've ever bought a house, you no doubt can recall how stressed out you felt and how you laid awake at night worrying about it. Imagine working in that environment every day, being responsible for a whole whiteboard full of loans.

 For more information, visit my Web sites: www.mortgage-helper.com and www.AskCarolynWarren.com.

Throughout this book you've read about the lies, the trickery, the nasty secrets, the shenanigans, the bait-and-switch tactics, and all the rest that goes on in this shark-eat-shark business. Imagine being a loan officer with high morals and integrity trying to compete, trying to make a living for your family in this environment. It's not easy.

These honorable loan officers work hard to be available to you any-time and anywhere you want them. I've heard some confess to taking a makeshift application while driving down the turnpike. They write on yellow sticky notes, ripped-apart cigarette packs, paper napkins, the back of golf scorecards, and even—according to one woman—on her arm with an eyeliner pencil. They pick up their cell phones to talk with you while they're in the airport, on a fishing boat, and running the track. They happily interrupt their personal time in order to accommo-date their clients.

Some loan officers give up their commission to do a "charity loan" every couple of months as a way of helping someone out and giv-ing back to their communities. In addition, nearly every loan officer who's been in business for more than a couple of years has a story about how they gave up their commission when interest rates rose, just to help out a client.

These good people are the real stars of the mortgage business. They rock! They deserve respect, and handwritten thank you cards, and letters of commendation to their bosses, and—most of all—your recom-mendation to others. Help keep the mortgage stars in business by refer-ring them to your friends and associates and by passing out their business cards. And when you smell a bloodthirsty, greedy loan shark, when you sense that something isn't adding up, when you see a bold-faced lie on your Final Settlement Statement, run like the wind in the opposite direction.

But if you've had the good fortune to work with a mortgage loan of-ficer who is truly extraordinary, please go to my Web site (www .AskCarolynWarren.com) and nominate him or her for my Mortgage Star Honor Roll. And let me know about your experience.

Conclusion

In my wildest, most hopeful dreams, enough people will read this book to cause a significant change in the mortgage industry. When the public knows how to shop for financing, they will have no reason to seek more federal regulations—which don't work anyway. The mortgage industry is already heavily regulated and yet financial rape happens every day.

The solution is simple, and the power is all in your hands: Stay away from unscrupulous lenders, no matter how charming they are. Give your business to the good, hard-working loan officers with integrity. Money talks louder than laws. If you agree, I humbly ask you to recommend this book to others. And I thank you for taking the time to read my point of view.

INDEX

Broker's Fee. *See* Origination Fee
Budget, personal, 15–16
  debt-to-income (DTI) ratio and,
    19–20
Buy-down rate, 116, 120

C

Chapter 7 bankruptcy, 7
Chapter 13 bankruptcy, 7
Charge-offs, 8
Checklist, surprise, 143–144
Civic professions, loans for people
  in, 169
Closing:
  costs, 161–162
  reasons a loan may not,
    189–193
  surprises, avoiding, 133–144
Collections, 8
Commission(s):
  how they work, 77–83
  what is fair, 86–87
Computerized underwriting,
  5–7
Condominiums, 177–179
Consumer Credit Counseling, 7
Courier fee, 102
Creative fees, 103
Credit:
  dealing with outstanding, 4,
    rating, 7–8
Credit challenges, how to get a
  loan with, 9–13
Credit life insurance, 44
Credit rating:
  boosting of, 3–20
  prequalification and, 3–20

Credit reports, 107
  trimerged, 4
Credit report up-charge, 108
Credit score:
  definition of, 6
  for conventional loans, 4
  needed for home purchase,
    4–8
  rating factors of, 5
  rip-offs and, 9–10
  selling of, 14–15
  sharing, 5
  steps to boost, 11–13
  rating, 6–7

D

Debt-to-income (DTI) ratio:
  criteria to calculate, 17–18
  defined, 17
  examples of, 18–19
  personal budgets and, 19–20
Denied loans, dealing with,
  183–187
Desktop underwriting (DU),
  definition of, 5–7
Direct lender:
  definition of, 56
  secrets of, 217–218
  yield spread premiums and,
    83
Discount fees, 105, 116–117,
  118–121
Discount points, truth about,
  115–117, 118–121
Document preparation fees,
  100
Document review fee, 102

224

CPSIA information can be obtained at www.ICGtesting.com
Printed in the USA
BVOW00n1658011013

332513BV00047B/42/P